The Buddha Was a Psychologist

The Buddha Was a Psychologist

A Rational Approach to Buddhist Teachings

Arnold Kozak

LEXINGTON BOOKS
Lanham • Boulder • New York • London

Published by Lexington Books
An imprint of The Rowman & Littlefield Publishing Group, Inc.
4501 Forbes Boulevard, Suite 200, Lanham, Maryland 20706
www.rowman.com

6 Tinworth Street, London SE11 5AL, United Kingdom

Copyright © 2021 The Rowman & Littlefield Publishing Group, Inc.

All rights reserved. No part of this book may be reproduced in any form or by any electronic or mechanical means, including information storage and retrieval systems, without written permission from the publisher, except by a reviewer who may quote passages in a review.

British Library Cataloguing in Publication Information Available

Library of Congress Cataloging-in-Publication Data

Names: Kozak, Arnold, author.
Title: The Buddha was a psychologist : a rational approach to Buddhist teachings / Arnold Kozak.
Description: Lanham : Lexington Books, [2021] | Includes bibliographical references and index.
Identifiers: LCCN 2021010183 (print) | LCCN 2021010184 (ebook) | ISBN 9781498535427 (cloth) | ISBN 9781498535434 (epub)
Subjects: LCSH: Buddhism—Psychology. | Psychology—Religious aspects—Buddhism. | Well-being—Religious aspects—Buddhism.
Classification: LCC BQ4570.P76 K697 2021 (print) | LCC BQ4570.P76 (ebook) | DDC 294.3—dc23
LC record available at https://lccn.loc.gov/2021010183
LC ebook record available at https://lccn.loc.gov/2021010184

Contents

Preface vii

Introduction xv

PART I: RECLAIMING THE BUDDHA FROM BUDDHISM ... 1

1 The Legend of the Buddha: History, Myth, and Hagiography ... 5

2 The Hermeneutical Buddha: What He Taught, What He Thought (Maybe) ... 23

PART II: THE BUDDHA'S PEDAGOGICAL PROJECT: THE ENNOBLING PRAXES (AKA FOUR NOBLE TRUTHS) ... 33

3 The First Ennobling Praxis: What is the Problem? ... 37

4 The Second Ennobling Praxis: Getting to the Root of the Problem ... 41

5 The Third Ennobling Praxis: Can the Problem Be Resolved? ... 45

6 The Fourth Ennobling Praxis: Resolving the Problem ... 51

PART III: MIND ON FIRE: THE BUDDHA'S PSYCHOLOGICAL MAP ... 59

7 Form: Brain Architecture and the Neuroplastic Forest of Self ... 73

8 Perception: Categorization ... 81

9	Feeling: Pain and Pleasure Drive Evolution's Primary Agendas (and Give Rise to a Sense of the One Having Pleasure and Pain)	87
10	Mental Fabrication and the Modular Self	97
11	Consciousness: Apparently Ubiquitous, Certainly Overestimated	109

Conclusion	115
Epilogue	125
Bibliography	129
Index	141
About the Author	149

Preface

I am sitting under a large red and yellow canopy, immediately ahead and at a right angle to where I sit is His Holiness the Dalai Lama. He is speaking in Tibetan and an English translation broadcast is eking out of a small boom box. In addition to the few of us huddled around this radio, we are surrounded by close to a thousand other Western faces from the United States, Europe, and Australia. Surrounding us are 10,000 maroon-clad and bead-adorned Tibetan monks, and surrounding them 250,000 Tibetans in exile—a sea of people in Bihar's arid landscape. We are in the town of Bodhgaya—the Buddhist pilgrimage site where the historical Buddha—also known as Siddhartha Gotama,[1] purportedly became the Buddha after sitting under a distant relative of the tree that sits besides an impressive, intricately carved stupa in the middle of town. The Dalai Lama is offering the bodhisattva vows and I am accepting them. It is 1985 and I am twenty-two years old. These vows enjoin an intention to work toward my own enlightenment as the best means of helping others. According to Tibetan Buddhist cosmology, life is a fraught cycle of birth and death, and enlightenment is a psychospiritual transformation that gives one the power to opt out of that ceaseless cycle. By doing so, one can dwell in a perpetual state of bliss—for eternity. The bodhisattva, though, eschews the ultimate release that might come upon death and takes another rebirth on earth to be helpful to those still suffering—forestalling personal wellbeing for the wellbeing of others. As a nascent psychologist, this approach appealed to me.[2]

A few years after this event in Bodhgaya, I was sitting in a ten-day silent vipassana meditation retreat led by S. N. Goenka. There, participants were expected to do what the Buddha urged his followers to do: "When one thing is practiced and pursued, ignorance is abandoned, clear knowing arises, the conceit 'I am' is abandoned, obsessions are uprooted, fetters are abandoned.

Which one thing? Mindfulness immersed in the body" (Thanissaro 1996, 100). Retreatants were—and still are—expected to meditate from early in the morning into the evening—some twelve hours on the cushion with some of those hours designated as sittings of strong determination—the challenge is not to move the body at all: not from restlessness, no shifting to get comfortable, leaving any and all itches unscratched. For the first three days, I was focusing as per instructions on the tip of my nose exclusively, building a foundation of concentration. I felt like a monk in the Buddha's time: "There is the case of a monk—gone to the wilderness, to the shade of a tree, or to an empty building—sits down folding his legs crosswise, holding his body erect and setting mindfulness to the fore. Always mindful, he breathes in; mindful he breathes out" (Thanissaro 2008). On the fourth day, the focus aperture widened to the entirety of the body. We were practicing the first of the Four Foundations of Mindfulness: It is quite possible that what I and the couple hundred other people were doing for these ten days bore similarity to what the Buddha and his followers did some 2500 years ago.[3]

This monograph is something of an ode to the Buddha—whose ideas have informed my entire adult life, even before, perhaps, as twenty years old is not quite adult. While I intend to honor the Buddha's legacy, I will also challenge conventional assumptions about his life, work, and their sequelae. The Buddha presented here is psychological not religious, human not divine, epistemological not ontological. Like a good psychologist, he wanted his work to be therapeutic—useful for alleviating suffering—a praxis, if you will, rather than philosophical speculation. That is the Buddha presented here. Admittedly, this representation is likely a fiction, as is probably any depiction of this figure.

En route from idealistic college graduate to doctoral psychologist to Buddhism and mindfulness author and teacher, I discovered that the version of Buddha presented in Tibetan Buddhism—indeed, all the different Buddhisms—might be quite different than the way he presented himself. This monograph attempts to reclaim the Buddha from the Buddhisms that he inspired. The story of Buddhism is a history of cultural and religious appropriation. I was surprised to learn that it took scholars until the middle of the nineteenth century to realize that disparate religions had a common source in the teachings of the Buddha.[4] The twenty-first century calls for a Western, indeed American, Buddhism that might be no Buddhism at all: materialistic, scientific, non-hierarchical. This version of Buddhism is also at risk for emulating other American "virtues" such as individualism, hedonism, and consumerism.[5]

Stephen Batchelor has proposed a secular Buddhism 2.0 to replace these ancient religions (Batchelor 2012). To go a bit further or a bit laterally, I propose a Buddha 2.0—the behavioral scientist Buddha.[6] The psychological—2.0—Buddha anticipated the evolutionary quirks that beset human creatures. Robert Wright claims that: "Buddhism's diagnosis of the human predicament is fundamentally correct, and that it's prescription is deeply valid and urgently important" (Wright 2017, xii) and makes his case by mapping the Buddha's teachings onto the findings of evolutionary psychology, defined as: "the study of how the human brain was designed—by natural selection—to misled us, even enslave us" (Wright 2017, 3). Indeed, many of Buddha's teachings can be situated in a contemporary, scientific, and Western framework (e.g., Flanagan 2011). Following Wright, the intent of Buddha's psychology could be captured in the hashtag #resistevolution.

The Buddha allegedly endeavored to undermine all of our fundamental assumptions about mind, self, and reality. His notion of radical empiricism—everything must be determined moment-by-moment without recourse to dogma—overturns conventional metaphysics and is a surprisingly modern approach. In my own life and meditation, I have sought to identify then set aside such assumptions: both metaphysical and personal. This letting go is hard—nay impossible—because metaphysics are heuristic—shortcuts to navigating through the complexities of perceiving the world and acting within it. At each turn, I must choose between regression to the familiar, comfortable, and limiting assumptions about mind, self, and reality or allow myself to venture into the alien, discomfiting, and boundless territory where mind is not just thoughts, images, and memories, where self does not exist as I had thought it existed, and where experience is much less stable and predictable than I would care to admit.

WHY I AM LEAVING THE MINDFULNESS MOVEMENT

As just presented, my Buddhist education started with His Holiness the Dalai Lama[7] and Tibetan Buddhism then settled into to silent, prolonged vipassana meditation, with a little bit of Zen sprinkled in. Since 2009 and the publication of my first book *108 Metaphors for Mindfulness* from the boutique Buddhist press Wisdom Publications, I have also taught the *dharma*—the collected wisdom of the Buddha.

My experiences with Buddhism and mindfulness provide a lens to view the cultural phenomenon—the explosive and controversial popularity of both mindfulness and Buddhism in America. A brief look at this phenomenon can help to make the case for the psychological Buddha that I will argue for in the remainder of this monograph. Mindfulness is no longer the province of the monastery and traditional Buddhist communities and has become a practice for non-affiliated individuals to undertake—at least 2 million of them (Morone, Moore, and Greco 2017). Meanwhile, over 3000 scientific articles on mindfulness have been published since 2010 (American Mindfulness Research Association 2017; Valerio 2016). Early Buddhist scholars like Thomas William Rhys Davids predicted that Buddhism would have a profound impact on the Western world, but he could not imagine the therapeutic, individualistic, and non-religious forms of Buddhism that proliferate today—chiefly as mindfulness-based interventions (or MBIs). In a devilish twist of fate, not only is mindfulness popular in the United States and the United Kingdom, it is going back to the traditional Buddhist strongholds of China, Korea, Japan, Sri Lanka, and Thailand as a standalone product (Cox and Webb 2015; Huang, Fay, & White 2017).[8] Mindfulness and other forms of meditation are a component part of positive psychology, spiritual psychology, mind–body medicine, cross cultural psychology, integral psychology, and integrative health care (Walsh and Shapiro 2006). Indeed, there has been a proliferation of MBIs (e.g., in addition to mindfulness-based stress reduction [MBSR], there is Mindfulness-Based Cognitive Therapy [MBCT], Mindfulness-Based Relapse Prevention [MBRP], and others).[9] I was an early adopter of mindfulness and I confess to some discomfort over the shape its popularity has taken, especially the hype that oversells the science (Dimidjian and Siegel 2015; Kozak 2018a), indeed that it has become a movement—as evidenced, in part, by a cover story in *Time Magazine*,[10] even a secular religion of sorts (Wilson 2014). Mindfulness can be found in many—perhaps all—sectors of society: healthcare, business, education, sports, military, and religion—of course, already parcel part of Buddhism (Gleig 2019), but influential in other religions such Unitarianism, Interfaith, and even the Episcopal church (e.g., Cooper 2017).

When I did the aforementioned vipassana retreat in 1989, mindfulness was not a household word. Jon Kabat-Zinn's bestselling book describing MBSR—*Full Catastrophe Living*— had not yet been published, and unless you read the 1982 *General Hospital Psychiatry* article on an obscure treatment called MBSR (Kabat-Zinn 1982) or one of Thich Nhat Hanh's books (e.g., *The Miracle of Mindfulness* 1982 or *Peace is Every Step* 1991[11]), you would probably never have heard of it. I was, thus, an early adopter of this now movement. As with all movements, there is a faddish tendency that distorts the original thing. Mindfulness has not been exempted from this bandwagon effect. To offer just one example: the Archetype brewery in Asheville, North Carolina, boasts the tagline: "Complex, mindful, living beer." Whatever could this mean? Another ironic example can be found in New Age guru and multimillionaire Deepak Chopra. Dr. Chopra made his fortune, in part, by selling Transcendental Meditation (TM), a different form of meditation. I was astonished to learn—from the original acquisitions editor for this book—that Dr. Chopra had gone over to the mindfulness side. She encouraged me to feature him in this book as a marketing hook. I do not think this caveat is what she had in mind.[12]

I've even contemplated *leaving the mindfulness movement,* but I am not sure what that means exactly. For all intents and purposes I have done just that, jumped off the mindfulness bandwagon. I decommissioned my website, I bequeathed my meditation studio to my protege, and with the exception of this monograph, I have not written "yet another mindfulness book." Even before departing, I was self-conscious about the movement. My bio includes the phrase that I was involved with mindfulness "long before it was popular." At the same time, I have not left of course, because I practice daily, still find it to be a valuable use of my time, and suspect that over time, even after the faddishness fades, mindfulness will demonstrate benefit in more rigorous scientific trials.[13] My personal practice is non-negotiable, invaluable for self-regulation and for the ongoing—if slowly accreting—cultivation of insight. However, and otherwise, I have moved away from offering mindfulness professionally.

Along with the mass popularity of mindfulness comes controversy—dharma wars—over the role of explicit ethics and Buddhist references in the teaching of mindfulness. Detractors note that while mindfulness is a way of paying attention, little attention gets paid to what is being attended to and worse, the focus on intrapsychic experience and individual responsibility could be a neoliberal form of subjugation: "Critics of mindfulness contest the extent to which mindfulness, as a therapeutic or social movement, is a revolutionary force for individual awakening and liberation, or a conspiracy to enslave individuals to consumer capitalism but making them individually responsible for their own suffering, distress, and well being" (Stanley, Purser and Singh 2018, 5; also see Purser and Loy 2013; Brazier 2013; Tan 2012; Purser 2019). Another critique of the popular rendition of mindfulness is that it appears to lack the quality of *appamada,* that gets translated as heedfulness, vigilance (Krägeloh 2018) or as diligence (Peacock 2014). "This 'recollective' aspect is obscured as soon as mindfulness is understood as simply being fully attentive in the present moment or remaining in a state of nonjudgmental awareness, neither of which would seem to have much to do with remembering something said or done in the past" (Batchelor 2015, 239). Batchelor, here, paraphrases Jon Kabat-Zinn's standard definition of mindfulness.[14] This recollection is not just of the moment or of oneself but can refer to the entire project of the Buddha's teaching. Taking mindfulness out of Buddhism is nothing short of McMindfulness—a light, fast-food version of transformative Buddhist practice (Purser and Loy 2013, Purser 2019).

The proliferation of mindfulness has been maligned for its superficial, amoral approach—The psychological perspective of the Buddha presented here might go some way at rendering these dharma wars moot. Those that decry mindfulness taken out of Buddhism would realize that—functionally—the Buddha did the same thing; those that shy away from mentioning the Buddha would be empowered to do so because he stands apart from Buddhism.

Despite problems with the mindfulness movement, Buddhist scholars, teachers, and practitioners would otherwise probably be toiling away in obscurity. Without it, I, and thousands of others, would not have had a career as a mindfulness-based psychotherapist or mindfulness-based stress reduction (MBSR) teachers. Without the Buddhist religions that have elaborated, extravasated, and expanded upon the Buddha's original teachings, his dharma would not have likely survived. Does the Buddhist baby—as it were—have to be thrown out with the bathwater? Take Zen for example: it was a reaction against orthodoxy, and over time instantiated its own traditionalism, became an animal far removed from the Buddha's project. Tibetan Buddhism is a colorful beast that is, thanks to the Dalai Lama, the most vivid image of Buddhism in popular imagination. But very little in the way of its practices or rituals resembles the Buddha's original project (e.g., ritualized imagery practices involving deities). Of course, the Dalai Lama espouses the Four Noble Truths and preaches compassion just as the Buddha did. Turning away from Zen and Vajrayana is not meant to question the potential value of mantra, tantra, and yantra. It is not to say that no improvement on the Buddha's original insights is efficacious. It *is* to say that if we want to have a true—if fictional—psychological Buddha then Buddhist religions have little to add.

Fictionalized or no, it is safe to say if the Buddha were around today, he would scarcely recognize the things people are doing in association with his name. He might be pleased to see people yearning for transformation, amazed at the science starting to confirm some of his observations, and dismayed over the sectarianism, dogmatism, and persistent metaphysics that characterizes much of Buddhism. The psychological Buddha did not want to be the charismatic founder of a religion, and yet this has been his legacy. The irony is that without these "corruptions" we would know nothing about him.

NOTES

1. While the future Buddha was known as Siddhartha Gotama, the name Siddhartha was added posthumously by some 500 years as part of the Buddha's hagiography (Peacock 2008).

2. Some thirty-five years later, I still construe myself as a bodhisattva even though I have rejected the underlying cosmology of rebirth and remote karma—i.e., one's deeds in this life determine one's fate in the next.

3. I will talk more about this retreat later in the book; I have written elsewhere that this was the single-most difficult *and* valuable experience of my life.

4. The modern conception of Buddha and Buddhism commenced about 150 years ago when Western scholars were first able to translate Pali, Sanskrit, and Chinese Buddhist scriptures. Yet, as Lopez (2013) clarifies, the West has known about the Buddha since the early part of the Christian Era: "Some of the Indians obey the precepts of Boutta; whom, on account of his extraordinary sanctity, they have raised to divine honors" (Saint Clement of Alexandra quoted in Lopez 2013, ix). For Saint Clement, the Buddha was Boutta one of the hundreds of corruptions of the Buddha's name. Some of my favorites: Boodoo, Daybot, Fotique, Sagamoni Borcan (a variation of Sakyamuni Buddha and what the Mongols called him), and Xocia.

5. Ironically, mindfulness is taking root in a culture notorious for self-indulgence, self-promotion, and self-aggrandizement. In the fervor to adopt mindfulness, the *culture of me* (Young-Eisendrath 2008) has invited in an empirical psychology that seeks to undermine that very sense of self that gives rise to that sense of "me." Many people turning on to mindfulness do not realize its roots in Buddhism and without extensive meditation practice may never get to the explicit insight that the self is not essential—not a soul seeking reunification with absolute consciousness. Even for those practicing Buddhism, the irony prevails—Buddhist religions have found a warm reception on the capitalist, materialistic soils of the United States and other Western developed nations (e.g., Seager 2012). It is counterintuitive that the self that wants to be a better self just might—if it is not too careful— meditate itself out of existence.

6. Of course, Batchelor's Buddhism 2.0 is predicated on a secular recasting of the Buddha and contains the idea, if not explicit, of a Buddha 2.0.

7. Prior to going to India, I attended the 1984 Inner Science Conference held at Amherst College; I was a junior in college myself then at nearby Tufts University. This conference was the precursor to the later Mind and Life conferences and featured Western scientists, physicians, and philosophers giving talks interspersed with lectures by His Holiness.

8. The mindfulness movement is part of the larger trend of meditation, yoga, and health consciousness. There are over 10 million meditation practitioners in the United States and over 100 million worldwide.

9. Another influential strain—without an explicit mindfulness moniker—can be found in Eckhart Tolle's *Power of Now* (2004), which extols of the virtues of a radical attention to the present moment.

10. This *Time* cover has been much maligned for featuring a blond, attractive white woman, wearing a tight-fitting white leotard.

11. Another popular and influential book, especially for me, was Jack Kornfield and Joseph Goldstein's influential 1987 *Seeking the Heart of Wisdom: The Path of Insight Meditation* (reissued in 2001 as a Shambhala Classic and then again in 2018 as a Shambhala Pocket Library edition).

12. TM and mindfulness share a common core of meditation practice, but their approach to mental focus is diametrically opposed. TM asks its participant to focus on a mantra—a repeated word or phrase. It is a concentration practice that attempts to tune out distractions to engender a state of peacefulness. Mindfulness includes a

concentrative component—most often on breathing, yet its aim is not filtering out distraction but bringing greater awareness to the momentary phenomena of the mind and the senses. If a state of peacefulness occurs that is an incidental benefit, not the aim of practice. TM is a yogic practice because it seeks to change state. While the Buddha was reputed to be prodigious yogi, mindfulness meditation seeks to increase awareness rather than produce an altered state of consciousness.

13. There are other vestiges where I remain engaged. I teach a fourth-year elective to University of Vermont Larner College of Medicine students on integrating mindfulness into their medical practices—for their personal wellbeing, to ameliorate some of the stressful effects of doctoring, as well as to cultivate a greater sense of clinical presence.

14. As just discussed, mindfulness can be a state governed by a certain kind of attention—variably defined—and it can refer to a set of meditation practices described in the *Satipathana Sutta*. These mindfulness meditations are known as *vipassana* or insight meditation (e.g., Goldstein, 2016, Rosenberg 2004, Rosenberg and Zimmerman 2013).

Introduction
The Psychological Buddha

Buddha. The name cannot be uttered without conjuring exotic associations: ancient, wise, Asian, sainly, and religious. For some mistaken few, a statue found in Chinese restaurants comes to mind, a fat, happy figure that is not the actual historical Buddha but the folklore Budai in China. For opportunistic others, "Buddha" is a trendy marketing icon: the Zen of whatever.[1] For millions of Asian Buddhists, the Buddha was, for all intents and purposes, a god—omniscient, superhuman, and spotlessly moral. No matter how multifarious, Buddha almost always represents something religious, spiritual, or both. Almost, but not always. Secular Buddhism seeks to separate him from the religions bearing his name. Buddha, then, takes the form of his representers and their purposes—savior, secularist—the words attributed to him can be used to support a multitude of positions. In this book, I present *my* Buddha, an idiosyncratic, likely fictional, iconoclastic version, influenced by my being a psychologist, one-time spiritual adherent, and current atheistic skeptic.

It is a bit of legerdemain to say that I am secularizing the Buddha's teachings because they already are—or appear to be before they were coopted by the religions of Buddhism. My Buddha invented mindfulness but I am not sure what he would think of its current popularity: Flattered? Frustrated? Furious? All of these after a fashion, I imagine. My Buddha was scientific—a cognitive–behavioral psychotherapist and an evolutionary psychologist—fascinated with how the mind works and dedicated to making life better through better use of awareness, a process that required wisdom, ethics, and meditative training to transcend the dictates of evolutionary programming.[2] My Buddha, like me, was also a spiritual seeker, skeptic, and dedicated to helping others. This psychological Buddha—Buddha, PhD, if you will: 1) was incredulous about metaphysical speculation, 2) advocated radical existential responsibility-taking (both positions 1 and 2 undermine religious dogma), and 3) his pedagogical curriculum was geared towards changing instinctual patterns of reactivity selected by evolution. The Buddha as psychologist, then, provides a lens to interpret the current controversies surrounding mindfulness and Buddhism—traditional and otherwise—as they proliferate in the West. At the same time, the anti-metaphysics, pro-responsibility, impulse-changing stance hews away the religious and mystical, leaving a psychotherapeutic project. Rather than cherry-pick passages that make my case, I will own the bias at the outset. I will cite sources that support my view recognizing that there are other sources that present a more religious view. I will not pretend that my interpretations are the true ones but, hopefully, they are compelling and, more importantly, *useful ones.* Since my Buddha looks like me—psychologist, psychotherapist, yogi, pedagogue—my rendering of him will appeal to people like myself who are secular, scientifically literate, skeptical, and self-reliant—people who do not like authority, tradition, and dogma, however expertly disguised.

For this modernized, psychologized, version of the Buddha, I rely upon scholars such as Richard Gombrich, John Peacock, Stephen Batchelor, Andrew Olendzki, and others. Also, I rely on my own interpretations from practicing various forms of Buddhism over several decades. A psychotherapeutic Buddha makes sense to me. Nearly forty years ago at the same time, I encountered the Dalai Lama and before dedicating myself to the Buddha's insight meditation, I practiced a form of yoga similar to the prevailing religion of the Buddha's time—the very religion he rejected. My guru-based Brahmanical practice of Siddha Yoga, a form of Kashmir Shaivism, was geared towards accessing—*atman*—the essential self—my *soul*—the ultimate self that we are exiled from by virtue of being embodied. Once accessed, my individual consciousness could be re-united, merged with the absolute, universal consciousness in a glorious homecoming of bliss. According to Shaivism, self-realization is understanding that atman and the rest of the universe are not separate entities—they represent a nondual awareness, a unity. These Siddha Yoga practices were effective at inducing altered states of consciousness but less successful at inspiring wisdom, at least for my young self. An immaterial soul is a comforting notion—there is something of me—the core part of me—that persists eternally, infinitely, absolutely. Some version of essence is found in virtually all religious systems from the Christian soul to the aforementioned atman. Indeed, an essential self or soul is a concept that 90 percent of world's population still believes in one form or another (Flanagan 2011). The Buddha is the outlier—he negated atman as will be detailed below—but it cannot be said that Buddhism is the outlier because soul has crept back in with the recrudescence of essence (e.g., Park 2012).

There might not be much harm in believing my essence can unify with a greater consciousness, after all the goal is a nondual form of awareness, yet in day-to-day life, essences lead to taking positions regarding others, tribalism, and warring. The essential self leads to the fundamental attribution error—*you* act badly due to your essence, *my* transgressions are situational. The problem with essence is the presumed duality that must be transcended, even if one eventually achieves a state of nonduality. Essence requires something apart and something enduring, ever-unchanging. The Buddha rejected essence because meditation showed him a ceaseless flux of phenomenon with nothing fixed or stable—no essential core. Atman for him seemed only a wishful mental construct—a metaphysical and, ultimately, unverifiable idea.

In 1989, I recapitulated the Buddha's discovery on my first vipassana (aka insight meditation, the source material for mindfulness meditation) meditation retreat. Focusing on momentary phenomenon *showed* me there was no core there—only energy, vibration, expansion, and contraction. I described an experience of intense knee pain that I experienced during a sitting of strong determination (meditation sessions where participants are encouraged not to move their posture at all):

> I turned my attention *towards* the sensations instead of away, which is where I instinctively wanted to go. After a week of practice, I had developed a level of concentration that allowed me to look precisely at my own bodily discomfort. My first approximation of that discomfort was that it was solid, intractable, brutal—like a railroad spike had been pounded into my knee. As I got closer to it with concentration, I noticed something else: oscillation, variation, and cessation. Within the discomfort there were moments of peace surrounded by moments of intensity. There was no "pain," only energy. The story of how awful it was dropped away, leaving only the bare experience of it. After that sitting, the tension in my muscles released; my body relaxed into the moment, and the rest of the retreat was free from that particular suffering. (Kozak 2015c, 3)

This insight was a gateway. It relieved me of the need to protect some essence—some *thing* that is my self. Instead I could participate in the flow of energy with curiosity, even wonder. This understanding of what the Buddha called not self (an-atman) was not conceptual, not a dictum to be believed; it was a direct experience.

During the span of some seven years from my time with Siddha Yoga to attending this retreat, I had covered some of the same ground that the Buddha had covered, if more modestly and without the years of ascetic deprivations. He spent time getting "high" with yoga masters—trying to reunite his atman with Brahma—but once he left those blissful altered states of consciousness, he found himself on the other side of ecstasy back in the mire of being—often referred to as *samsara* or worldly existence. More specifically, these rarified states did not resolve the big existential problems: why is life so difficult; how do we make sense of life given sickness, old age, and ultimate death? I too, found sweet relief from the burdens of life when ensconced in my guru's love but once separated from that state of grace, I was back in my own version of existential uncertainty. I did not know it at the time but I was looking for a more durable method for addressing the challenges of being an embodied, intermittently conscious being, and I found that in vipassana meditation. I am happier now that I do not feel metaphysically deficient by being estranged from the absolute. Everything fluctuates—states come and go, nothing is exempt. The Buddha did not have a guru and neither do I, any longer, although I look to Buddha's legacy for inspiration, guidance, and connection. The Buddha is my role model not my deity. It is hard not to sanctify him, as Asians have done for millennia (Lopez 2013) though, almost impossible not to make him into a salvific master. I try to counteract this god-making by remembering the Buddha's flaws. He was precocious, yes, exceptional, yes, yet very human at times, as will be explored in the next part.

I am fond of the Buddhist religions: I have practiced in Zen temples; I received teachings from His Holiness the Dalai Lama in the very place that the Buddha purportedly awakened. I am grateful for these institutions for without them, the teachings of the Buddha would most likely—almost definitely—have been lost. They have been faithful guardians of the dharma, even as they have urged that wisdom into religious forms. Despite my affections, I am suggesting that for the purposes of a psychological interpretation of the Buddha, we can skip over Buddhism. I am not saying that improvements could not have been made over the past 2500 years, that, for example, the imagery-driven practices of Vajrayanic dzogchen (Khenpo and Surya Das, 2008) might not be highly efficacious. I am not implying that the historical innovations of Bodhidharma, Nagarjuna, and Dogen are not important, they are just not relevant for the scope of this monograph.

THE BUDDHA AS PSYCHOLOGIST

The opening lines of the Dammapada are: "All experience is preceded by mind,/Led by mind,/Made by mind" (Fronsdal 2015, 1). I am not the first to suggest that the Buddha was more of a psychologist than a philosopher, metaphysician, or preacher (Arch and Landy 2015; Batchelor 2012; Brach 2002, 2012; Carmody 2015; Olendzki 2010, 2016; Ryan and Rigby 2015; van Vugt 2015). There is a growing literature on mindfulness and psychotherapy (e.g., Germer et al. 2016; Hayes et al. 2011, 2016; Germer and Seigel 2014; Orsillo and Roemer 2011; Roemer and Orsillo 2010; Segal et al. 2013, just to include the citations from the titles on my own bookshelf) and Buddhism and psychoanalysis (e.g., Jennings 2011; Magid 2002; Safran 2005; Young-Eisendrath and Muramoto 2003). And while there have been many mentions of the Buddha as psychologist, there has been no in-depth treatment of this issue. I was surprised that a search of book titles with "Buddha" and "Psychologist" yielded nothing. Representing the *Buddha before Buddhism* (also the catchy title of Gil Fronsdal's 2016 book) suggests that the Buddha was *more* interested in the practical benefits of his teachings (e.g., Mikulas 2018; Peacock 2014) rather than asserting the nature of ultimate reality as his Brahman cohort was fond of doing and as is the wont of most religious founders, prophets, and messiahs. And he was not just a psychologist, he was, perhaps, the world's first psychologist, long before there was such a thing (Peacock 2014). Of course, long before contemporary scholars noticed the Buddha's psychology, the Buddha spoke of the mind and behavior. The opening lines of the *Dhammapada,* the most famous of Buddhist poems are explicitly psychological. Mind does not just precede experience it *leads* it, indeed *creates* it. The Buddha realized: "My gosh, how long have I been fooled, cheated, & deceived by this mind!" (Thanissaro 1999, 84). He exhorted anyone who cared to listen: *know* this mind, learn how to *work* with this mind, make this mind into a good *leader*, and like a good craftsman, a *skillful* fabricator of experience.

Not everyone agrees with the Buddha-as-psychologist formulation: "The Buddha, it could be said, did not teach religion nor did he teach psychology or philosophy. The Buddha taught dharma" (Kearney and Hwang 2018, 288). Dharma is a problematic term, having some currency in English vernacular (e.g., the television show *Dharma and Greg*) without much clarity on its meaning. Dharma can refer to the collected teachings of the Buddha and what those teachings point to—truths, realities, and principles of experience. Dharma is also a mind state, which confuses the issue. By asserting universal truths, dharma has epistemological baggage as well—it has a different look and feel than the science of psychology. Some of dharma's truths can be experienced subjectively (first person empiricism) and many might be hard to submit to rigorous experimentation (Popper's World Three). Nonetheless, it is hard for me to reconcile dharma in its broader sense as anything other than applied psychology. For the Buddha, dharma was the reliable fundamentals of embodied human existence, just as light and sound perception are the underlying psychophysics of experience, if you will. The dharma is, then, the Buddha's *Principles of Psychology* and much weightier than William James's ground-breaking two-volume edition. The Buddha viewed these dharmic principles, such as dependent origination (*paticca samuppada*), as elemental forces, similar in their function to gravity. They were detectable, predictive, and inviolate. To make dharma its own special category only seems to mystify what is otherwise a set of straightforward—and testable—claims. The Buddha's science is a first-person introspective process aimed at clarifying empirical phenomenon. Now, we can use third-person science in conjunction with first-person perception to verify the Buddha's claims (e.g., Young 2016). I would like to think that he would approve because it extends his project beyond the means and needs of his time.

Like a good psychologist, the Buddha was curious about the phenomenological present. He focused on three things—the hallmarks of existence— 1) the subjective sense of being alive (*dukkha,* Pali, *duhka,* Sanskrit), 2) the objective sense of how things are constantly changing (*anicca,* Pali, *anitya,* Sanskrit),[3] and 3) the nature of self (*anatta,* Pali, *anatman,* Sanskrit). The Buddha famously said: "I teach suffering and the end of suffering" with suffering being the most common translation of the Pali term *dukkha.* A problem arises at the outset: translating dukkha. The presumption is, typically, that there is a one-to-one word correspondence between the Pali and English terms, but dukkha refers to a wide range of experiences. "Suffering" as a translation suffices: it covers much ground but does not capture all of its meaning and misses the pervasive, edgy, and sneaky quality that is also dukkha. Dukkha has also been translated as stress (e.g., Bhikkhu Bodhi's translation of the Pali Canon; e.g., Bodhi 2003, 2012), dissatisfaction (Bernhard 2013), dis-ease (Pali Dictionary), and anguish (Batchelor 1998). All of these are correct and none of them are complete: "There is no word in English covering the same ground as Dukkha does in Pali. . . . Misery, distress, agony, affliction and woe are never right. They are all much too strong & are only mental" (Pali Dictionary). The trouble stems from forgetting the rhetorical intent of the term—it is one of the Buddha's principle metaphors. The word was extent but he applied it in a new way. The Buddha appears to have recognized the polysemy of the concept he wished to convey and chose a metaphor to express it based on the contrast to *sukha,* which means pleasant or agreeable.[4] *Du* can mean "asunder, apart, away from" or "bad, woe" and *akkha* meaning an axle such as one found on an oxcart. The Buddha may have been conveying the sense of something being off, like a broken axle or a bad wheel on an oxcart. Unawakened life is the metaphorical equivalent of traveling on that cart such that each moment is colored by that broken axle. It does not matter if that cart (i.e., experience) is painful or pleasurable—the wheel is still broken—the rider wobbles, shakes, and bounces up and down at the whim of the malfunctioning axle and the rutted, potholed, washboarded dirt road the carts travels over. This metaphor could be extended to the wheel itself. If the wheel is bent, it can likewise distort the ride. Like a bicycle wheel that is out of true, the Buddha sought to "true" the wheel to get it rolling more smoothly. An alternate etymology is offered by Peacock when he parses dukkha into *dus* (dirty, difficult, hard) and *kha* (space, atmosphere, sky). The result is a "bad space" or "difficult situation" (2008, 210). Peacock connects dukkha to the Wheel of Life (a map of rebirth scenarios; see below) since dukkha referred to the hole in a wheel where the axle went: "This metaphorically referred to the failure of the 'wheel of life' to run smoothly when under the influence of 'ignorance'" (2008, 210).

The enduring highlight from the Buddha's forty-five year teaching career appeared early on, encapsulated in the Four Noble Truths, his very first lecture. A thumbnail sketch: The starting point is dukkha: something is off; life is difficult. This is so because of how we are constituted and how we manage our thoughts, feelings, and behaviors. If the mind does not take account of impermanence, including impermanence of self, then dukkha is generated as the Buddha cautioned: "People grieve what they take as "mine"/—No possession exists forever" (Fronsdal 2016, 63). The Buddha identified three metaphorical fires that afflict the mind: desire (*raga*), aversion (*dosa*), and confusion (*moha*) over the three hallmarks—what they are and how they work—drive dukkha. The fires, though, can be put out, and this typically requires a combination of wisdom, ethics, and meditative practice.

The Buddha's model of mind can be viewed as empirical—grounded in experience—and natural—it does not require supernatural explanations, concepts, or—importantly—beliefs. The Buddha was a determinist, each experience arises from what came before. Yet, while everything is determined, there is some kind of awareness mediated by agency that can participate in the causal chain of events or what the Buddha called "this-that causality."[5] Thus, we are both determined and determining. Every moment presents the stuff that one must deal with: the energies at play, the challenges to be negotiated. Dukkha and its causes covers the first and second noble truths. The third suggests that participating in the deterministic flow of experience without succumbing to the fires along with a full appreciation of impermanence and non-essentiality of self can bring about a state of cessation: *nibbana* (Pali)—aka *nirvana* (Sanskrit). The fourth truth is a set of eight interrelated practices, ideals, and recommendations that guide thinking, action, and practice that facilitate the process of cessation—putting out the fires. These eight include wisdom (attitudes), behavior (ethics), and training (meditation, e.g., mindfulness).

Muddying the Psychological Waters with Spirituality

Caroline Brazier (2014) makes frequent reference to the Buddha's teaching as spiritual in nature: a "spiritual process" leading to "spiritual transformation" or "spiritual breakthrough." I wonder what she means by this and I have to keep wondering because—of course—it is not operationally defined. I also wonder why it is necessary to invoke spirituality. Spiritual often refers to something that cannot be measured or described or that transcends ordinary human consciousness. But I do not think any of these apply to the Buddha's teachings. It is cleaner—and still accurate—to replace one with the other: a *psychological process* leading to *psychological transformation*. If there was nothing *spiritual* in the Buddha's teaching, there is plenty of *spirit* in the Buddhist religions—precisely because they *are* religions and not strict therapeutic enterprises.

The Buddha's dharma can appeal to the zealous, the pious, and the skeptical—all at once. It is easy to conflate the dharma with religion and also, apparently with psychology. Mikulas (2018) in a chapter titled "Buddhist Ethics, Spiritual Practice, and the Three Yanas" is a case in point. Mikulas first orients the reader to the Buddha's psychology and then reviews the religious traditions of Buddhism including Theravada, Mahayana, and Vajrayana, losing the psychological thread. Moving even farther from psychology, he emphasizes the role of faith in Mahayana. He also makes the following claim: if "essential Buddhism [the teachings of the Buddha before the Buddhist religions] is psychology not religion, then ethics can be understood as a major factor influencing personal/spiritual growth. Ethical behavior is part of an overall spiritual practice that affects body/mind/spirt. Ethically good behavior improves biological health, psychological well-being and functioning, and awakening" (Mikulas 2018, 103). With the exception of awakening, none of these terms are defined and the definition of awakening is cursory. I am also unclear how the psychological grounding of the Buddha's teachings makes it spiritual (also undefined as was the case with Brazier). The Buddha was concerned with behavioral and psychological change, so perhaps we can uncritically accept personal growth as a desired outcome. Mikulas's conflations are typical in the literature; it is hard for psychology to stand by itself in the Buddhist world.

Krägeloh (2018) counterpose mindfulness as a "science of happiness" with Buddhist "salvation" and I wonder if this is a distinction without a difference. The Buddha had a soteriology but one explicitly geared toward happiness or, perhaps, more accurately, the absence of dukkha, which when taken to an extreme fosters the ultimate happiness—nirvana. The Buddha sought a means to address dukkha—he did so by creating a "science" of happiness comprised of knowledge, commitment, effective action, and rigorous practice (the four ennobling praxes to be covered in part II).

To avoid committing the same errors of omission, I need to clarify my use of terms. Psychology is the study of subjective experience, motivation, behavior, emotion, and other domains of experience. Philosophy also takes these as its subject. Psychology, though, seeks to verify ideas through scientific experimentation, whether via qualitative or quantitative methods. In similar fashion, the Buddha employed a method of qualitative introspective analysis—a first-person empiricism. He encouraged his followers to do the same. Spiritual refers to intangible things and so does psychology, so non-material is not very useful as a distinction. Spirituality is one of those terms—like pornography—that is difficult to define and is often left to being recognized when one sees it. I use the term with great hesitation. For me spirituality is a willingness to transcend one's selfish interests to be concerned for something larger than one's individual life, such as the welfare of others.[6] In my sense of spirituality, there is no intelligence in the universe, at least not one that is anything other than indifferent to my existence.[7] When others use *spiritual* I cannot vouch for what they mean. I have been accused of being a rationalist and I welcomed that as a compliment. The same colleague issuing this characterization also mentioned that science has its own metaphysics. I countered that it is more of an issue of physics than metaphysics; at the same time, he is also right. Science does have metaphysics or, perhaps, more accurately, axiology. It values the rational over the irrational, the true over the false, progress over stasis, skepticism and critical thinking over certitude and dogma. I embrace scientific axiology. Its values overlap with my values: I was trained as a behavioral scientist and I've promoted scientific literacy (Diamond and Kozak 1994; Herreid and Kozak 1995).

NOT SELF: THE CASE AGAINST ESSENTIALISM

Buddhism is notorious for its claim that there is no self. For example, the Buddha might have said: your self is more like a river or a fire than a fixed thing. This no-self proposition is one of the most difficult concepts for a Western audience to understand (Kozak 2011b; 2015a). Olendzki points out, "Nothing is so cherished in contemporary culture as the self, so much so that one might even say it acts as the organizing principle around which all contemporary culture is patterned. And nothing is quite as uniquely Buddhist as the critique of this idea" (Olendzki 2016, 109). It is often misconstrued that the Buddha said there was no such thing as self, that any sense self was delusion and should be abandoned. The Buddha might have said: there is no physical "you"—what you regard yourself to be arises out of what you perceive, what you feel, what you think, what you are aware of. A more careful reading shows that he did not deny that there were selves but rather that he argued for two things: 1) the self—whatever it might be—is misapprehended—seen to be more than it actually is and 2) self is fabricated by the mind, nothing more than an epiphenomenon. This misconstrued self is reified. Reification takes the abstract and makes it concrete, it is a process of fabrication—a synthetic, constructive process, in one sense of fabricating. But, fabrication also has another sense—lying. This reified self, this self-as-noun is a lie—and should not be believed. The self-as-noun takes ownership over things and with that staking of possession, a world of attendant anxieties. Proprietary objects need to be cared for, protected, repaired if damaged, worried over—will they be lost or stolen? will they wear out, break? will I stop enjoying them?

The Buddha did not articulate a developmental model of self but if he had, the realization of anatman would have been the culminating stage.[8] From phenomenological investigations of his interior experience, he found that his self as subjectively perceived was not as stable, enduring, or autonomous as he thought it was. Self is fabricated in both the sense of being constructed *from* and distorted *by* language, culture, and biology. Without deliberate, dedicated, and disciplined intervention, self concepts will be erroneous and give rise to a sense of being out of sorts with the world in each moment of existence (contributing a large measure of dukkha). The Buddha recommended a praxis that could fundamentally alter self concept and liberate individuals from the psychological pain that it otherwise causes. The Buddha recognized that the problematic—folk psychological—root metaphor for self was that of a thing: that the self is mistakenly perceived as being "closer to wood than wave" (Kusserow 2019). Atman was thing-like in its essentialness even though it was immaterial. After all, while not tangible, souls are nouns. But for the Buddha, this objectified noun-self was the chief source of unhappiness. Instead of thingness, he offered a new metaphor—self-as-process. For him, self was more like a flowing river or a raging fire—always changing:

> In his view, the more closely we examine ourselves, the harder it becomes to find anything that we can pinpoint as a fixed entity. The human personality was not a static being to which things happened. Put under the microscope of yogic analysis, each person was a process. The Buddha liked to use such metaphors as a blazing fire or a rushing stream to describe the personality; it had some kind of identity, but was never the same from one moment to another. (Armstrong 2001, 111–12)

Preeminent mindfulness teacher Joseph Goldstein likens self to a complex weather event:

> Imagine for moment a great summer storm. There is wind and rain, thunder and lightening; but there is no storm apart from these elements. "Storm" is simply the concept or designation for this interrelated mix of phenomena. In the same way, when we look more closely at what we are calling "self," we see a constellation of rapidly changing elements, each one of which is itself momentary and insubstantial. (Goldstein 2016, 181)

This verb-self has access to a more enduring and durable form of happiness not available to the noun-self.

While the flickering fire captures the inessential, changing nature of self, fire served another metaphoric purpose for the Buddha: It described the mind's condition—ablaze with desire, fear, and confusion, the so-called three fires. The mind on fire cannot see itself as an ever-changing process, thinks of itself as the *one* that things happen to, the subject at the center of yearning and aversion. Gombrich further elucidates the Buddha's metaphor:

> He derived inspiration from Vedic speculation about fire, and saw it as a non-random process which was appetitive and yet operated without an agent, simply coming to an end when the fuel ran out. He took this as a model both for consciousness and more generally for how the life and experience of a living being could be self-generating processes for which it was otiose to posit any additional, unchanging entity to act as an agent. (Gombrich 2009, 196)

A person is a tangible entity—a body occupying space. But unless we make self synonymous with this body, the entailments of self are always abstractions—a psychological entity, or group of entities: public self, private self, hidden self, etc. The abstraction that characterizes self requires metaphors to flesh it out, so to speak. Not-self says there is no *one* but, instead, a complex of stories that fuel dukkha. There is, of course, the subjective experience of a concretized self, a mistaken sense of enduring self, a misconstrued—otiose as Gombrich warned—personage who seems to stand outside of the phenomenal flow of experience—the very core of my self, the most intimate sense of being myself. The Buddha said "no"—no matter how compelling it seems—there is no such self.[9] There is only that flow and we are at our best when we are in concordance with that stream of momentary experiences.

The Buddha negated atman—or any notion of fixed self—because 1) it was a speculative metaphysical construct and 2) he noted, from his personal phenomenological investigations, that self could not be found anywhere in the mind, i.e., there was no introspective empirical data to support the existence of a self. Again, the Buddha did not deny that there were persons or even that there was a self (Wright 2017), only that this self did not conform to the essentialist, folk psychological, and spiritual conventions of the day. Rather, he denied that self could be located in space and time as a discrete object. Despite its fluidity and non-locatability, the self becomes reified, which leads to a large measure of the variance in human misery. The Buddha's insight into not-self opens the way to its transformation: we got ourselves into this mess and—with some insight and hard work—we can get ourselves out of it.

Fronsdal (2016) translates *bhava* as becoming and I would clarify this as the process of self-making—giving the self (atman) an existential status. Self-making is a process of reification, taking the self-as-verb and making it into self-as-noun. "To live without clinging to self is to live without clinging to any states of becoming. It is also be free from anxiety about what will happen at the moment of death" (Fronsdal 2016, 45).

Language, Metaphor, and Self

A variety of literary giants have recognized the power of metaphor to shape experience. George Eliot in Middlemarch said, "All of us, grave or light, get our thoughts entangled in metaphors, and act fatally on the strength of them." Robert Frost warned, "Unless you are at home in the metaphor, unless you have had your proper poetical education in the metaphor, you are not safe anywhere." The late Princeton psychologist Julian Jaynes emphasized, "For metaphor is not a mere trick of language, as it is so often slighted in the old schoolbooks on composition; it is the very constitutive ground of language" (Jaynes 1976, 48). When it comes to the mind, linguist George Lakoff and philosopher Mark Johnson claim: "It is virtually impossible to think or talk about the mind in any serious way without conceptualizing it metaphorically" (Lakoff and Johnson 1999, 235). Geary points out that "Metaphor is a way with thought long before it is a way with words" (Geary 2011, 3). C. S. Lewis, reflected that "When we pass beyond pointing to individual sensible objects, when we begin to think of cases, relations, of mental states or acts, we become incurably metaphorical. We apprehend none of these things except through metaphor" (Lewis quoted in Geary 2012, 169). Metaphors are not just used as literary devices but are integrated into the very structure of language and every concept the human mind generates.

The Buddha's preference was to proceed via metaphor: "Very well then, my friend, I will give you an analogy; for there are cases where it is through the use of an analogy that intelligent people can understand the meaning of what is being said" (Thanissaro Bhikkhu 1999). One way to understand the Buddha's teaching of not-self is that our implicit sense of our selves operates through the same principles as metaphor. The Buddha had a better metaphor than the ubiquitous folk-psychological one for self: verb instead of noun, wave instead of wood, after all wood can burn. As discussed in the previous section, the Buddha's primary observation was that misapprehending the nature of self was the principle cause of suffering, misery, and dissatisfaction. We do not realize that the we are addicted to telling stories, starring ourselves—the "Me Movie" (Kozak 2016) as it were—and that our fortunes rise and fall with its dramas. No matter how good the movie is, it cannot change the fact that there is no solid, essential actor in the lead role. Through the same mechanisms that make literature exciting, we influence our own consciousness making us "storytelling animals" (Gottschall 2012). Gottschall reflects: "How bizarre is it that when we experience a story—whether in a book, a film, or a song [or our own mind]—we allow ourselves to be invaded by the teller. The story maker penetrates our skulls and seizes control of our brains. . . . Squatting there in the dark, milking glands, kindling neurons" (2012, xv). Looking at the self from the vantage point of metaphor, if self-identity is a solid object or even an immaterial yet immutable soul, then it might be subject to the same forces that physical objects are subject to—gravity, mass, inertia. If the self is a thing, it has features like a container and things can be put into and taken out of it, such as painful memories.

The Buddha skillfully manipulated language to encourage a different way of seeing things. The late Galway Kinnel spoke of what it is to be a poet when he said, "Poetry is somebody standing up, so to speak, and saying, with as little concealment as possible, what it is for him or her to be on earth at this moment." Not only did the Buddha use satire, metaphor, irony, and other poetics—he taught through poetry (Fronsdal 2016). The Buddha used these tools to teach dharma—his revelation, a simple yet direct psychological insights into how the mind worked and at the same time an intervention to cure the tendencies of mind that give rise to unsatisfactory existence.

The Buddha was a master at minting metaphors and he used this capacity as *upaya*—skillful means. By tailoring images to his audience, he was able to reach farmers with farming metaphors and kings with royal ones. The Buddha had an uncanny sense of using the familiar to provide a bridge to the unfamiliar: "The Buddha's skill in teaching the Dharma, demonstrated in his ability to adapt his message to the context in which it was delivered. Parables, metaphors, and similes formed an important part of his teaching repertoire, skillfully tailored to suit the level of his audience" (Keown 1996, 118). Keown's sentiment is echoed by Batchelor when he said, "The Buddha had a great sensitivity to the power of metaphor (Batchelor 2009). Gombrich also points out that "The sermons are chock-full of analogies, similes, and metaphors. Indeed, what else would one expect of a thinker who had concluded that language could give pointers, but could not by its nature give exact expression to the truth about reality?" (Gombrich 2009,165). The Buddha also favored lists.[10] About 1000 metaphors[11] appear in the Pali Canon addressing 568 concepts. Earth images were used 41 times, fire 58 times, air 32, and water 114—pools, the sea, floods, and rivers. Animals included elephants, cows, lions, horses, snakes, deer, birds, camels, goats, wolves, watchdogs, cats, and mice (Hecker 2009). The Buddha also communicated visual metaphors such as when he turned a vessel upside down, grabbed a handful of leaves, picked up dust in his fingernail. The Buddha was also sensitive to events in his environment and would incorporate images into his teaching such as jackals howling, a log floating down the Ganges, or moths flying into the flame.

The Wheel of Life is a traditional Buddhist image. For millennia, Buddhists have interpreted it literally without—apparently—considering if the Buddha might have meant it metaphorically. The Wheel is a guide to the afterlife, mapping out where one might be reborn. There are six options: into a hell realm; as a hungry ghost, creatures with ravaging hunger and pinhole mouths that will not permit food; as an animal; as jealous, titan-like gods; in a celestial heavenly realm; or another human birth. Only if one's karma is good can there be a hope of another human birth. Countless Buddhists, past and present, have taken the Wheel as truth—bad karma will send you to hell or bring you back as a hungry ghost in the next life (Kozak 2011a). Psychoanalyst Mark Epstein views the Wheel of life more fruitfully as metaphor such that each of the realms is a reflection of the emotional states we find ourselves in now. It is a comprehensive model for neurotic suffering replete with fear, aggression, lust, and self-inflicted misery (Epstein 1995).

The Buddha was acutely aware that the language we used constrained the concepts we embraced and the experiences we have. Later Buddhists in the Ch'an tradition recognized the limiting constraints of language and sought to circumvent them through koan[12] practice—propositions or short stories that defy logical analysis, i.e., that are contradictory, paradoxical. The storytelling animal assumes a central agent who acts on things inside and outside of itself. "The structure of Indo-European languages, including both the Pali used to express the core teachings in the early texts and the English used to translate and interpret them today, are patterned around assumptions of agency and of subject/object relationship that do not easily yield alternative formulations" (Olendzki 2016, 110–11). Olendzki continues:

> Indo-European languages are largely built around nouns that take on modifiers and are subject to the action of verbs. This yields a habit of mind that is accustomed to construing the world as an edifice of persons, places, and things that exist, each with a defining essence, and to which can be attributed various qualities. . . . All nouns are an artificial construction of language, useful on conventional levels of discourse but inadequate as tools for looking closely at the nature of reality. (Olendzki 2016, 111)

Nouns "create islands of meaning upon a constantly shifting sea of becoming. . . . We have no acceptable way to say that one *selfed* yesterday, is *selfing* as we speak, but will try not *to self* as much next week. . . . Self is a noun that cannot be verbed" (Olendzki 2016, 112). Despite these linguistic limitations, it can be useful to think of *selfing* as a process—what we undergo automatically when we do not question the nature of self. *Selfing* is what happens when we project ownership and identification onto experience and attach to the results, i.e., liking and disliking, pushing and pulling, craving, and clinging.

The Buddha also recognized that words are not accurate reflections of reality, it appears to pin otherwise fluid things down in time and space. Of course, the things that words point to, like everything else, are empty of essence, and this is another limitation of language (Gombrich 2009). The Buddha recognized that categories were necessary in the conventional sense and also limited in how they map to reality. A metaphor is sometimes more accurate or at least more compelling than conventional descriptions—like fire. The mind burns; how to put these fires out?

THE FIRE PROBLEM:
"THE WAY OF PUTTING THINGS AS BEING ON FIRE"

The Buddha was a fire spotter—he was ever alert to the spark of flame. He saw that his fellow humans were, combustible, afire, running high fevers; he was also a fireman—providing the tools to put the fires out—the water of dharma, the flame retardant of wisdom, the common sense to know that *if I don't put fuel on this fire, it is going to go out.* This fire-fighting tendency was present from the very outset of his Buddhahood:[13]

> I have heard that on one occasion the Blessed One—while staying at Uruvela on the bank of the Nerañjara River in the shade of the Bodhi tree, newly awakened—was sitting in the shade of the Bodhi tree for seven days in one session, sensitive to the bliss of release. After the passing of those seven days, on emerging from that concentration, he surveyed the world with the eye of an Awakened One. As he did so, he saw living beings burning with the many fevers and aflame with the many fires born of passion, aversion, & delusion. (Thanissaro 1999)

He is very specific about the three sources of fire and they are all psychological. In the quote above, the three are presented as passion, aversion, and delusion. These are the translations of raga, dosa, and moha. Alternate English renderings of these terms include, instead of passion: desire, lust, greed; instead of aversion: hatred, disgust; instead of delusion: ignorance, confusion, stupidity, even intoxication. While all the translations of moha revolve around the notion of cluelessness, given moha's multiplicity, like dukkha, it might be best to use the Pali term. Moha implies either not caring or not knowing—or both—what a predicament we are in; how urgent the consequences are of remaining blithe to the crisis of being alive. Putting out his own fires was integral to the Buddha's personal transformation under the Bodhi tree—as we will see later in part I—and crucial to the very process of his becoming the Buddha—and likewise, central to his praxis. The therapeutic goal is to diminish the fires, to put them out if possible, as he had done on a fateful night under a fig tree and for the seven days thereafter.

Thus I heard. On one occasion the Blessed One was living at Gaya, at Gayasisa, together with a thousand bhikkhus.[14] There he addressed the bhikkhus. "Bhikkhus, all is burning. And what is the all that is burning?" The eye is burning, forms are burning, eye-consciousness is burning, eye-contact is burning, also whatever is felt as pleasant or painful or neither-painful-nor-pleasant that arises with eye-contact for its indispensable condition, that too is burning. Burning with what? Burning with the fire of lust [raga], with the fire of hate [dosa], with the fire of delusion [moha]. I say it is burning with birth, aging and death, with sorrows, with lamentations, with pains, with griefs, with despairs. (Ñanamoli Thera 1993)

The Buddha is being himself—a masterful metaphorical pedagogue. The Buddha is yelling "Fire" in a crowded house. He is not trying to get the monks to disperse, they sit listening with rapt attention. He is, rather, trying to rouse them from complacency. To inspire them to become firemen themselves, ready to put out the flames that afflict them. Fire is ubiquitous, omnipresent, inescapable. It is not an occasional fire, an incidental fire, a random fire; it is all-consuming, unrelenting, tireless. There is no escape. It is *everything*. He was referring to the five senses, everything the eye sees, the nose smells, the ears here, the skin touches, and the tongue tastes—any contact with the objects of perception sets in motion the gears of pleasure and pain, the desire to have or to avoid, the fear that we may not get what we want or that what we have—that we want—will not last. He breaks each of the sense organs down into their constituent components. Whatever the eye sees, whatever it makes contact with burns. Evolution is the source of this fire—but the Buddha could not have possibly known this; he only knew we had certain tendencies. These proclivities make creatures desire things like sex and food, makes them single-pointedly driven by this craving to acquire them, and once satisfied to quickly tire of that pleasure, to start the pursuit over again. Indeed, "Craving fuels suffering the way that wood fuels a fire" (Keown 1996, 49). Evolution also equipped creatures with a deep-seated aversion to unpleasant things. Pain is a powerful motivator. As brains got more complex the types of objects that occasioned attraction and repulsion expanded to include mental objects, narrative-based wishes, and imagined losses and gains. The creatures that became language-using humans evolved from a limited repertoire of conditioned impulses to varying degrees of narrative self-awareness, thus compounding the burning problems of desire, craving, or clinging. While all creatures are driven by lust and hate, only humans—apparently—can be afflicted by moha[15] (delusion, ignorance, confusion) because this particular issue requires reflective self-awareness. Although we do not know for certain—elephants have a rather sophisticated emotional life (Safina 2015), they may have a modicum of moha, perhaps even the octopus (Godfrey-Smith 2017).

I might reconfigure the Fire Sermon like this: *The story has been told. The Buddha—the great psychologist—gave a lecture to his followers numbering 1000. Everything is burning, he said, your senses—what you see, hear, feel, taste, and smell—your desires—pleasant and unpleasant, every experience that you have had, are having now, and will ever have, unless you awaken and extinguish those fires. The mind burns with the fire of attraction, the flames of repulsion, the conflagrations of confusion. It starts burning the moment you're born, grows hotter as you age, and flares with the anticipation of death. Each sorrow, regret, pain, and loss, every despair, anguish, and misery smolders—ready to explode into dukkha.*

The Buddha's metaphor accords with contemporary fire metaphors that can be found in everyday language (Lakoff and Johnson 1987). Both the concepts of lust and anger—the first two of the Buddha's fires—utilize heat.

ANGER IS FIRE:

Those are *inflammatory* remarks.
She was doing a slow *burn*.
He was breathing *fire*.
Your insincere apology just added *fuel* to the fire.
After the argument, Dave was *smoldering* for days.
That *kindled* my ire.
Boy, am I *burned* up!
He was *consumed* by anger.
(Lakoff and Johnson 1987, 388)

LUST IS HEAT:

I've got the *hots* for her.
She's an old *flame*.
Hey baby, *light* my *fire*.
She's *frigid*.
Don't be *cold* to me.
She's *hot* stuff.
He's still carrying a *torch*.
She's a *red hot* mama.
I'm *burning* with desire.
He was *consumed* by desire.
(Lakoff and Johnson 1987, 411)

Reckoning with these fires, then, is the challenge the Buddha's followers confronted. He had managed to put the fires of his mind out. He taught a method so that others could likewise extinguish their fires: "Seeing this [fire], monks, the instructed disciple disregards all feelings and sensations whether they be pleasant, unpleasant or neither pleasant nor unpleasant, as well as all mental formations and consciousness of such feelings and sensations. Disregarding them he becomes dispassionate, and through dispassion he become free, and in this freedom he then knows, 'I am free'" (Penner 2009, 53–54).

When the Buddha says: "it is burning with birth, aging and death, with sorrows, with lamentations, with pains, with griefs, with despairs" he cites a mixture of life events and psychological states. To see—to be an embodied being—is to be limited by biology and embedded in time. We are born, inexorably decay, and then expire. Subject to impermanence, dukkha follows (e.g., suffering, sorrows, lamentations, pains, and griefs). The Buddha's aim is therapeutic; like a physician, he wants to understand the cause of the suffering. Staying with the fire metaphor—the mind burns because it is kindled by the three fires.[16] Whether it is the fire of lust or hate—we—all beings—are caught in this push–pull dynamic. The third fire—moha—speaks to the nature of being: "When he finds estrangement, passion fades out. With the fading of passion, he is liberated. When liberated, there is knowledge that he is liberated. He understands: Birth is exhausted, the holy life has been lived out, what can be done is done, of this there is no more beyond" (Nanamoli Thera 1993).

The process is involuntary. Contact kindles fire: "The ear is burning, sounds are burning. . . . The nose is burning, odors are burning. . . . The tongue is burning, flavors are burning. . . . The body is burning, tangibles are burning" (Nanamoli Thera 1993). A fire deprived of fuel can appear to have gone out—the coals look ashy, there is no smoke—yet the embers may still have life in them, as a strong blow of air might reveal. The Buddha did not believe that the fire could be extinguished beyond rekindling in this lifetime. He also did not claim—like his Brahmanic counterparts—that fire was eternal. Apparently, the Buddha did claim that after death, his fire would be extinguished irrevocably—known as *paranirvana*. But to know this is to speculate on something he could not possibly have known and, thus, contradicts his otherwise anti-metaphysical predilection. Fires need sustenance or *upadana* (Pali) to keep burning. Without sustenance—without fuel keeping the fires of the mind going—there is calming. The Buddha clarified:

A great blazing fire
unnourished grows calm
and though its embers exist
is said to be out (Thanissaro Bhikkhu 1999)

Clinging, attachment (or contingency as discussed below) is the quality that fuels the three fires. "Fire, when burning, is in a state of agitation, dependence, attachment, & entrapment—both clinging & being stuck to its sustenance. Extinguished, it becomes calm, independent, indeterminate, & unattached: It lets go of its sustenance and is released" (Thanissaro 1999, 38).

The five aggregates are the five processes that comprise mind—the totality of individual psychology. Courtesy of evolutionary psychology, these five follow the dictates of survival, not optimal happiness—e.g., the aggregate of feeling craves pleasurable experiences and fears painful ones. These five are often referred to as the "clinging aggregates"—they are the mind faculties that drive the fires, are their fuel. Thanissaro Bhikkhu prefers Buddhaghosa's translation of "unbinding" for nirvana ("nir" is a negative prefix combined with "vana" that translates to binding) to Gombrich's "extinction" because it connotes the freedom that comes when the fires go out—or become embers, of course, since they do not diminish entirely. Unbinding—liberation, awakening—is the Buddha's goal: "Just as the great ocean has but one taste, the taste of salt, even so does this doctrine & discipline have but one taste: the taste of release" (Thanissaro 1999).

Translating nirvana as unbinding, the goal is "estrangement" from the sources of the fire. In another version estrangement is rendered as "disenchantment" (Thanissaro 1997). Both of these seem to work well. Estrangement, though, suggests repudiation (and much repudiation sounding language can be found throughout the Canon). To sidestep this sense of revulsion (and the aversion that may accompany it) the moment of estrangement/disenchantment can be seen not as a turning away but a breaking of *contingency*, disrupting the evolutionarily encoded link of pleasure to objects of desire and the avoidance of pain. The Buddha is not saying "don't see"; he is saying do not allow seeing to trigger desire and aversion—do not be fooled by the process of seeing into thinking that there is an essential self who sees and who needs to see this something-in-particular in order to be okay. Without fresh fuel, the fires goes out.

In another fire text, "The Exposition on Burning," the Buddha provides this explanation on the danger of desire:

> And what, bhikkhus, is the Dhamma exposition on the theme of burning? It would be better, bhikkhus, for the eye faculty to be lacerated by a red-hot iron pin burning, blazing, and glowing, than for one to grasp the sign through the features in a form cognizable by the eye. For if consciousness should stand tied to gratification in the sign or in the features, and if one should die on that occasion, it is possible that one will go to one of two destinations: hell or the animal realm. Having seen this danger, I speak thus. (Bhikkhu Bodhi https://suttacentral.net/sn35.235/en/bodhi)

Here, the Buddha ratchets up the fire metaphor, extending it to the image of being stuck in the eye with a hot poker. That pain, however horrible, pales in comparison to the psychological pain imposed by "grasping"—making oneself contingent on what the eye sees, what the ear hears, what tongue tastes, etc. The contingency is spelled out here: "For if consciousness should stand tied to gratification in the sign or in the features." The choice appears to be binary: be non-contingent and experience nirvana (with its attendant bliss and freedom) or be contingent and go to hell, whether actual or symbolic. The Buddha amplifies the warning with details:

> Not understanding these fires, people
>   —fond of self-identity—
>   unreleased from the shackles of death,
> swell the ranks of hell,
>   the wombs of common animals, demons,
>   the realm of hungry shades. (Thanissaro Bhikkhu 1999, 15)

As previously mentioned, I prefer to see these references to rebirth in hell, animal, and hungry shades as metaphors—although adherents to Tibetan Buddhism, for one, would take these statements literally. The Buddha's hyperbole is masterful here. Today's vernacular of a "sharp stick in the eye" pales in comparison to his "red hot iron pin" but the logic is reversed. The red hot iron pin is preferable to grasping. To grasp is to be consumed in fire, immolated by passion, burning in a living hell. But the Buddha was not content to rest on his laurels from this brilliant metaphor, so he continued: The ear gets lacerated by a "sharp iron stake"; the nose gets its laceration from a "sharp nail cutter burning, blazing, and glowing"; the tongue gets a sharp razor; and the body gets a "sharp" spear—*burning, blazing, glowing*" (Bhikkhu Bodhi 2000).

> And if someone were to ask you, Vaccha, "This fire burning in front of you, dependent on what is it burning?": Thus asked, how would you reply? . . . I would reply, "This fire burning in front of me is burning dependent on grass & timber as its sustenance. . . . If the fire burning in front of you were to go out, would you know that, 'This fire burning in front of me has gone out'"? . . . yes. . . . And if someone were to ask you, "This fire that has gone out in front of you, in which direction from here has it gone? East? West? North? Or south?": Thus asked, how would you reply? . . . "That doesn't apply, Master Gotama. Any fire burning dependent on a sustenance of grass & timber, being unnourished—from having consumed that sustenance and not being offered any other—is classified simply as 'out' [unbound]." (Thanissaro 1997)

Gombrich points out that fire concerns, "The totality of experience," so when the Buddha said, "Everything, O monks is on fire," he wasn't being hyperbolic. The fire metaphor is also meant ironically since fire rituals—*yagna*[17]—play such an important role in Brahmanism. "The Buddha juxtaposes the three sacrificial fires (brahmanism) with the fires of passion, hatred and delusion" (Gombrich 2009, 112). The Brahmanic fire was the province of the god, Agni.

As the one fire has entered the world
and becomes corresponding in form to every form,
so the Inner Soul of all things
corresponds in form to every form,
and yet is outside.
(Thanissaro Bhikkhu 1999)

For the religion informed by the Vedas and Upanishads, fire was a positive force—representing the eternal, the soul, the life force. The Buddha's metaphor turns the Brahmanic love affair with ritual fire on its head. Instead of the sacred medium of priests, fire represents the forces that afflict; instead of purification, there is torture. When the mind is caught up in obsession, addiction, jealousy, and other related states, Gombrich (2009) points out there are *upadana-khanda*—"blazing masses of fuel."

Reactivity or contingency is driven by greed and hatred but the third fire—moha—is more of a result of misapprehensions regarding the three marks of existence: dukkha, impermanence, not-self. Contingencies can be expressed as *if then* statements. *If* I feel pain *then* I cannot be okay, cannot be happy. If I feel pain, then I must change my circumstances—at any cost. Take the example of an itch. It is unpleasant and urges us to change the situation by scratching it. That is all well and good unless you cannot reach the itch or to scratch will make your condition worse. Then, the dukkha of the itch is compounded. If the pain is work, financial, or social uncertainty, let us say, then there may be no way to change circumstances to provide a sense of certainty. Moha gives rise to much reactivity and that reactivity is predicated upon neither understanding nor accepting the three hallmarks. The Buddha said, "No sense desires adhere to one/Whose fires have cooled, deprived of fuel/All attachments have been severed" (Olendzki 2016, 17). That is—absent reactivity. Furthermore, "Just as if a great mass of fire of ten . . . twenty . . . thirty or forty cartloads of timber were burning, into which a man simply would not time & again throw dried grass, dried cow dung, or dried timber, so that the great mass of fire—its original sustenance being consumed, and no other being offered—would, without nutriment, go out" (Thanissaro 1998c). While the legends of instant enlightenment are idealized, a more practical approach is to mitigate the fires, not eliminate them entirely:

> These fires are not to be extinguished but regulated. Since emotions appear to be rooted deep in our limbic system as the legacy of biological evolution, regulation might be all that is possible and feasible. Rather than suffer fires that erupt and engulf us, we might learn how to adjust our inner airflow to enable them to become like the steady blue flame of a Bunsen burner. In this way, perhaps, we could discover how to burn like miniature suns. (Batchelor 2015, 211)

By taking fire as his target, the Buddha communicates two important points. One: the power of craving and clinging is formidable—akin to not just ten cartloads of timber but forty, and perhaps more. We do not start from ground zero; we are born on fire. Two: notwithstanding our inborn legacy, we play an active role in the burning of that fire. It is up to us whether we add unnecessary fuel or not.

TAKING EXISTENTIAL RESPONSIBILITY BY RELINQUISHING DOGMA

Refuge in beliefs is the easiest and most readily available way to abdicate existential responsibility. The problem with spiritual doctrines is untestable metaphysics; the problem with metaphysics is the need to believe—to take a position without an evidentiary foundation. It is as if instead of the line from a *Few Good Men*: "you can't handle the truth!" the Buddha feared: "you can't handle freedom!" People want rules, just like kids need limits. To be responsible, context must be considered in every instance, which means in every instance one must be attuned to the demands of the moment and interpret what will be the beneficial course of action. In this sense, the dharma is only a guide not a formula or a rule-bound approach. During the Buddha's time—and still very much in evidence today—people abandoned their agency to dogma, priests, and gods. Gombrich reflects: "A great deal of modern education and psychotherapy consists of making people aware that they are responsible for themselves. In fact, we consider that it constitutes a large part of what we mean by becoming a mature person. It is amazing that someone should have promulgated this idea in the fifth century BC, and hardly less remarkable that he found followers" (Gombrich 2009, 14). Dogma can take the form of rules, rituals, and beliefs, and it can also take the form of philosophical argumentation—particularly around metaphysics. Questions about the ultimate nature of reality are irresistible. Dogmatism provides refuge because it reduces the shocking complexity of the world to dualistic concepts where one can find comfort. Sitting with the ambiguity of the world without taking a premature stand requires a sophisticated level of epistemological development (e.g., King and Kitchener 1994).

The ultimate ontological question is "it is" versus "it is not." In brief, the Buddha says:

> This world, Kaccana, for the most part depends upon a duality-upon the notion of existence and the notion of nonexistence. But for one who sees the origin of the world as it really is with correct wisdom, there is no notion of nonexistence in regard to the world. And for one who sees the cessation of the world as it really is with correct wisdom, there is no notion of existence in regard to the world. This world, Kaccana, is for the most part shackled by engagement, clinging, and adherence. But this one [with right view] does not become engaged and cling through that engagement and clinging, mental standpoint, adherence, underlying tendency; he does not take a stand about my self. He has no perplexity or doubt that what arises is only suffering arising, what ceases is only suffering ceasing. His knowledge about this is independent of others. It is in this way, Kaccana, that there is right view. All exists: Kaccana, this is one extreme. All does not exist: this is the second extreme. Without veering towards either of these extremes the Tathagata teaches by the middle. (Bodhi 2003, 544)

Further, the Buddha offers these lines of poetry that emphasize the wisdom inherent in relinquishing metaphysical speculation: "Nowhere does a lucid one/hold contrived views about *it is* or *it is not*./How could he succumb to them/having let go of illusions and conceit?" (from the Chapter of Eights (Atthakavagga), Batchelor 2015). The Buddha warns, "One who dwells in 'supreme' views/and presents them as final/will declare all other views 'inferior'—/he has not overcome disputes" (Batchelor 2015, 132).

The Buddha's middle way between the extremes of "it is" and "it is not" is not concerned with the ultimate truth of things because such truth has no bearing on practice. We know from contemporary physics that things at the quantum level are not as they appear at the Newtonian level and that matter is mostly comprised of space. If all the space was taken out of all the atoms of the universe, the remainder would be an object the size of a bowling ball! The Buddha did not know about quantum subparticles and it might not have mattered if he did because considering quantum ultimates does not have any bearing on putting one foot in front of the other because those feet do their work in the Newtonian middle world where gravity and other forces are predictable (Dawkins 2008).

The notion of space or "emptiness" can be heuristic for appreciating the constructed nature of things but there is no substitute for experiential insights stemming from meditation practice. If I meditate for a prolonged time with earnestness, I might notice that my mind contributes the sense that things have essences—*there's* me *remembering, there's* me *anticipating, there's* me *enjoying a sense of calm, there's* me *getting annoyed by an itch*. When I guide the mind away from telling these mini-stories, as one does with mindfulness practice, I experience the unfolding of each moment without any sense of ownership—or to put it another way, there are things being experienced, no pronoun is necessary: *I* am seeing versus *there* is seeing. There is no essence of me that does the noticing or the experiencing; there is just noticing and experiencing.

Did the Buddha have some privileged *access* to the nature of reality or did he just have a profound *insight* into the way *his* mind worked? Access implies something ontological while insight implies something epistemological and nonprivileged—anyone can do it. Stephen Batchelor agrees:

> Much of the later history of Buddhist epistemology, philosophy, and metaphysics is taken up with discussions about such topics as *pramana* (valid cognition), *anumana* (logical inference), and *yogipratyakasa* (yogic perception), terms that are foreign to the discourses. Without demeaning the richness of philosophical and other insights gained by such developments, I suspect that they were achieved at the cost of losing sight of the skeptical and ethical pragmatism of Gotama's dharma. (Batchelor 2015, 321)

Dogma is appealing because it gives followers a clear set of rules to follow as Batchelor explains: "People adopt inflexible views as a comforting defense mechanism when they find themselves threatened and overwhelmed by forces they cannot control" (Batchelor 2015, 44). When defenses prevail, beliefs are calcified and independent thinking is bypassed. Adherence to dogma is a convenient way to circumvent the existential responsibility the Buddha advocated.

Dogma is a short-cut, a cheat against the psychological homelessness that such radical responsibility-taking demands. To be homeless is to leave one's cognitive home: "The body, Householder, is the home of consciousness; one whose consciousness is chained by lust for physicality is called one who wanders about in a home" (SN, 22.3. iii 9–10, Fronsdal 2016, 27). Rejecting doctrine was a big ask in the Buddha's time and it remains challenging today. We like to have structure. We adore heroes, superstars, and project Messianic hopes on our presidential candidates—all cheats against a radically free existence. The goal, then, would be to get out of this home by not taking refuge in views, self-making through taking positions, feeling superior to or more pure than others. The twin themes of the early Buddhist poem, the *Book of Eights:* sensuality and taking positions are the chief sources of self-making: we fabricate an identity through desire and ego. Again, to be free from conceptual entanglements is to undertake the harrowing tasks of making oneself homeless.[18]

Dogma is not only an attempt to hoodwink responsibility, it can also be seen as an attempt to cheat against impermanence. That is, by hiding behind beliefs couched as certainties—whether rationalized by tradition, truth, or the word of god or Buddha—one is seemingly protected from the vicissitudes of an uncertain existence. Without dogma, one is on a dynamic cutting edge of experience in every moment of life. It is comforting to take refuge in absolutes; the psychological Buddha recognized this trap and took a different approach.

The Buddha recognized there is no firm resting place that can extinguish existential insecurity; we stand on that uncertain ground with either anxiety—when resisted—or equanimity—when accepted. A more modern example of this stance can be found in this Rilke's quote: "Each experience has its own velocity according to which it wants to be lived if it is to be new, profound, and fruitful. To have wisdom means to discover this velocity in each individual case" (Baer 2006, 10). The ideal "velocity," as it were, of each experience is available in any given moment. It is typically obscured by a mind that is at once volatile in its reactivity and fixed in its rigidity. With such alternating volatility and fixity, the mind cannot attune itself with the flow of experience.

The Buddha did not think the dharma required the person of the Buddha to be understood, practiced, and realized. Practitioners were, famously, islands unto themselves. Self-reliance means you have to work it out yourself without priests, temples, and sacred texts. The Buddha's teachings appealed to wealthy merchants of the Bronze Age in northern India because they were portable and emphasized self-reliance. The untrained mind was unwieldy and inflicted harm. The trained mind was wieldy, beneficial, and entailed "great happiness" (Bodhi 2012, 267). The dharma is also democratic because individuals are responsible for their experience and behavior and that responsibility remains the same whether one is "high" or "low" born (Gombrich 2009).

Despite all his emphasis on self-reliance, the Buddha's community of followers—numbering in the thousands—was factious. The monks clamored for more structure than the Buddha provided. They did not like the moral ambiguity that taking personal responsibility insisted upon and thus "reformers" such as the Buddha's cousin Devadatta had a lot of support because they pushed for more strict adherence to rules. Dogma reduces the world to black and white dualities. This is comforting, especially in times of chaos, uncertainty, and transition. Many political figures have exploited this vulnerability by pushing dogmatic rhetoric (insert your favorite fascistic dictator here). The Buddha intended to enfranchise people with the dharma not to create Buddhist franchises.

CALL ME BY MY NAME: WHAT TO CALL THE BUDDHA

As part of this effort to re-secularize the Buddha, he might need a different name. Stephen Batchelor prefers his family name, Gotama and this is a safe choice. The honorific title Siddhartha could also work but carries the association with Herman Hesse's book of that title that is not, as some mistakenly assume, a fictionalized biography of the Buddha. We do not know the Prince's first name before he was the Buddha. Like Batchelor's suggestion for a Buddhism 2.0, I need a Buddha 2.0—that could be his name, though an awkward construction. Assuming that the Buddha was an actual person—he would have been given a name by his parents— His father was Sudhadona, his mother, Mahamaya and he was raised by his aunt Prajapati after his mother died soon after childbirth. Perhaps he was named Krishna, Ram, or Govinda, Devandra, Vikas, Arjuna, Kumar, Unni, or Subramanaim. The namelessness of the Buddha probably contributes to his mystique as if he were destined to Buddhahood (which of course he was prophesized to become according to myth). To reclaim Buddha from Buddhism, it would help to unveil this mystique—the humanize Gotama as an exceptional, perhaps, but ordinary human being. But, there are other ways to demystify the Buddha and much of this book is devoted to that task. Therefore, I will refer to him simply as the Buddha, not the enlightened one or the Awakened One, not Lord, Shakyamuni, or the Tathagata—the one who has gone forth. After all this, I am still partial to *Buddha* despite all its historical, cultural, and rhetorical baggage but Buddha* with the asterisk denoting caveats might be technically more appropriate. Buddha* is how the Buddha of myth, perhaps of history, certainly of hagiography could be presented here. Buddha* is my Buddha, a synthetic, idealized, and pragmatic Buddha. Since Buddha* is a distracting usage, read all plain references to Buddha as denoting Buddha*.

Buddha is also safe because it is a generic term that carries the meaning: "Awakened one." According to Buddhist lore, there have been many past Buddhas and there will be many future Buddhas. We could land on "the historical Buddha" to be specific to Gotama, but that, like Buddha 2.0 or Buddha* is a mouthful. Much of the issue with "Buddha" has to do with its conflation with Buddhism, but if we are successful at disentangling Buddha from Buddhism, we can come to have a new appreciation for this ancient term.

There is also an issue of timing. Gotama became the Buddha when he was approximately thirty-five years old. Prior to that, he was just the young prince. I could delineate any reference prior to his awakening event as the "Buddha to be," but here again the extra words are a burden to the reader. For simplicity, there is the Buddha. Before his awakening he was the pre-Buddha, the Buddha-becoming and if I refer to his earlier life he was technically not yet the Buddha. To complicate the matter further, at some point—perhaps between the ages of twenty-nine and thirty-five, he considered himself to be a bodhisattva—a Buddha in training, as it were. Buddha covers all of it.

OVERVIEW

This monograph proceeds with an introduction and three parts. The introduction has made the case for the Buddha as psychologist rather than philosopher, rather than founder of the one of the world's religions. The Introduction covered the Buddha's basic ideas such as suffering, not self, and existential responsibility. The Buddha taught—and apparently *thought*—through metaphors (Gombrich 2009). One of the Buddha's most famous sermons or lectures (to be more secular) was the Fire Sermon. This lecture is an exemplar of his project writ large: a skeptical, psychological, and entirely secularly compatible and empirically verifiable paradigm. The Buddha proclaimed: *The mind was on fire.* It was then in the Iron Age and it remains ablaze in the Digital Age.

To make the historical Buddha founder of Buddhism into Buddha, PhD, licensed psychologist, cognitive-behaviorally oriented group and individual psychotherapist (e.g., Tirch, Silberstein, and Kolts 2015), practical theoretician, he will first need to be rescued from Buddhism. This can be accomplished by exploring Buddhist history, hagiography, and hermeneutics. Part I titled "Reclaiming the Buddha from Buddhism" explicates a skeptical, secular version of the Buddha, stripped of saintliness, supernaturalism, and piety. Chapter 1 "The Legend of the Buddha: History, Myth, and Hagiography" asks if there was a historical Buddha, and if so, what do we know of this figure? To what extent are the Buddhist scriptures of the Pali Canon the words of the Buddha? How can his teachings be interpreted? What were the rhetorical styles and possible intents of his pedagogy? Once separated from Buddhism, the Buddha can claim mindfulness and mindfulness can claim the Buddha without any cultural or religious baggage. The need for a rescue mission makes it seem that Buddhism is the bogeyman that must be banished. However, without the Buddhist religions and their dogma, ritualization, and sanctification that helped to preserve the Buddha's insights over millennia, those insights that would likely have disappeared into obscurity. Chapter 2 "The Hermeneutical Buddha: What He Thought (Maybe)" explores the Buddha's aversion to metaphysical speculation and his insistence on taking responsibility for one's decision making without reverting to dogma.

Part II, "The Buddha's Pedagogical Project: The Ennobling Praxes (aka Four Noble Truths)" focuses on the Buddha's pedagogical legacy. Like all the Buddha's pedagogy, the fire metaphor is intended as praxis—ideas have no value by themselves and gain currency only to the extent that they can be applied to immediate experience. Praxis was one the epithets of Aphrodite signifying *action*—and the Buddha's most famous teaching—the Four Noble Truths—can be re-rendered as a set of actions (Batchelor 2012). But, perhaps, "action" is not pointed enough as a term because a simple application of effort is not enough to master each of the four. There must be something more akin to devotion or commitment for them to be anything more than an intellectual preoccupation. I will use the term *praxis* because it implies more than a casual action and should be read to entail devotion, commitment, responsibility, and a therapeutic intent. Each of the chapters in this section takes up one these praxes. Chapter 3 "The First Ennobling Praxis: What is the Problem?" adopts a medical metaphor—diagnosis, etiology, prognosis, and prescription—to understand these truths or praxes that the Buddha had identified the problem, he diagnosed the human condition: we suffer, become dissatisfied, feel anguished, saddled with sorrow, miserable, unsettled, as if a fire burns within us. Chapter 4 "The Second Ennobling Praxis: Getting to the Root of the Problem" considers the cause of humanity's great problem: We like and we dislike; we identify with experience; our well-being becomes contingent on having or not having. Each reaction, each push and pull against experience adds fuel to the fire. Chapter 5 "The Third Ennobling Praxis: Can the Problem be Resolved?" Considers prognosis: can the fires be put out or at least significantly reduced? The Buddha was confident—based on his own introspective efforts—that the fires could be attenuated. This is the state of nirvana. Chapter 6 "The Fourth Ennobling Praxis: Resolving the Problem" touches on the eightfold process the Buddha recommended as the treatment plan for the ailing patient, with a focus on mindfulness. The Buddha was not just a fire spotter, standing in a fire tower surveilling the landscape for danger. He was also a firefighter, offering tools for putting out these fires. And like a good firefighter, he also taught prevention. Some portion of these fires is inevitable—constitutionally due to our status as embodied beings subject to the laws of physics—but other aspects can be modified. The Buddha taught his adherents how not to put more fuel onto the fire.

Part III: "Mind on Fire: The Buddha's Psychological Map" considers the five aspects of the Buddha's mind model, known as aggregates. The Buddha suggested both the urgency to confront and then provided the means to transcend the dictates of evolutionary programming. The brain's evolutionary psychology has features that once had adaptive value to early humans that are either vexing or unnecessary or both for modern humans, e.g., we no longer have to relentlessly hunt or forage for our food and so no longer "need" the feelings that drove those behaviors for our ancestors. These evolutionary vestiges are the targets of the Buddha's intervention (e.g., The Four Noble Truths) that address: relationship to desire, the attribution of essences to things, others, and ourselves, and the perception of a unitary (essential) self. These vestigial evolutionary features can be mapped onto the five aggregates that the Buddha mentioned in his Fire Sermon—his psychological map or model of the mind. In the introduction to this part, I will briefly map his claims onto evolutionary psychology (e.g., modularity, affect), neuroscience (e.g., brain architecture), and the cognitive science of language (e.g., metaphor). Chapter 7 "Form: Brain Architecture and the Neuroplastic Forest of Self" considers the brain's form and how its architecture enables and constrains experience. Chapter 8 "Perception: Categorization" details how the tendency to make categories, while adaptive, has limiting consequences, especially for citizens of the Information Age. Chapter 9 "Feeling: Pain and Pleasure Drive Evolution's Primary Agendas (and Give Rise to a Sense of the One Having Pleasure and Pain)" argues that the process of desire creates our sense of self and suggests that if we are less attached to—that is, less identified with, not as contingent upon—these desires that we can experience a different sense of self. The challenge is to counter those genetic tendencies. Chapter 10 "Mental Fabrication and the Modular Self" addresses the narrative mind—mental contents—along with the modular theory of mind that claims there is no unitary self but a collection of self modules, each with its own function. Chapter 11 "Consciousness: Apparently Ubiquitous, Certainly Overrated" touches on the faculty of consciousness and how much of mental life is unconscious, which further undermines the case for a special, unitary, essential self.

The conclusion wonders what experience would be like if language and the categorical tendency could be set aside. From the naturalized perspective, the Buddha's notion of nirvana can be more accurately seen as hacking into our evolutionary programing to deliberately transcend its dictates (and constraints to some degree). Nirvana, while aromatic with transcendental implications in popular imagination and in much of Buddhist history, does not require a metaphysical explanation yet would have to be constrained by the limits of the system it is trying to self-hack.

Even though these ideas were formulated some two-and a half millennia, ago, the Buddha was prescient in highlighting much of what mind scientists study as noted Buddhist scholar Richard Gombrich makes clear:

> I certainly do not intend to claim that the Buddha anticipated all the discoveries of modern psychology. . . . Nevertheless the similarity between some of his ideas and the picture painted by modern cognitive psychology is striking. Nowadays perception is regarded as an activity, a kind of doing. Moreover "Perception is inherently selective," which means that it cannot be dissociated

from volition. Both of these propositions would have the Buddha's complete assent. (Gombrich 2009, 197)

Despite this prescience, the naturalization and secularization of Buddhist psychology remains controversial. Controversy, notwithstanding, it is possible to naturalize Buddhism or return to the "nature-compatible" original ideas of the Buddha before they become the core of Buddhism. A natural Buddhism reclaimed from institutionalized dogma, then, would likely meet the Buddha's "complete assent."

An epilogue likewise wonders what the Buddha would think if he were to see how his teachings were being used today.

NOTES

1. A Google search on "Zen of" reveals too many examples to include here. The top ones are: The Zen of Python (computer programming), Zen of Steve Jobs, Zen of Everything (with the subtitle A Zen take on love, life, and everything else), Zen of Creativity, Zen of Slow Cooking, Zen of Weightlifting, and the Zen of Business. This list could go on for pages.

2. It is hard to discuss evolution without resorting to what sounds like teleological terms. Evolution *builds* things into organisms; it *designs* them. This languaging is a short-cut to the more cumbersome explanation of the basic genetic mechanism: genes, with the assistance of sex, replicate. Mutations that function as adaptations have more copies and are thereby preserved, ones that do not, do not. Evolution is a mechanical process; no intentions are required.

3. Pali terms will be used predominately. The exception is the Sanskrit anatman that is the converse of the well-known Sanskrit atman. The first instance of a non-parenthetical Pali or Sanskrit term will be italicized. Further instances will not.

4. Sukha/dukkha cover the full range of positive/negative. Sukha ranges from feeling okay to bliss. Dukkha ranges from not feeling okay to extreme suffering.

5. The reader of Buddhism will find this causal construct described as "dependent origination" or *pratitya-samutpada* defined as a complicated scheme of twelve processes in that causal chain. Many teachers (and scholars) seem to regard these steps as veridical and valid, yet I have always found them confusing. As did Robert Wright: "I won't run through the exact sequence of twelve conditions, partly because some of them are, for my money, a little murky" (Wright 2017, 218). After the first few steps (contact gives rise to), the sequence devolves into silliness. Indeed, Richard Gombrich regards them: "as a chain of absurd, meaningless changes which could only result in the repeated death of anyone who would reproduce this cosmogonic process in ritual activity and everyday life" (Gombrich 2009, xi). Why might this be so, given the Buddha was otherwise astute in his delineations? The Buddha was quite fond of lists and if one is teaching on a near daily basis for forty-five years, one needs to mix-up the pedagogy, as it were. Creating such numbered schemes was likely one way of doing this (employing stories and parables and metaphors was another). Thus, there

are the *four* Noble Truths, the *three* hallmarks of existence, the *three* fires, the *eightfold* Noble Path, the *seven* factors of awakening, and the *twelve* steps of the *pratityasamutpada*, etc. Given the ambitiousness of the twelve-step scheme, the Buddha might have had to fudge the data, if you will, to make them all fit. As any pedagogue knows, teaching the same material over and over again is boring. My teaching was rich in metaphors—many original to my work and others borrowed from the Buddha and other teachers. Each metaphor highlights and hides some aspect of reality. Like metaphors, these lists highlight and hide and should be viewed as pedagogical devices rather than explicit blueprints to reality.

6. My spiritual development has been a process of becoming a better version of myself—less reactive, more wise, compassionate, and loving, while feeling happier, grateful, and gratified. At least those are the aspirations. My spirituality does not set the body against the spirit—the body *is* the spirit. Carnal pleasures are not frowned upon as long as they do not become the basis for self-making contingencies (as will be explored further below in part III).

7. My spirituality does not require any sentient mystery out there in the larger universe—no universal consciousness, no intention, no Universe with a capital "U."

8. Self Determination Theory proposes two precursor stages to the realization of not self: The me and I selves. The me-self is in play when: "When one is not able to bring an openness to the perception of events, and is constrained by feelings of defensiveness, rigidity in thinking, or other preconceptions in order to protect or enhance the 'me-self,' there is a higher likelihood of feeling more controlled forms of regulation, including external regulation and, in particular, introjected regulation marked by feeling of internal guilt, pressure, or compulsion" (Rigby, Schultz, and Ryan 2014, 227). The I-self takes "concerns the inherent integrative tendencies of people to understand, grow, and create coherence in their experiences. Whereas regulation by the me-self is often associated with externally controlled behaviors, integrated 'I' regulation is manifest in behaviors that are more fully self-endorsed and wholehearted, tending to be both higher quality and more positively experienced" (Ryan and Rigby 2015, 246).

9. "This suggests that, instead of being a metaphysical assertion that there is no self, the teaching on not-self is more a strategy, a technique of perception aimed at leading beyond death to Unbinding [nirvana]—a way of perceiving things that involves no self-identification, no sense that 'I am,' no attachment to 'I' or 'mine'" (Thanissaro Bhikkhu 1999, 71).

10. The thirty-seven of the Samagama Sutta (MN 104): Four Foundations of Mindfulness, Four Right Strivings, Four Spiritual Power bBases, Five Faculties, Five Powers, Seven Enlightenment Factors, and Eightfold Path. In addition to these thirty-seven, there are the Three Hallmarks of Existence, Four Noble Truths, the eight *jhanas* (*dhyanas*, Sanskrit) (four and four), and the twelve links in paticca samuppada.

11. Metaphor can be used as an umbrella term for language devices that help us to understand one thing in terms of another to include simile, synecdoche, and metonym. Much of what appears in the Canon is simile.

12. The purpose of koan is to "tease the mind outside normal linguistic structures into profound non-verbal depths" (Hinton 2012, 123). Koans help the practitioner to

transcend the self-as-metaphor to get closer to *Tzu-jan:* "thought appearing out of emptiness and disappearing back into it" (Hinton 2012, 79).

13. "The Way of Putting Things as Being on Fire" is the English translation of the Pali for what is colloquially known as the "Fire Sermon" (Gombrich 1996).

14. One thousand monks listened to this lecture and upon conclusion they all—apparently—became enlightened, which is taken to mean that they had transformed—in an enduring way—their psychological functioning such that it was no longer dictated by desire, no longer ignorant of how the mind worked, and no longer attached to what would be colloquially termed "self" or, more technically, a transcendent essence or soul. Would that it be so simple. Throughout the discourses, the Buddha often exhorted and his followers often experienced spontaneous results. Perhaps things are different now in the Information Age, where attention spans are notoriously shorter, or perhaps these are idealized depictions of the Buddha's teaching prowess and the monks' receptiveness. Nonetheless, moving toward an awakened way of being is difficult, and it seems that change typically cannot be effected by exhortation—if that were the case, scores of my psychotherapy patients would count themselves among the enlightened (and myself as well). In contrast to the Fire Sermon, Majhima Nikaya 26 presents a more realistic view of the awakening process: "This dharma I have reached is deep, hard to see, difficult to awaken to, quiet and excellent, not confined by thought, subtle, sensed by the wise. But people love their place: they delight and revel in their place. It is hard for people who love, delight and revel in their place to see this ground: 'because-of-this' conditionality, conditioned arising. And also hard to see this ground: the stilling of inclinations, the relinquishing of bases, the fading away of reactivity, desirelessness, ceasing, nirvana" (translated by Stephen Batchelor, Batchelor 2017, 17–18).

15. Technically, though, animals do suffer from moha because they—like the run-of-the-mill person—misconstrue the nature of self, among other things. Their lack of understanding, though, must be of a different order and only we can use words and thoughts to nudge ourselves in the direction of putting out the fire of moha.

16. Much of contemporary understanding of and exposure to Buddhism is through the Mahayana forms, for example, Tibetan Buddhism, Zen. Interestingly, these Buddhist religions developed for over a millennia after the Buddha all but forgot about the fire metaphor (or ignored it). Instead of three "fires" there were three "poisons." It is telling that the Mahayana forms of Buddhism changed the three fires into the three poisons. As chemical process metaphors go, fires have very different entailments than poisons: fire destroys tissue; poison corrupts it—as if a soul was being stained, polluted, contaminated. Poisons gets at the toxic nature of greed, hatred, and confusion but misses all the metaphorical nuances of the Buddha's extended fire metaphor and moves awakening from a psychological to a mystical footing. If the Buddha's project is to shift from ontological to epistemological perspectives, purity is problematic. The Brahmins of his day were obsessed with purity and all their beliefs, rituals, and virtues were aimed at purification. But such entanglements make the purity-seeker vulnerable to disappointment. Purity is more of an ontological state—free from defilements, like toxins. Or purity is externalized through gods, gurus, the absolute. It is ironic, then, the later Buddhists would go back to this purity obsession.

17. I had an encounter with a similar fire that the Buddha lampooned with his metaphor in October, 1985. I arrived in Ganeshpuri India to the Gurudev Siddha Peeth ashram. The third anniversary of the Swami Muktananda's *mahasamahdi*—that is, death—was quickly approaching. I was part of a work crew cleaning the *yagna mandap*—the enormous, open-air structure that would host the upcoming celebration with some 3000 participants. My job was to clean the soot from the white-painted aluminum surfaces. These ashes were the remnants of the last fire ceremony that had been held there—*yagna*—the sacrificial, everlasting fire, home to the eternal Hindu god Yagni. Even when the fire was not burning, it was quiescent, waiting for its latent power to be ignited by Sanskrit prayers, scattered rice, and orange, yellow, red, and pink powders. It was to these fires and their underlying metaphysics that the Buddha ironized his fire metaphors. Fire was a language that his Brahmanic cohort could relate to and it was by no means assured that they would catch the anti-metaphysical turn the Buddha was taking (Gombrich 2009).

18. James Wood's in *The Nearest Thing to Life* (2015) coins the neologism, *homelooseness* that points to this difficulty of relinquishing identity through ideas. Similarly, "Exile is strangely compelling to think about but terrible to experience. It is the unhealable rift forced between a human being and and native place, between the self and its true home: its essential sadness can never be surmounted" (Edward Said "Reflections on Exile" cited in Wood 2015). In contrast to this conventional view of exile, the Buddha relished such estrangement and offered a different kind of home.

Part I

RECLAIMING THE BUDDHA FROM BUDDHISM

This part goes back in history to find solid footings for the Buddha or at least attempts to do so. Securing the Buddha is a complicated task—who was the historical Buddha? What evidence supports his existence? What did he actually say? How do we differentiate myth from reality? Whatever he said or whatever words are attributed to him were not written down for hundreds of years after his alleged death and none of those early documents survived. These questions remain rhetorical—there is no way to know with certainty what is "original" to him and what was added later, and for what purpose. The task of winnowing the myth by presuming that anything non-supernatural is a biographical datum is a hermeneutical assumption, one without incontrovertible evidence to support it.

To fully appreciate the Buddha's psychological contributions he must be reclaimed from the Buddhist religions that have persisted, metamorphosed, and disseminated his teachings over the past 2500 years (Batchelor 2012; Keown 1996; Trainor 2004). To accomplish this, some history, hermeneutics, and hagiography must be discussed. Stephen Batchelor's (1997) classic *Buddhism Without Beliefs* was a bold secular Buddhist statement. More recently, he calls for a "complete secular redefinition of Buddhism" (Batchelor 2012). To bring this about, he goes back to the Buddha's original teachings—the Four Noble Truths and reinterprets these as a set of experiential tasks rather than ontological statements about reality. This shift from the ontologic to the pragmatic facilitates the transformation of Buddhism from the "belief-based metaphysics of classical Indian soteriology (Buddhism 1.0) to a praxis-based, post-metaphysical vision of the dharma (Buddhism 2.0)" (Batchelor 2012, 87). Batchelor continues: "The secularisation of the dharma that seems to be currently underway might not, as its critics bemoan, be a further indication of the terminal watering down and banalisation of the

Buddha's teaching, but rather a sign of the waning power of the orthodoxies that have held sway for the past two thousand or so years" (Batchelor 2012, 106).

Until the nineteenth century, Buddhists were viewed as idolators. While this may have been Christian bias and misunderstanding, there is no doubt that the people of Siam, Mongolia, and other countries with Christian missions regarded Bouton, Siaka, Godama, or whatever name he was known by as superhuman, as a God (Lopez 2013). However, he was not the intercessory of Christian faith: "there is no intelligent divine being who judges of human actions as good or bad, and rewards or punishes that as such;—this indeed is practically the same as having no God" (William Erskine (1773–1852) quoted in Lopez 2013, 166). Scholars by the early nineteenth century recognized the Buddha more accurately: "Boudou is a distinguished philosopher, a sage born for the happiness of his fellow creatures and for the good of humanity" (Michel Jean Francois quoted in Lopez 2013, 168). While Buddhism was roundly condemned by the Europeans, they began "to distinguish between the ancient founder and his modern followers, *as if the Buddha bore no responsibility for Buddhism*" (Lopez 2013, 169 emphasis added). I agree that the Buddha is not responsible for what has been done in his name and he must be rescued from the religions to once again become that "distinguished philosopher" or psychologist that he might have been.

A Buddha-centric praxis would necessitate the following claims about its soteriology: 1) All of the Buddha's propositions ought to be filtered through hermeneutics, hagiography, and history. The words attributed to the Buddha ought to be interpreted through the very vehicle of those words—the Pali Canon, and an imagined rendering of his pedagogical intentions, i.e., should the Buddha be taken literally and to what extent can the discourses be regarded as his veridical teachings? 2) The application of the Buddha's teachings ought to be *experiential.* Metaphysics, ontology, and epistemology ought to yield to praxis grounded in individualized introspective and behavioral experiments and, to the extent possible, tested in third-person science. 3) Following the Buddha's wisdom ought to lead to e*xistential responsibility.* Individuals interested in Buddha distinct from Buddhist orthodoxy ought to commit to an individualized, experiential, and empirical approach. That is, they would reject existential short-cuts and metaphysical refuges in doctrine, dogma, and abstruse philosophical debates. Practitioners relinquish elitist ontological pursuits. They recognize the futility of metaphysical speculation (e.g., the debate between the mind only school within Tibetan Buddhism). Dogmatism is undermined if the Buddha's pedagogical approach was metaphorical, satirical, poetic, and ironic. 4) The Buddha's project ought to be *grounded* in a rational, scientific worldview. The Buddha—if he existed—might have been an extraordinary man, but he could not have been a deity. He was a human being. He most likely did not have powers, perform miracles, or do many of things later ascribed to him. Any salvation earned for himself and his followers came as the result of hard work and intelligence rather than faith or superstition. The Buddha, like any other human being, had his share of psychological issues, e.g., his mother died just after giving birth to him (Epstein 2013). His penchant for monasticism might reflect an avoidant personality. 5) Practice ought to be *pragmatic*. The Buddha was friends with peasants and kings alike. As beggars dependent on the charity of the community, the Buddha and his followers were pragmatists. The Buddha had no apparent scandals but he remained friends with kings, such as the patricidal Ajatasattu, even as they were involved in the many bloody wars that marked that turbulent era in northern India. The Buddha and his followers were protected by these kings and their armies, and he apparently made concessions to continue the support he and his community needed to survive.

Chapter 1

The Legend of the Buddha
History, Myth, and Hagiography

HISTORICAL CONSIDERATIONS

Buddhism—one of the world's great religions—is actually a collection of religions that share a common lineage to the teachings of the Buddha, who lived between 2500 and 2600 years ago. The Buddha is generally, and problematically, regarded as a historical figure. Buddhist scholar Maurice Percheron proclaimed: "The Buddha actually existed; he is as historically real as Ramses II, Plato, or Alexander the Great" (Percheron 1960, 6). More recently, Buddhist scholar Hans Penner is circumspect. He points to the lack of historical evidence that supports the existence of the Buddha—there is none from his actual time (Penner 2009). Penner does not question that there was a Buddha, just that there is no artifact to support him other than a large body of circumstantial evidence and posthumous literature. The typical scholarly argument is that he *must* have existed—the Canon appears to be the work of a single individual—but Penner cautions that this does not qualify as historical evidence. Reading Penner's caveat regarding the received tradition of Buddhist scholarship came as a shock—my assumed certainty of the historical Buddha was suddenly undermined. Yet, after a brief moment of dismay, I started to feel liberated—since the Buddha is not established fact—all renderings are fictionalized to some extent, as is my depiction of him as a psychologist.

TRANSMIGRATION OF BUDDHISM

The history of Buddhism has been a history of migration and transformation, as the forms of Buddhism traveled farther East, building upon, elaborating, and changing the earlier conventions. The Buddha has always been represented according to the fashions and particulars of geography—the specific local cultures and religions that embraced his teachings. The Indian Buddhism that arose after the death of the Buddha was different than what the Buddha taught in his lifetime. Indian Buddhism went to China and from China it went to Tibet and Japan and throughout East and Southeast Asia. Each location contributed its own metaphysics, rituals, and doctrines. The core of the Buddha's teachings might have been retained—for example, the Four Noble Truths—then elaborated upon wildly. Practitioners of Vajrayana perhaps do not know that "The original teachings actually denied all theology, all dogma, and even the idea of divinity" (Percheron 1960, 5).

READING THE CANON

Theravadan Buddhists consider the Pali Canon to be sacral—the confirmed words of the Buddha as memorized by his faithful attendant Ananda and others and corroborated at the First Council (Mu Soeng 2020). There are several leaps or linkages of faith that must be taken to read the Canon as the words of the Buddha. First, there must have been the person of the Buddha who spoke these words. Then, these words had to have been memorized and recited accurately for hundreds of years before being written down. Then, what had been written down had to survive nearly 2000 years to become the Canon. Richard Gombrich admonishes: "The gross fact remains that almost all our evidence for the texts of the Buddhist Canon comes from manuscripts and that hardly any Pali manuscripts are more than about five hundred years old. The vast majority are less than three hundred years old" (Gombrich 1996, 9). Since none of the original copies of that initial transcription exist, we must assume that the converging of Pali and Sanskrit to Chinese texts—these documents also no more than 500 years old—provide the best estimate of what he might have been said. The historical Buddha is a retrofitted image from these later, convergent texts. What was omitted and what accreted over time is unknown—scholars like Gombrich and Bachelor and Mu Soeng have made guesses as to what might have been more original and, thus, more authentic by looking for discrepancies, consistencies, and other tells. "But no particular passage can ever be proven to be original" (Ven. Cintita Dinsmore cited in Mu Soeng 2020, 4). Another issue is politics—the Canon likely served power as the basis of authority in the religious communities that formed after the Buddha's death (Mu Soeng 2020). Each of the extant forms of Buddhism has its own received tradition, whether from the Canon or other sacred texts. What might have been the original genius of the Buddha—the signal—often gets lost in the noise of orthodoxy.

THE BUDDHA'S MYTH

The early life of the Buddha is elusive. His biography[1] is constructed out of fragments found in the Pali Cannon and other sources. It is a grand story of mythic proportions, replete with magic, infinite time, and deity worship—of the Buddha himself.[2] The entire universe bowed to his presence from the moment of his birth. He comes out of his mother's side walking and talking: "I am born for enlightenment for the well-being of the world; I am the first in the world, I am the best in the world. This is my last rebirth in the world of becoming" (Penner 2009, 22). The gods revel in his arrival. They have prophesized this coming Buddha and he will be able to do things for mankind that even they cannot do. Much of this biography defies credulity from a modern, Western, scientific standpoint. The scholarly tendency is to extract the historical Buddha from the "noise" of his mythology, winnowing out the nonrational, superstitious, and supernatural elements found in the Buddha's biography. Then, certain "facts" can be accepted as unproblematic, such as his leaving the palace at age twenty-nine and becoming enlightened at age thirty-five.

Doing so may bring another set of problems. Hans Penner, decrying the contemporary tendency to rationalize the Buddha's history has instead embraced the glorious, technicolor mythology on its own merits.[3] Penner suggests: *Read this literally, the people of the Buddha's time did.* It is a fantastical tale with its own cosmology that not only defies credulity but also violates every known law of physics. Time does not exist in linear or comprehensible fashion—an eon is 10,000,000,000,000,000,000,000,000,000 years, and there have been a lot of them—it is eternal for all intents and purposes. Penner warns not to interpret the myth as history, not to read between the lines but to see it as a mythic universe of oppositions. He also asserts that Buddhism is inappropriately Buddha-centric, ignoring the role of Universal Monarchs[4]—buddha-like rulers who are not monastic renunciants and what—according to prophecy—the young prince would have become if he had not become the Buddha. But numbers such as—ten octillion beg to be read as symbolic—a number so large that rationality must give way to a sense of non-linear, cyclical time. Before Penner delves into his analyses of the myth later in his book, the reader is supposed to enjoy the first section that the recounts the Buddha's story—it *is* as entertaining as it is unbelievable.

SUMMARY OF THE MYTH

A brief and selective précis of the Buddha's mythology—a biographical skeleton sans supernatural elements—can help to highlight the need to rescue, reclaim, and relieve the Buddha from the Buddhisms that have swallowed him up, elevated him as their titular symbol. The Buddha's origin story proceeds as follows: The future Buddha is born, his mother dies within a week[5]; he is prophesied to become a great king (actually a Universal Monarch) or saint. His father fearful of the latter protects the prince from the existential realities of life—we are asked to believe—until he is twenty-nine years of age. Once he discovers these realities, he leaves his heavenly palace life to find enduring spiritual truths—answers to life's most fundamental difficulties. He spends six years practicing extreme yogas and ascetic practices until he is emaciated and on the verge of death. He is given a meal, which he accepts and then with renewed strength, he sits down under a fig tree and vows not to get up until he has accomplished his goal—discovering these truths. He meditates through the night tempted by desire, ego, and attachment—vanquishing them by morning. After a period of continued meditation, the now Buddha—literally, an awakened one (from *buddho* to awaken)—sets out, wondering if he can help others with his insights. After wrestling with the question, he decides to teach—for forty-five years he travels around the Gangetic plane, giving lectures, attracting followers, managing a large community. He dies at age 80 without having named a successor; he wants his teachings to be enough.

MYTH: FOUR SIGNS

This great prince, this omniscient, walking-talking newborn, we are asked to believe, has never seen an old, sick, or dead person until he is twenty-nine years of age—no dead relative, servant, or member of court.[6] Nonetheless, once he discovers the realities of sickness, old age, and death[7] he also discovers the virtues of renunciation in meeting a wandering mendicant. One might be able to uncouple oneself from the ravages of desire—or so the wandering ascetics and dedicated yogis tried—but there is nothing to be done about sickness, aging, and death.[8] While his father might have been able to engineer keeping all saints, swamis, and sadhus out of the Buddha's sights, he could not have possibly protected him from sickness, old age, and death. There were family members and servants within the walls of the palaces. Not to mention animals, such as the swan that his cousin Devadatta nearly fatally wounded and that would have died except for the young prince's intervention. The future Buddha certainly understood the dramas of prey and predator, for most creatures, living things were food. Yet this was not enough to shake the prince out of complacency. Percheron attempts to address his lack of awareness by the following sleight of hand: "He had heard of disappointment, pain, and death, but to him these were words he understood only in an abstract way. They were words that referred to things grownups ordinarily

The Legend of the Buddha 9

prefer to ignore—or to pass over in silence. They were empty words, and he never suspected that, one day, he too would learn their tragic meaning" (Percheron 1960, 73). It might be possible to accept this attitude from a boy, a teenager, or even a very young man, but such an attitude persisting at twenty-nine, again, defies credulity. Percheron schemes further by elaborating the king's efforts to keep the prince in pleasure: "By official decree, everything that could evoke age, illness, and death he ordered banished from the palace. . . . Let a dancer betray a trace of weariness and she was withdrawn; a servant was dismissed if her plaited hair showed a touch of gray. A faded flower or a dead leaf was taboo. No lamp could flicker low for lack of oil" (Percheron 1960, 92). The young prince, living in a "dream world of pleasure" was put into a protective bubble, as if his immune system could not tolerate the slightest irritant. His was a world of suspended animation. Yet, despite Percheron's efforts to rationalize through this narrative device, it still defies sense. If dancers and servants just disappeared for no reason, this might have caused greater consternation for the prince, spurring a different kind of existential dread. Perhaps he was too blissed out, drunk on new love to notice. Perhaps, but if he had been so ensconced in sensual delights, then he probably would not have been distressed by a sign of fatigue or a gray hair. Not only this, but we are also asked to believe that the King was able to maintain this charade—to avert the young man's attention to nature's violence and decay for over ten years! The reader is also asked to believe that the young man engaged in unrelenting carnality and—yet despite such prodigious sexuality—did not conceive a child for eleven years. To pull off this charade—or attempt to—the myth must truncate time—ten years pass as if a day. It is interesting how the mythic narrative shifts from the superhuman proportions (e.g., vanquishing his rival suitors) to the almost subhuman—the not yet Buddha is so beholden to the flesh that he has given up his agency. The reader is forced to believe the unbelievable or can simply accept the Four Signs—sickness, old age, death, and a wandering holy man—as a narrative device that propels the story forward.

MYTH: THE BUDDHA'S ALLEGED CRISIS

At the age of twenty-nine, the Prince is finally determined to leave the palace for a little fresh air. The King orders the streets cleared: "No heaps of filth were visible, no beggars or cripples no butchers blocks where the meat disappeared under a cloud of flies, no chained slave gangs digging ditches, no scavengers bent under their heavy slop barrels, no funeral processions" (Percheron 1960, 97). These royal efforts are to no avail; an old, decrepit man slips out of the crowd and into the prince's path. The not so young man is shocked—dumbfounded—he does not know what he is seeing (never mind that his chariot driver Chana readily knows the answer). The future Buddha starts to panic: "Oh, Chana, Chana, are there may like this? Could it happen to me? Could I suddenly be struck down by the same sickness. . . . Suddenly or little by little?" (Percheron 1960, 101). This brilliant, superhuman (e.g., as evidenced by his athletic exploits) is naive when it comes to the most basic facts of life—in a sense, he is an existential idiot, bearing the innocence of a three-year-old rather than someone who is almost three decades old. Even as a narrative device to move the story forward, I find this unsatisfactory yet it also leaves me wondering whether there is some more sinister rationale for this ploy—a justification of the Buddha's familial irresponsibility, perhaps. The plot needs to have a reason for the reader to believe that he would give up everything—wealth, power, beautiful wife, and newborn child. Sickness, old age, then death—the trifecta of misery—precede his exposure to a wandering yogi, who embodied a supreme placidity. The prince requests his leave from his father; the king doubles down on surrounding the prince with pleasure—again, to no avail. The Prince musters his courage to renounce everything he has known. To do so, he resorts to grandiosity: "His heart beat in unison with all those hearts that were suffering in the world outside, and he felt within him the strength, which only a man at the peak of happiness can possess, to undertake a task from which even the gods had turned away, knowing that they were impotent to save anyone from affliction" (Percheron 1960, 112). He will not remain flaccid. He—empowered by the gods, surpassing the gods—will discover the existential cipher and deliver the entire world from the ravages of anguish and misery, birth, and death.

MYTH: GOING FORTH

One can read extensively about the Buddha and rarely find an author question the validity of the four signs fable (see Kozak 2011b for an exception). After seeing these four signs, the prince mounts his horse Kanthaka and leaves the palace on his spiritual quest. We really do not know why—especially—the Buddha is called to find the way beyond suffering other than he has been preordained by the gods. If that conceit is set aside, all that is left is a burning passion—he is going to do it at any cost—without any particular explanation. The reader is asked to accept that the Buddha is special but he certainly is not the first person to be disturbed by the ephemerality of existence. He leaves his wife and newborn son behind and sets out into the forest. Leaving home at this time, not even middle-aged, is odd and against custom. Consider Chana's final plea once he realized his lord is committed to leaving: "How can you talk about helping people and, in the same breath, desert them. No master, enjoy the pleasures of life a while longer. Learn to know the child who will soon be born, carry him to the temple, present him to the gods, give him brothers. . . . Later, when your beard has grown gray, when your arms are less strong but you mind is strengthened by experience, then place your eldest son on the throne and go meditate in the forest. You can find the way to save us all from suffering then" (Percheron 1960, 113). This is the most sensible line in the entire story. It was the custom of the day and is still practiced in India—one fulfills their worldly duties before becoming a spiritual seeker. And again, the reader must abide by the Prince's specialness. Still, there is a contradiction here: If time is indeed eternal—as it is been presented—what is the big deal if he waits twenty years? It is not as if there was some particular urgency to his arrival or his mission—it is always been so: life is difficult, suffused with stress, laced with loss. Epic-worthy grandiosity—a holy anointed mission—is the only way to justify his premature departure. Not only an inflated sense of importance but a utilitarian philosophy—*the ends justify the means*—must prevail as well: "The time has come to leave this bediamonded cage and seek the Truth. For the sake of man's well-being I must find it" (Percheron 1960, 113). *It is okay for me to inflict pain on all those who love me because I am going to save humanity.* First, he could not have known that with certainty that he would be successful (the assurances of the gods notwithstanding). It was a monstrous, reckless risk. Second, and perhaps more importantly, it is inconsistent with the principles he would later teach.

Given these considerations—the bizarre timing of his leaving, the convoluted self-importance—I think there must have been a more prosaic reason: he was desperately unhappy. He left as much to escape as to realize a divine mission. He was a lost soul in search of himself. He was an exile as much as an incipient savior. But he was a talented, prodigious, highly intelligent lost soul (he seems a lot smarter once we bypass the nonsense about the four signs). He was destined to accomplish something great, something that would change the world and have a lasting impact on humanity. During his self-imposed exile, he does intensive yogic practices for six years. En route to his later near death experience from starvation—he might only eat a grain of rice with a little mud—he studies with the great gurus of his day—Arada Kalama and Udraka Ramaputra in particular—quickly mastering their techniques. He finds the gurus and their methods insufficient, not a thoroughgoing solution to the great existential problem. He is exposed to the yoga philosophies of his day such as atman—the spiritual essence—and *tat tvam asi*[9] (thou art that). Despite his initial encouragement that the fourth of the four signs inspires— the peaceful-at-heart ascetic he sees—the aspiring Buddha is not impressed with the gurus available to him: they seem more impressed with their own powers than attaining enduring liberation from life's existential challenges. Being the prodigy that he was, he seeks to push himself beyond, and starts his years of severe asceticism. He meditated in harsh conditions—on exposed rock—amidst tigers, monkeys, and other wild beasts. He was—apparently—undeterred, undaunted, untouched by external—or internal—conditions. The ascetic credo avowed that mortification of the flesh leads to transcendence. The body is an obstacle, something to be subdued—starved, pierced, stressed beyond normal capacity. But no matter how far the yogi goes in conquering the body, this transient state cannot persist: the soon-to-be-Buddha objects that no matter how high a yogi might get, there is an eventual return to baseline; nothing is eternal, perhaps not even the gods. He realizes these meditative highs are only a temporary solution, a stop-gap to the big existential problem. He wanted something more enduring, something that got to the root of the problem. Conquering the body, it would turn out, was futile because the body was not the culprit. Flesh does not have to be broken into submission, but the desires of the mind do have to be. Despite this insight into the ephemerality of asceticism, and although nearing-Buddha-hood, he became a victim of his own success and succumbed to the *joys* of deprivation. He was so engrossed in his meditations that he forgot or chose not to eat—his ribs protruded, his eyes sucked into their sockets—as many statues of the Buddha depict. But he pulled himself back from the edge, started to eat more and opined that "nothing in nature mutilates itself in seeking a better way to live"[10] (Percheron 1960, 137). He also begins to realize that solitary meditation was not the entirety of the path—it must include service to others. Whether he is successful or not, he is getting very close. Strengthened by the rich—by the standard of a grain of rice—meal offered by Sujata, he's got a date with a fig tree later that night: "Then Guatama crossed his legs, so that each foot rested under the opposite thigh. He closed his eyes, and in a firm voice, he pronounced an oath that the gods, the trees, the birds, and the earth could call to witness. 'Let my skin wither, let my hand waste away, let my bones crumble but until I have gained Supreme Enlightenment, I will not stir from this spot'" (Percheron 1960, 146). His evening is about to be crashed by his ubiquitous nemesis: "Mara, king of demons, waits for us on both sides of the road" (Ikkyu in Messer and Smith 2015).

MARA AS THE REPRESENTATION OF SELF

Mara is not the devil, not the embodiment of evil but the representation of desire and all of its shortcomings—a proxy for the forces of evolution that compel us to do the things that we do: search for food, eat that food, crave more food (replace food with sex, materials objects, fame, fortune). Mara knows that he has met his match—a prodigious yogi sitting under a fig tree.

Nevertheless, Mara marshals superhuman god-like forces of deadly destruction toward the dedicated yogi, and the soon-to-be Buddha remains unmoved. He tempts the Buddha with everything he has got: egoism, pride, vanity, pleasure, ecstasy. Even the temptation of love fails, the almost-Buddha-by-the-dawns-early-light counters that personal love pales in comparison to a universal love of all humanity. Nothing that Mara throws at the Buddha including a razor-edged discus can touch him, everything—spears, arrows—turn to flowers. Mara's final temptation is the Buddha's own reflection. The Buddha sits facing this image enticed by the belief in a permanent self—his essential soul. And again, the Buddha, transcends Mara's tricks, sees through the illusion. He touches the ground so the earth can witness his triumph.

The Buddha of myth is omnipotent; the psychological Buddha has insight into the impermanent nature of self and the causes of suffering as all-powerful—if there is no essential self, if everything is always changing, then adversity—including losing or not getting what we desire—cannot touch you. This supreme insight makes the Buddha invulnerable, immune, inviolate. Mara's inability to touch the Buddha is the litmus test for liberation. The Buddha went from one extreme—indulgence—to another—deprivation—and at the age of thirty-five in what is now Bodhgaya, India, he formulated a compromise between these polar opposites. The Buddha's myth can be seen as a teaching parable that sets up, in dramatic fashion, the core principle of his teachings: The Middle Way. He ate a meal, sat down under a fig tree, and proceeded to meditate through the night. To cling to the pleasures of this world, and even his own identity—his essential self—is futile. The Buddha conquers Mara and becomes a Buddha—an awakened one—much to the delight of the Hindu gods. He is not the first Buddha, mind you, but one of countless others to proceed him and to follow him into never-ending time.

MYTH POST-ENLIGHTENMENT

Once Mara is vanquished, the Buddha realizes there is no "builder of his house." His sense of self and its wellbeing has been based on false assumptions and perceptions. He rests in nirvana: "Death bringing birth is no more, for desire is crushed!" (Percheron 1960, 160). This insight makes a metaphysical assertion if interpreted literally, but if he is talking figuratively about the birth of craving in any given moment, a more psychological interpretation is available. True to the mythic origins of the Buddha, once he becomes illuminated, the world changes around him as if a ripple of goodness has swept over the earth where bad people became good and good people became even better. What was a solitary, introspective triumph gets mythologized into a salvific, grandiose, screed. The gods rejoice—the very same ones and their priests who the Buddha would later reject as speculative and unnecessary. To cover its own myth-making tracks, this great accomplishment must justify the means taken to achieve it. The now Buddha's grieving wife also feels the ripples of his enlightenment and ceases to grieve. All is good in the end.

After this glorious, life-altering night, the Buddha continues to work—that is, meditate—for seven weeks in perfect stillness. He has another profound insight during this period, something rather obvious and mundane rather than mystical or supernatural: whatever happens in any given moment has preceding events that cause it—i.e., dependent origination, the Buddha's positivistic, mechanistic causal insight: *because of this, that*. He challenges the traditional view of karma that actions in past lives determine everything such as illness or misfortune. This reframing of karma suggests that the Buddha was more concerned—perhaps only concerned—with causality within the context of a lifetime. The Buddha's ethics contrasted to those prevailing during his time. Karma was understood as action and any action generated karma—like a grimy film that collects on the skin. The Buddha's radical idea was that actions were not enough—intentions had to accompany those actions to generate karma. By making this distinction, the Buddha moved karma from the realm of religion to the purview of psychology (Gombrich 2009).

The Buddha worried, although, that his insights would not be understood by the average person, that a teaching mission would be pointless, exasperating, or an embarrassing defeat—a strange thought for one so illuminated and grandiosely confident earlier in his life. To the rescue comes Brahma the Creator who beseeches the freshly minted Buddha to embark on his pedagogical journey. Again, it is ironic that Brahma was not only excited at the awakening that would undermine belief in his world-creating godliness but helps the Buddha get his message out into the world.[11]

The Buddha ventures out and encounters a monk named Upaka, who is impressed by the Buddha's radiant countenance and enquires about his teacher lineage. The now Buddha disavows having had a guru. He is a self-made man, an autodidact of perfection. He, although god-like in his power, denies being a god and simply says he has awakened—*buddho*. Thus, *buddha* can be read as one who has awakened. This latter depiction is far less grand—and less problematic. If the Buddha's accomplishment is so rare and requires god-ordained omnipotence and if his intention is to recruit others into having a similar experience, how would this be possible if he is without peer—even among the gods? If his insights are the result of wisdom mixed with hard work, rather than divine preordination, then awakening could be available to just about anyone.

A LIFE OF SERVICE

Finding a psychologist in the mythic biography of the Buddha's long and illustrious career is by no means guaranteed, the Buddha of lore is also busy performing miracles:[12]

> On one occasion the Blessed One was traveling along the road between Ukkattha and Setabya, and Dona the brahman was also traveling along the road between Ukkattha and Setabya. Dona the brahman saw, in the Blessed One's footprints, wheels with 1,000 spokes, together with rims and hubs, complete in all their features. On seeing them, the thought occurred to him, "How amazing! How astounding! These are not the footprints of a human being!" (Thanissaro 2005b)

Over his long career, the Buddha is portrayed as an irresistible charismatic force: virtually everyone who encounters his personage or his teachings abandons their former life to follow him—including his now seven-year old son.

After his enlightenment, the anti-prodigal son, as it were, returns to his home of Kapilavastu. Broken-hearted father and wife wait for him expectantly. They both get speeches about former lives, past Buddhas, and a love that transcends the senses and familial bonds. It is the perfect setup for one who has abrogated his familial obligations. Of course, his wife falls into line, becomes a disciple, gives up her attachments. His father kneels too. The Buddha's return to his home city is—it seems—apologia. The ends have justified the means once again. The psychologist in me sees this scene as an expression of ambivalence, along with its justification. This magico-omnipotent, miracle wielding Buddha has a antisocial streak in him—he's ruined individual lives[13] and stressed communities. Unlike many psychopathic gurus of today, he is not exploiting that material wealth for himself but vilifying it—throwing it on the fire to be destroyed. Do not worry—it is not his own doing. It is the will of the gods—obeisant to the cycles of time—since he is done this all before. Justification: the Buddha's spiritual "treasure," unlike actual treasure, endures—power and wealth are impermanent.

AN IGNOBLE END TO A NOBLE LIFE

Toward the end of his life, the Buddha chided his followers to be islands unto themselves, not to succumb to sectarian affiliations, not be lax with their meditative disciplines. The entire history of Buddhism could be seen as a dismissal of or meandering from these injunctions (until, for example, the meditation revivals by Ledi Sayadaw in the early twentieth century; Braun 2016).

The Buddha's oft-quoted parting speech: "You should live as islands unto yourself, being your own refuge, with no one else as your refuge, with the Doctrine [dharma] as an island, with the Doctrine as your refuge" (Penner 2009, 96). This bold statement of self-reliance appears at odds with the grandiose Buddha, the Perfected One. Now he demurs, human-like[14] at the very end. And the final utterance: "Now monks, I declare to you: subject to decay are all conditioned things—strive on untiringly" (Penner 2009, 110).

MAKING SENSE OF THE BUDDHA'S MYTHOLOGY

The Buddha is born, not vaginally—and thus dirtily—and not even through a c-section, instead he emerges from the relatively clean side of his mother—the same side that she was impregnated by a white elephant's tusk. He hits the ground talking and walking. The Buddha vacillates between holiness and humanity, grandiosity, and uncertainty. He is at times megalomaniacal, if benevolent. This Buddha is sent by the gods on this holy mission. He is later protected by the gods as he later vanquishes the vanquisher: Mara, the tempter, who overran the chief of the gods—Sakka (also known as Indra). Thus, the Buddha is not just god-like, he appears to be more powerful than the gods themselves[15]. Then, shortly after his miraculous birth, he seems to forget his divine decree altogether. He becomes a human being—extraordinary, yes, but amnestic. Suddenly at the age of twenty-nine, as if hearing voices—to be the savior of humanity—his pre-ordained plan is set in motion. He is on a collision course with the image of sickness, old age, and death. Once he becomes the Buddha, some of the grandiosity returns: he is inviolate to human violence: "It is an impossible thing, one that cannot occur, that someone should deprive a Perfected One of life by violence, that a Perfected One should be killed by any act by anyone besides himself" (Penner 2009, 88).

Why does narrative coherence matter? It's an epic myth after all, not a factual treatise. Perhaps I am just nit-picking the Buddha's origin story. This myth might not be problematic except for the fact that it informs the contours of Buddhism and how we envision the Buddha today; it reeks of epistemological and ontological commitments—ones that are at odds with a psychological Buddha. The myth asks a lot of the reader—the suspension of credulity, the adoption of the Buddha's superhumanness godliness. This divine image is at odds with the brooding, lugubrious boy, who would steal into corners of the palace compound to meditate, it diverges from the thoughtful compassionate meditator under the rose apple tree.[16]

The Buddha grows up in an idyllic period of harmony: "the people were happy as if they lived in paradise" (Penner 2009, 23). If life had been so ideal, why did the Buddha want to go forth? If the reason was his only—late—discovery of sickness, old age, and death, it is not satisfying as a narrative device. There must be some other compelling reason, one such as homosexuality, perhaps. If the Buddha was gay, then solitude, mendicancy—with its sanctioned celibacy—relieved him of sexual otherness, and might explain why it took so long to sire a son—his carnal contact with his wife might not have been as frequent as the myth leads the reader to believe.

It is curious that after his god-ordained birth magic, the Buddha's life becomes rather ordinary. He has human concerns such as whether people will be able to understand him. If we were to believe that the Buddha really was superhuman, then it would seem that he would have less doubt—what happened to the confidence he had when he was born? His doubts, however, do not translate into modesty. He is, after all, a self-made man: "I am victorious over all, omniscient, undefiled, freed from all craving, gaining liberation and wisdom by myself alone" (Penner 2009, 41). Later on he says: "If there be anyone, Sir, to whom such enlightenment might be rightly attributed, it is I. I verily am perfectly and supremely enlightened" (Penner 2009, 73). Here, he is the Buddha—Lord Buddha to millions of believers.

The Buddha's project caused great social upheaval and disrupted communities as he had his own family—all of a sudden droves of young men (and old men) were—to borrow Timothy Leary's phrase—tuning in, turning on, and dropping out. He was changing the social fabric: young men were taken from mothers and wives to join his order, villages were beset—stressed by having to feed these possessionless, begging monks.[17] The Buddha's influence was more devastating than a pandemic. The Buddha dismisses everyone's concerns; they should be grateful instead. That is, do not complain; consider yourselves lucky—all these social parasites will provide these communities with great merit, wisdom, and holiness.

The Buddha is married to the most beautiful woman in the kingdom. Let us re-imagine this eleven years period of nuptial bliss. It is tedious. Onerous. Even if his sexual preference had not been for a male courtier, the endless passion with Yashodhara would have been exhausting, draining, even boring—after a while. He would have known, long before the momentous exposure to sickness, old age, and death, that blissful, unrelenting pleasure was empty, unable to provide lasting gratification. Realizing the dissatisfactions of the senses seems a more interesting narrative vehicle because it is psychological. He does not need an inane existential revelation. Instead he discovers, moment-by-moment, climax-by-climax, sumptuous meal by boundless banquet that the pleasures of experience are fleeting, insubstantial, and—ultimately—not a reliable source for happiness. There had to be something else—his identity could not nurture itself on the temporary abatement of lust, hunger, and pain or the delight of a graceful flower. A psychological motivation is more compelling, not just because it is more believable, but because it is insightful rather than fatuous—it accords with what people experience every day.

The Buddha was clever because he was able to put together observations in novel ways that no one had been able to do before. Just like an artist who creates something never created before: Van Gogh's painting strokes are not that difficult to replicate, but he was the first to conceive—and execute them. Like Van Gogh, I am at once struck with appreciation for and recognition of the obviousness of what has been created, and a sense, of course, "why didn't I think of that?" The Buddha tied things together—like an artist who arranges painted furring strips into a variegated circle, metal pins configured to the pattern of a face, or casts colored resin inside of a toilet paper roll to create negative space sculptures—things right in front of our noses. The Buddha took readily observed things and put them together in novel ways. Hyperbole is not necessary; epic gymnastics are not required to appreciate his accomplishment.

An alternative, more realistic scenario is that the prince was not a prince at all but the son of a wealthy, powerful nobleman. He was raised with privilege, skilled in athletics, inclined toward meditation. Like many, he lost his mother in childbirth, although he would have been too young to remember and too oblivious to develop attachment trauma from that loss, it may have carried symbolic weight later in his life. He was well versed in the existential facts of life, having travelled and studied abroad. The sybaritic benefits of palace life were endearing but unable to fulfill deeper yearnings. He was bored, restless, and felt trapped by the rigidity of court life. He was chastened by relentless hedonism—he found it somehow lacking. To satisfy his father, he would need to produce an heir. This does not happen until he is twenty-nine even though he has been having constant contact with his beautiful wife. But perhaps there was not as much fornication as the myth leads one to believe. Perhaps he liked to cross dress in his Aunt Prajapati's saris. Perhaps. If the Buddha was a flesh and blood human being pursuing a psychological project, then he would have flaws, shortcoming, and blindspots. The Buddha relied upon avoidance of the world as a principle strategy for affect management, thus simplifying the range of temptations[18] that confronted him and his followers. Renunciation was, perhaps, a short-cut, an easy way out through the much more difficult gauntlet of practicing non-attachment in the process of material daily life.[19]

NOTES

1. Biographies of the Buddha did not come until 400 years after his death, and the most famous of which the *Buddhacarita* dates from the second century CE (Lopez 2013).

2. Take this excerpt from the *Flower Ornament Scripture*—the root text for all East Asian Buddhism (Cleary 1985)—as an example: "At one time the Buddha was in the land of Magadha, in a state of purity, at the site of enlightenment, having just realized true awareness. The ground was solid and firm, made of diamond, adorned with exquisite jewel discs and myriad precocious flowers, with pure clear crystals. The ocean of characteristics of the various colors appeared over an infinite extent. There were banners of precious stones, constantly emitting shining light and producing beautiful sounds. Nets of myriad gems and garlands of exquisitely scented flowers hung all around. The finest jewels appeared spontaneously, raining inexhaustible quantities of gems and beautiful flowers all over the earth. There were rows of jewel trees, their branches and foliage lustrous and luxuriant. By the Buddha's spiritual power, he caused all the adornments of the enlightenment site to be reflected therein" (Cleary 1985, 55).

3. Penner (2009) does not distinguish between rebirth and magical, supernatural feats. Rebirth was the prevailing worldview in brahmanic India and it is no surprise that the Buddha's myth relies heavily on rebirth and that such stories—as in the Jataka Tales—which were enshrined by Ashoka on every available architectural surface he could find or make. The magical Buddha—the peer of the gods—might have been a later embellishment.

4. The mythic rendition of the Universal Monarch Vessentara, for example, portrays an individual more concerned with the perfection of mental states than with flesh and blood individuals, such as family members. Vessentara who says, "Omniscience is a hundred times, a thousand times, a hundred thousand times more precious to me than my son" (Penner 2009, 16). This claim sounds suspiciously similar to the Buddha's attitude toward his own son, whom he abandoned just after his birth.

5. "As is usual in the birth of all Buddhas, Gotama's mother died when he was seven days old" (Penner 2009, 23). As a consolation prize, she goes to Tushita Heaven, where the young prince—soon to be Buddha—just came from.

6. According to Batchelor (2011), the future Buddha's father, the King, was more of a magistrate and, thus, the Prince was more like a privileged kid from the elite ruling class. Unlike the myth where he never left the palace walls for twenty-nine years (on the face of it contradictory because there were three palaces the family frequented), he might have attended college in Taxila—what is modern day Iran.

7. Life, rather than death, is the problem because life implies sickness, old age, and death (Dukkha-dukkha). Death only begets more life in rebirth cosmology, but life itself is difficult. "Suffering enters the world in the umbilical cord of the infant" (Penner 2009, 156). The list of existential realities would often include birth along with sickness old age, and death in the Buddha's later teaching.

8. The metaphysic of rebirth, though, does offer a long-term solution: if you can become an *arhat*—literally, one who is worthy; someone who has accessed nirvana—you can step out of the cycle of birth and death.

9. I am familiar with this phrase—*Tat tvam asi*—thou art that—from my Bhakti yogi days. My guru's motto was a variation on this: *God dwells within you as you.* I sat on the cool polished marble floor, yearning for a connection. My visual field pulsated with a blue light, a sign that my shakti—divine spiritual energy—had been

activated through the guru's grace. I had been a lost soul—a *jivan*—seeking liberation—*mukti:* Atman reuniting with absolute consciousness. I aimed for unity from duality. None of these metaphysics prevailed at my first vipassana retreat. I did not see the blue lights, but I did notice how my body was comprised not of muscle, bone, and sinew but of pulsing, oscillating, vibrating energy. I discovered that my sense of self derived entirely out of narrative striving—the stringing together of memory, commentary, and anticipation. I experienced another awareness that did not require words, that abided with the energy of the body that had lost its solidity (and the excruciating pain that had been tormenting my knee for days). The difference between these two experiences might seem subtle—they were both self-transcendent; they were both "spiritual"; they were both intense and life altering. But the first presumed a kind of deficit, while the latter suggested a pre-existing wholeness that I was then able to access. The first required the intervention of a powerful guru, the second was self-orchestrated. The earlier involved striving for something beyond myself, the latter was a relinquishing of striving, letting go into the non-contingent, non-self-making flow of experience.

10. The story of Sujata and the golden dish that floats upstream where the Buddha famously predicts that if the dish *did* go upstream he would become enlightened and if it did not he would not belies a modesty missing from his earlier grandiose predictions.

11. Brahma's actions can only be explained by a later Brahmanification of the Buddha's story—e.g., the Buddha was the ninth incarnation of Vishnu—a process that at once corrupted the Buddha's atheistic message and helped to preserve it for the ages.

12. These include different spiritual powers and were not limited to the Buddha himself, but his disciples as well: Flying, clairvoyance, taming a wild drunk rampaging elephant, restoring severed limbs, etc. Apparently for the mythic Buddha, such powers were by-products of holiness and not ends to themselves. There are only occasional miracles and superhuman powers like curing a plague in the city of Licchavi, flying across the landscape and up to heaven, etc. The Buddha's powers seem to amount to cheap parlor tricks, a bit of flying, appearing and disappearing, teleportation; and he is not the only one with superpowers, Mogallana can fly too.

13. When he takes his son Rahula to join the order of monks, he does not consult the boy's mother or grandfather, who has been his father in the Buddha's absence. The Buddha does realize his mistake and makes a rule about getting parental permission to take children, but he does not return Rahula, leaving his family bereft, yet again.

14. More evidence of the Buddha's humanity is his peevish, almost mean teasing of Ananda who did not pick up on his hints about living to 100 instead of 80, the Buddha therefore dies at 80 when he was prepared to live much longer. The mythic Buddha is also misogynistic; the presence of women such as his aunt and stepmother adversely affected Buddhism's career as a "pure religion" reducing its reign from 1000 to 500 years.

15. Perhaps this is the benefit of realizing not-self—one becomes more powerful than all the gods and devils—who must thereby, by logic, be extensions of self.

16. Of course, the story of the rose apple tree is also tainted by mythic magic. Somehow the young prince loses his handlers and is watching the planting festival under the shade of a rose apple tree alone. He is disturbed that worms are maimed during the plowing. He later falls into a state of blissful meditation. The sun is so impressed with the boy's ardor that the shadow cast by his small sitting body does not move as he meditates through the day.

17. Of course, in the cosmological system of the Buddha's myth, his throngs of monks are not parasites because giving gifts of food and lodging to them brings great merit to the gift giver, ensuring happy rebirths. This megalomaniacal Buddha is also doctrinaire: Those that follow false doctrines do not go to the heaven of the thirty-three gods but are reborn in hell.

18. Take for example the Buddha's views on sex: "Haven't I in many ways advocated abandoning sensual pleasures, conquering sensual perceptions, subduing sensual thirst, destroying sensual thoughts, calming sensual fevers? Worthless man, it would be better that your penis be stuck into the mouth of a poisonous snake than into a woman's vagina. It would be better that your penis be stuck into the mouth of a black viper than into a woman's vagina. It would be better that your penis be stuck into a pit of burning embers, blazing and glowing, than into a woman's vagina. Why is that? For that reason you would undergo death or death-like suffering, but you would not on that account, at the break-up of the body, after death, fall into a plane of deprivation, a bad destination, a lower realm, hell. But for this reason you would, at the break-up of the body, after death, fall into a plane of deprivation, a bad destination, a lower realm, hell" (Thanissaro 2013).

19. The Buddha's avoidance was not limited to material but relationships as well. Making secure connections to parental caregivers during infancy and childhood is the parlance of attachment theory (e.g., Bowlby 2014). This attachment should not be confused with the Buddha's form of attachment—clinging, craving. The Buddha's avoidant maneuver is canonical—he abandoned his wife just after she gave birth to their first son. If he had not left infant Rahula in the hands of his wealthy grandfather, the Buddha might have also been considered a deadbeat dad. The Buddha takes his avoidant attachment style to an extreme in the Rhinoceros Sutta: "As a deer in the wilds/unfettered/goes for forage wherever it wants/the wise person, valuing/freedom/wanders alone/like a rhinoceros." He chooses the solitary image of the rhinoceros as the emblematic metaphor for monastic life. What the Buddha has apparently not considered or simply omitted is that at some point, this rhinoceros would have had to couple in order for there to be any rhinoceros at all. The monastic should not desire offspring, living socially in free society has too many entrapments, too much temptation for self-making. The Buddha eschews sympathy for friends, spouses, and children. But such dispassion cannot be the image for a fully realized human being but a cold automaton. It is almost like the caricature of Freud that American psychoanalysis became. Freud sat face to face with his patients. True, they sometimes laid on the couch but the rarified image of the analyst sitting behind the analysand—the blank screen—out of view is, likewise, sterile.

Chapter 2

The Hermeneutical Buddha
What He Taught, What He Thought (Maybe)

Buddhology is an imprecise discipline. We know of the Buddha mostly from the text of the Canon, with all its limitations; it is all that we have. Perhaps the Canon does contain the words of the Buddha, perhaps these are only partially his words. Perhaps the entire thing—some 16,000 pages—is confabulated. While physical, incontrovertible evidence is lacking, scholars read a coherent body of ideas in this multitude of texts—contradictions, inconsistencies, and lacuna notwithstanding. It is possible, as many Asian Buddhists do, to accept the stories of the Buddha's life and the episodes in the Canon as literal truth. That is, as far as we can tell—this is the Buddha speaking and he meant what he said literally.

Whatever the Canon represents, it has been a living, evolving document: "If the Canon, a vast body of material, was produced over many years—and to suppose otherwise seems to fly in the face of common sense—it is not surprising if misunderstandings or diverse interpretations arose in the process" (Gombrich 1996, xii). Commentaries exist, as well, but those commentators were written eight or nine centuries after the Buddha and about half a millennium after the time, in the first century BCE, when the Canon was first committed to writing.

Rahula Walpola wrote the classic *What the Buddha Taught*. Gombrich, playing on that title, wrote his book: *What the Buddha Thought* as a reading of the Buddha's mindset. Gombrich turns the literal reading of the Buddha upside down. Instead, he gives a hermeneutic interpretation of what the Buddha might have meant. The traditional literal Buddha gives way to sarcasm, irony, and metaphor.

Putting aside the question of historical authenticity, Gombrich asserts that the Buddha's words cannot be taken literally and much of the misunderstanding surrounding Buddhism stems from scholars doing just that: "As is his wont, the Buddha accepts the tenets of his brahman predecessors only to reinterpret them—one might say, to ironise them" (Gombrich 1996, xi). Penner (2009) says to read the myths as literal—as they were meant; Gombrich contends that the Buddha's words ought to be read as satire. Secularists rationalize the fantastical parts of the canon as later additions—religious embellishments. However, the Buddha might not have intended his lectures to be taken literally. If this is the case, then we do not have to see the fantastical parts of the Canon as later embellishments but as the Buddha's favored pedagogical devices. When he talked about his past life as Vipassi who lived for 80,000 years and presided over 6.8 million monks, he did so for some instructive or even artistic purpose. In other words, the embellishments might have been the Buddha's own.

THE BUDDHA ESCHEWED METAPHYSICS: EPISTEMOLOGY OVER ONTOLOGY

Most of the founders or promulgators of the world's great religions were ontologists—they taught the nature of the cosmos and humanity's place within it. The Brahmans of the Buddha's time believed in a cosmic order where the individual contained divine essence—the atman—that was separated from the tripartite Godhead: Brahma the Creator, Vishnu the Maintainer, and Shiva the Destroyer. Brahmanic soteriology is one of reunification—merging one's essence back into the pure, blissful, consciousness of the universe. The Abrahamic religions see humans as having an original sinful, flawed essence and consequently repentance, obedience, and subjugation to God the Father are soteriological imperatives. Much of Buddhism can be seen as "An immense metaphysical apparatus, a mythology without boundaries" (Eugene Burnouf quoted in Lopez 2013, 197). Yet, the great Buddhist scholar Eugene Burnouf could separate Buddha from Buddhism: "It is certainly not without interest to see Buddhism, *which in its first organization* has so little of what makes a religion, end in the most puerile practices and the most exaggerated superstitions" (quoted in Lopez 2013, 204, emphasis added). Daniel Lopez resonates with Burnouf when he says: "He [Buddha] is an anomaly in a culture devoted to priest craft, hierarchy, metaphysics, and myth" (Lopez 2013, 210). The Buddha, unlike the founders of the other world religions, did not appear to have a religious intention, but in fact, an anti-religious one. Ever the pragmatist, he thought that ontological speculation was a waste of time; instead one should devote oneself to self-development. The nature of the universe was irrelevant; a human's place in the universe was, likewise, besides the point, other than humans *did* live within the cosmos.

The Buddha did not allow his followers the consolations of dogma, ritual, speculation[1]—as most religions do—but he did, though, permit three refuges: awakening (buddha), truth (dharma), and community (*sangha*)—the obvious and uncontested point that individuals worked on their own salvation while part of a larger group. Awakening was the possibility realized by the Buddha himself. His experience is, admittedly, an $N = 1$ experiment. Dharma—as discussed before—has dual meaning: 1) the collected teachings of the Buddha as found in the Pali Canon and 2) the natural principles that these teachings refer to, e.g., the absence of an essential self. Here, the Buddha established himself as a naturalist.[2] Therefore, there is no additional need to naturalize dharma because that is what the Buddha meant by truth—natural lawful principles of experience, such as this follows that, this causes that (e.g., Flanagan 2007). In the Buddha's time, the laboratory was the individual, the empirical crucible of the solitary practitioner in the community of like-minded people working toward awakening. Now, the laboratory can be groups of individuals, scientific subjects contributing to group means, effect sizes, and probably coefficients.

The psychological Buddha advocated a praxis aimed at the radical transformation of the person. He could have engaged with metaphysical debates and questions (as the Tibetan Buddhists do today). However, given his experience with *samvega,* he saw no value in it. The term samvega (sam+vega) was used somewhat rarely by the Buddha in the Pali Canon. Its linguistic root *vega* means "shock," "impulse," or "wave." According to Thanissaro Bhikkhu, it is an emotion that was felt as an "absolute terror" by the young Gotama when he contemplated aging, illness, and death in the midst of an otherwise comfortable life. Despite the narrative convolution of those signs, discussed in the previous chapter, Samvega gets more to the underlying point of the story device. Thanissaro describes it as "oppressive sense of shock, dismay, and alienation" (Thanissaro 2011). These feelings are accompanied by disgust at having been so complacent—not having taken the existential realities of life more seriously, and thus having wasted so much time dwelling in moha. The startling, unsettled feelings give rise to a sense of urgency to do something about the situation. For the prince, it was to leave the palace in search of a greater truth—an enduring solution to the oppressions of sickness, old age, and death.

Given the problematic nature of the four signs incident, instead of all at once, the Buddha's experience of samvega was likely a gradual accumulation of dis-ease, disgust, and disquiet. Whether slow or gradual, it does not matter; the experience of samvega, however it arrived, was a sufficient motivating force to send the Buddha out of the palace and into the forest to seek a remedy that was not merely intellectual.

For the Buddha, the urgency was now. He ridiculed, lampooned, and satirized intellectualization, theorizing, and the speculations of metaphysics.

This distaste for metaphysics is powerfully portrayed in his dialogue with Malunkyaputta who—like many of us—wanted to figure out life's big questions, and he wanted to know the Buddha's position on a host of ontological issues. Malunkyaputta asks the Buddha the following questions: "Is the world eternal? Finite? Is the soul the same as the body? Whether a tathagata (the term the Buddha often referred to himself as; meaning 'one thus gone') exists after death?" The Buddha took issue with these questions, demurs, and finally asks him in return: "Why have I left your questions unexplained? Because they are of no benefit and do not lead to nirvana. What I have explained is the Four Noble Truths, because they are beneficial and lead to nirvana" (Gombrich 2009, 167). He then launches into an extravagant speech about the perils of metaphysical speculation. To make his point, he provides examples ad nauseam with absurd levels of detail—once again showing his penchant for irony, satire, and metaphor:

> It is as if a man had been wounded by an arrow thickly smeared with poison, and his friends and kinsmen were to get a surgeon to heal him, and he were to say, I will not have this arrow pulled out until I know by what man I was wounded, whether he is of the warrior caste, or a brahmin, or of the agricultural or the lowest caste. Or if he were to say, I will not have this arrow pulled out until I know of what name of family the man is; or whether he is tall, or short, or of middle height; or whether he is black, or dark, or yellowish; or whether he comes from such and such a village, or town or city; or until I know whether the bow with which I was wounded was a chapa or a kodanda, or until I know whether the bow-string was of swallow-wort, or bamboo fiber, or sinew, or hemp, or of milk-sap tree, or until I know whether the shaft was from a wild or cultivated plant; or know whether it was feathered from a vulture's wing or a heron's or a hawk's, or a peacock's; or whether it was wrapped round with the sinew of an ox, or of a buffalo, or of a ruru-deer, or of a monkey; or until I know whether it was an ordinary arrow, or a razor-arrow, or an iron arrow, or of a calf-tooth arrow. Before knowing all this, verily that man would have died. (Jennings 2010, 39–40)

The human condition, like the man wounded by an arrow, is curable—but only if treatment is applied efficiently. If there is delay, hesitation, or obstructing doubt, the patient may bleed out. The Buddha's position could not be clearer. It is not enough for the Buddha to just make the point, he drives the point home, pounds it into the ground. He does this, I think, because the pull for the "run-of-the-mill" person—("How very fearful, scary, abhorrent, detestable, and sickening is the state of an ordinary person"; Ledi Sayadaw cited in Braun 2016, 130)—toward speculation is so strong; without constant vigilance, one will lapse into the false certainty of metaphysical belief.

> There is the case where an uninstructed, run-of-the-mill person . . . does not discern what ideas are fit for attention, or what ideas are unfit for attention. This being so, he doesn't attend to ideas fit for attention, and attends [instead] to ideas unfit for attention. . . . This is how he attends inappropriately: "Was I in the past? Was I not in the past? What was I in the past? How was I in the past? Having been what, what was I in the past? Will I be in the future? Will I not be in the future? What will I be in the future? How will I be in the future? Having been what, what will I be in the future?" Or else he is inwardly perplexed about the immediate present: "Am I? Am I not? What am I? How am I? Where has this being come from? Where is it bound?" (Thanissaro 1999, 72)

Assuming responsibility for one's meaning-making without resorting to metaphysical speculation, at all times, in every moment, is hard, very hard.[3]

The cosmologies of the Buddha's time presumed reincarnation—the essence was that atman passed from one life to another. Whether the Buddha shared this as a personal belief, it was given in his teaching as the cultural lens from which he spoke. Given the primacy of rebirth in the prevailing beliefs of the time, it would have been an easy target for the Buddha's ironic satire. As Gombrich (2009) has speculated, even if not meant as satirical, talk about past lives was just the lingua franca of the time. The Buddha certainly referred to his past lives—in great detail—but it is not clear that he did so in a literal way. Here is an example:

> When the mind was thus concentrated, purified, bright, unblemished, rid of defilement, pliant, malleable, steady, & attained to imperturbability, I directed it to the knowledge of recollecting my past lives. I recollected my manifold past lives, i.e., one birth, two . . . five, ten . . . fifty, a hundred, a thousand, a hundred thousand . . . many eons of cosmic contraction & expansion: "There I had such a name, belonged to such a clan, had such an appearance. Such was my food, such my experience of pleasure & pain, such the end of my life. Passing away from that state, I re-arose there. There too I had such a name, belonged to such a clan, had such an appearance. Such was my food, such my experience of pleasure & pain, such the end of my life. Passing away from that state, I re-arose here." Thus I remembered my manifold past lives in their modes & details. (Thanissaro 2008)

The Buddha is either omniscient or embellishing with colorful rhetoric. A "hundred thousand" lifetimes *sounds* hyperbolic. The Buddha lived eighty years but say he only averaged fifty years across these births, that would amount to some 5 million years of existence. Since homo sapiens have not been around for 5 million years, it is safe to assume this statement takes poetic license. Whatever the case, these past lives references can become dogmatic stakes in the ground for people looking to believe, for those who cannot handle the existential burden of radical freedom (which is pretty much everyone).[4] The Buddha's account of past lives asks the reader to set aside conventional cosmology for a vastly different order of space-time. Indeed, the Canon is rife with fantastical references. Analayo (2018b) points to the mention of fish that are seven miles long and kings that lived 300,000 years. The Buddha's followers may well have accepted these claims literally but it is a big ask for a modern reader.[5] The passage above about past lives could be read, instead, as poetry. Then, its hyperbole can be seen as a creative device. Then—as Gombrich has suggested and I agree—these past lives descriptions are metaphorical vehicles. Multiple births, birth, and rebirth in heaven or hell is a description of this life—here and now. An unwholesome mind generates bad consequences; a wholesome mind, good ones.

Rebirth and remote karma (i.e., across purported lifetimes) were and remain metaphysical speculations without conclusive evidence (Analayo 2018b). Elsewhere, the Buddha took a more cautious tone: "Those who believe that all experience is caused by what was done in the past Sivaka, surpass what can be known by themselves and what is accepted as true in the world. Therefore, I say that those wanderers and Brahmans are mistaken" (Bodhi 2003, 1279). This is a very modern view. Actions have consequences *and* operate with known mechanisms. In the Buddha's day, little formal knowledge of psychology, biology, and physics was available, but much could be inferred from direct, common sense experience—*what the world agrees upon*. An earlier version of the Buddha's story, *The Noble Quest*, makes no mention of the Buddha having attained powers of clairvoyance into his past lives, but another version, *On Fear and Dread*, does feature these powers and may serve the later purpose of the Buddha's hagiography: he is god-like, omniscient. The Buddha also rejected metaphysical speculation as it pertained to causality. The prevailing view of karma saw causality in a cosmic scheme of checks and balances. All actions planted seeds that would take fruit in this or future lifetimes. Like the poison arrow, and his admonition to Sivaka above, the Buddha saw remote karma as speculative:

> There are cases where some feelings arise based on bile. You yourself should know how some feelings arise based on bile. Even the world is agreed on how some feelings arise based on bile. So any brahmans & contemplatives who are of the doctrine & view that whatever an individual feels—pleasure, pain, neither-pleasure-nor-pain—is entirely caused by what was done before—slip past what they themselves know, slip past what is agreed on by the world. Therefore I say that those brahmans & contemplatives are wrong. (Thanissaro 2005)

The Buddha observed that actions have consequence and that each seed will bear fruit, perhaps in the immediate ensuing moment or perhaps at a later time—but in *this* lifetime. An omniscient person could trace the entire interconnected, intricate causal chain that gives rise to each present moment experience. The Buddha articulated a psychological mechanistic theory known as conditioned arising (*paticca-samuppada*). The Buddha said *Evam sati idam hoti:* "It being thus, this comes about" or "things happen under certain conditions," i.e., "processes subject to causation" (Gombrich 2009, 131). This is known as the Chain of Dependent Origination. The Buddha on "this-that causality" said: "Let be the past, Udayin, let be the future. I will show you the *dharma*: when this is, that comes to be; with the arising of this, that arises when this is not, that does not come to be; with the ceasing of this, that ceases" (Batchelor 2011, 131).

Anything to do with rebirth may simply be cultural context and has no direct bearing on the Buddha's praxis—the process of awakening—except to the extent that it is a metaphor for cause and effect in one's own experience— in this lifetime with its ceaseless cycles of waking and going to sleep, eating and getting hungry, being in pain and being released from pain. The The Buddha was, it would seem, an extraordinarily intelligent meditation prodigy and a dedicated teacher. Strip away the hagiography and we can see a master pedagogue who used multiple rhetorical devices to teach his followers. When the Buddha is viewed through this pedagogical lens, a different sense emerges—not someone to be revered, admired certainly, but someone, rather, to be emulated.

THE BUDDHA BEFORE BUDDHISM

Conformists do not become revolutionaries. The Buddha was like a base jumper.[6] He leapt off a mountainous cliff with a wing suit but without the parachute that base jumpers require. Or, perhaps, the Buddha did have a parachute but chose not to use it. His wing suit was enough—responding to immediate conditions: thermals, wind, approaching crags—without panicking and without resorting to pulling the cord of the metaphysical refuges of essence, soul, and self.[7]

The *Book of Eights*—an anthology of sixteen poems—is believed to be among the Buddha's first teachings; they give a glimpse at the *Buddha Before Buddhism* (Fronsdal 2016)—an exemplar of primitive Buddhism: "We do not yet have a clear understanding of when many of these texts were composed . . . we know very little about the genesis of the early Buddhist teachings" (Fronsdal 2016, 138, 146). Many texts may have been composed long after the Buddha was dead. It is also not clear when the canon was "closed" to additions. It was supposedly first written down in the first century BCE, but it may not have been until the commentaries of the fifth century CE that all additions were made (Fronsdal 2016). Finding the early Buddha is similar to Gombrich's project of understanding not just what the Buddha taught (vis-a-vis Rahula's famous book) but what the Buddha *thought*. The *Book of Eights* sounds and feels secular *and* psychological.

The Buddha that appears in these verses favors the practical over the ideological, the psychological over the metaphysical, peace and equanimity over clinging and strife. The *Eights* stand on their own as a pedagogical statement without reference to the Buddha's most well-known teachings, such as the Four Noble Truths. While there is an "eight" in the title, this work lacks the familiar quality of lists. Its lack of numerical structure suggests its early origin but Fronsdal points to the most compelling evidence—that other well-established early texts reference the *Book of Eights*. Therefore, this series of poems gives an unusual insight into the nascent mind of the Buddha—the Buddha before he become institutionalized—and corrupted—by his followers. Fronsdal imagines that "Many of the rest of the surviving teachings [that is, the balance of the Pali Canon] could be considered elaborations, adaptations, and digressions from these early foundational teachings" (Fronsdal 2016, 10).

The Book of Eights has four recurring themes: not being attached to beliefs, not engaging with sensual desire, the qualities of a seeker, the curriculum for seekers. The first theme was radical for the Buddha's time and remains radical today in a world of sectarianism, racism, fake news, and alternative facts. The Buddha set out to differentiate his teachings from the doctrinal, ontological, ritualistic Brahmanic religions of his day. The Buddha distinguished his teaching from a plethora of other radical anti-traditional teachings as enumerated in the Samannaphala Sutta. These philosophies included variations of fatalism (actions are predetermined, actions have no consequences), materialism, and ritualistic agnosticism. He also had to compete with them (Mu Soeng 2020). This Buddha is not an intellectual, not interested in theory for theory's sake, not interested in conceptual minutiae. And while he was non-intellectual, he was not anti-intellectual as his teachings are astute and complex. He was, rather, as just discussed, against speculation without any immediate benefit. The practices he advocated were accessible without being arcane (with some notable exceptions like the twelve steps of paticca-samuppada).

THE "GREAT ONE'S" ORDINARY LIFE

Despite the mythological grandeur of his entry into the world—trumpeted by the gods as he was—he exited it in a rather ignominious fashion. At age 80, he was decrepit, living on the margins of society, no longer radiant or sharp. His body was failing and uncomfortable and he likely died of mesenteric infarction disease (and not food poisoning as is widely recounted, Batchelor 2015). Even before he reached older age, the Buddha complained of his energy and well-being. This image of him (rendered in multiple independent sources) is not particularly glorious and therefore likely reflects a more accurate portrayal (Batchelor 2015). After forty-five years of teaching, the Buddha's final words were, "Now, then, monks, I exhort you: All fabrications are subject to decay. Bring about completion by being heedful" (Thanissaro 1998). In another translation his last words are "Well now bhikkhus, I say to you: things fall apart, tread the path with care" (Batchelor 2015, 282). This admonition captures much of his teaching. Anything fabricated, which is everything experienced, is subject to decay, i.e., impermanence. To be heedful—mindful—is the path to self-transformation.

However, over time, the Buddha's ordinariness gave way to a grander vision. "By the time the Mahayana came into being, the Buddha had been dead for several centuries, and as the accounts of his life became more exaggerated and embellished, he came to be thought of as a semi-divine being" (Keown 1996, 59). Furthermore, "The major Mahayana sutras, such as the Lotus Sutra[8] (AD c.200) embark on a drastic revisioning of early Buddhist history. They claim, in essence that although the historical Buddha has appeared to live and die like an ordinary man, he had, in reality, been enlightened from time immemorial" (Keown 1996, 62). A more human vision of this Buddhahood makes the path more accessible than the idealized one presented in much of traditional Buddhism.

NOTES

1. The Buddha eschewed speculative metaphysics, and while his approach was epistemological, it still contained a basic metaphysic—non-harmfulness is desirable. His approach was ethical: actions have consequences, and we should incline toward beneficial outcomes. Relatedly, happiness is better than misery or if not better, preferable. It is hard—impossible—to think without metaphysics of some sort (e.g., Taylor 2012). Why is wellbeing better than pain? Why is goodness better than harm?

2. "The mere fact that Karl Popper and the Buddha agree about something proves nothing. Nevertheless, as a historian I find it interesting that they broadly agree about essentialism" (Gombrich 1996, 3).

3. For example, Jon Kabat-Zinn often speaks of intrinsic wholeness as an argument for and a result of mindfulness practice but this is a "bold metaphysical claim for which there is no scientific evidence and no chance of any such evidence" (Kearny and Hwang 2018, 296). This notion comes from Mahayana elaborations on the Buddha's teachings, which of course influenced Jon Kabat-Zinn since he practiced

Korean Zen. Intrinsic wholeness is a religious claim and a good example of backdoor metaphysics.

4. There is another problem with taking this passage literally. Who or what is reborn in each instance? If there is no essence that is self (as will be explored in detail later), then what could possibly persist?

5. To reject rebirth as preposterous, I might be succumbing to confirmation bias, as Analayo (2018b) has cautioned. He presents evidence for phenomena that are difficult to explain within current scientific paradigms. A lack of understanding might not be that surprising or problematic given that the brain is the most complex thing in the known universe and our understanding of it is—as any self-respecting neuroscientist would have to admit—superficial, preliminary, and cursory. We simply do not know what it is capable of. The brain's connectivity is, in some sense, *eternal*—if you started counting the connections aloud at the beginning of time, you would still be reciting them at the end of time. Strassman believes that near death experiences are hallucinations fueled by the pineal gland (Strassman 2001). The vast literature on psychedelic drugs also testifies to the types of experiences the brain is capable of producing (e.g., Pollan 2018). The key issue is whether the brain is the producer of consciousness (the materialist, biomedical view) or whether the brain is a tuner of consciousness that is somehow a fundamental property of the universe—take for just one example, the "mind stone" featured in Marvel's *Avengers Infinity War* and other films. Addressing this question is beyond the scope of this book.

6. For those of you who are unfamiliar, base jumping is the most dangerous recreational activity where people jump off high places with nothing but a wing suit and a parachute. It is far more dangerous than skydiving because of the terrains (jumping off a mountain instead of an airplane) and the shorter distances before hitting the ground.

7. Notice how I am using a metaphor here just like the Buddha used metaphors with his audiences. If I am being successful fostering a sense of understanding with this image, then I am using skillful means just as the Buddha did.

8. Mahayanists as depicted in the *Lotus Sutra* fueled the Buddha's hagiography. Here, the Buddha was enlightened before he sat down under the fig tree—his qualities ordained rather than earned, and what people saw twenty-five centuries ago was merely an emanation of the eternity that the Buddha was.

Part II

THE BUDDHA'S PEDAGOGICAL PROJECT

THE ENNOBLING PRAXES (AKA FOUR NOBLE TRUTHS)

Building on the ground covered in part I, part II looks at the Buddha's basic pedagogical project—his foundation course in introductory psychology, if you will—its principles, plangent with metaphors—fire, primary among them—as found in his most famous of teachings—what is commonly known as the Four Noble Truths: "Whoever in the past, the present, or the future, becomes fully awakened to things, says the Buddha, does so by becoming fully awakened into, what? . . . By becoming fully awakened to the Four Noble Truths" (Batchelor 2009).

Lopez (2013) clarifies that a better translation would be "the four truths for the noble" (226). While Peacock (2008) recasts "The Four Noble Truths" as the "Four Ennobling Truths," which shifts the emphasis from the nobility of its truth claims to the ennobling effect of practicing them. The transition from noble to ennobling makes sense because it is not clear the Buddha was making ontological or even epistemological claims with the four; they are praxes: situated in the moment rather than being *right* or *true* in any abstract manner. The Buddha's psychological approach can be viewed as bottom-up, derived from empirical, body-based wisdom and not driven by a top-down set of rules derived from dogma, tradition, authority—even the authority of the Buddha himself.

Upon becoming awakened, the Buddha had a major insight regarding dukkha: that it was pervasive and related not only to the big ticket existential facts of life (sickness, old age, and death) but to desire—why we want things we do not have; how we are afraid to lose the things that we do have. His first lecture was given in Sarnath to his previous five ascetic companions.

The Buddha's praxis is captured in his saying: "Both formerly & now, it is only dukkha that I describe, and the cessation of dukkha" (Thanissaro 2004).

The Buddha's invitation is to live life with intelligence (e.g., seeing into the nature of self more accurately) and living deliberately (skillfully) in such a way that dukkha is minimized. Wisdom and ethics are necessary but not sufficient because one also needs to train the mind so that it can execute the insights and disciplines in a structured manner (during meditation) and in life off the cushion. Batchelor sees the four as experiential hypotheses to be tested rather than epistemological claims. No beliefs are required. Adjectives of "right," "true," and even "noble" color these practical elements with an elitist religiosity. However, Batchelor points out that "noble" (*ariya*) was not in the Buddha's original description, another one of these later add-ons that lends a "polemical, sectarian and superior tone" (Batchelor 2012, 92), shifting the focus from the direct experience of doing the tasks to an abstract set of metaphysical considerations (Batchelor 2015). The use of the term "truth" invites an epistemological endeavor—to know the truth can lead to belief, elitism, and dogmatism. Batchelor argues that "nobility" invokes not just epistemological propositions, but metaphysical ones. So, instead of "truths" to be believed, Batchelor recommends "tasks" to be completed. Thus we get:

Suffering (*dukkha*) is to be *comprehended*[1] (*parinna*)
The arising (*samudaya*) is to be *let go* of (*pahana*)
The ceasing (*nirodha*) is to be *beheld* (*sacchikata*)
The path (*magga*) is to be *cultivated* (*bhavana*). (Batchelor 2012, 99)

A GREAT DOCTOR

The Buddha's first discourse can be rendered in a medical metaphor with each of the four corresponding to diagnosis, etiology, prognosis, and prescription or treatment plan. However, the medical metaphor is not in the original version: "The overall result of employing medical diagnosis to express his awakening is that this first teaching points directly to a psychological, or perhaps even therapeutic, attitude toward *dukkha*" (Analayo 2018a, 45, emphasis original). It is a useful metaphor and one that is consistent with the Buddha's self-description as a physician[2] and the dharma as healing medicine: "The Buddha said, 'O bhikkhus, there are two kinds of illness. What are those two? Physical illness and mental illness. There seem to be people who enjoy freedom from physical illness even for a year or two . . . even for a hundred years of more. But, O bhikkhus, rare in this world are those who enjoy freedom from mental illness, even for one moment, except those who are free from mental defilements'" (Rahula 1974, 67). It is an especially apt metaphor today, given the birth of secular mindfulness in the medical setting (e.g., Kabat-Zinn, 1990). "A good doctor can cure your disease but only a great doctor can show you that you were never sick" (Shinzen 2016). The Buddha was both a good doctor in "curing" the disease of dukkha and also a great doctor in that the cure involves the cessation of particular mind activity that reveals a more healthy state that was there all along—nirvana. The Buddha's teachings could be seen as removing the conditions that impair health rather than restoring an unhealthy body to a state of health.

It cannot be overemphasized that the Buddha's one and only concern was praxis: the pragmatic realization of awakening. Famously, and again, "The Buddha said that just as the ocean has only one flavor, that of salt, his teaching had only one flavor, that of liberation" (Gombrich 2009, 162).

NOTES

1. Thanissaro translates these as *comprehended, abandoned, realized*, and *developed* (Fires, 73).
2. The Buddha as physician was not just a metaphor. He actually did have some medical knowledge and cared for the sick and encouraged his followers to do the same. "Whoever would tend to me, he should tend to the sick" (Batchelor 2015, 228).

Chapter 3

The First Ennobling Praxis
What is the Problem?

The Buddha declared the first of his propositions: "Truth of suffering (Dukkha). What, O Monks, is the Noble Truth of Suffering? Birth is suffering, sickness is suffering, old age is suffering, death is suffering. Pain, grief, sorrow, lamentation, and despair are suffering. Association with what is unpleasant is suffering, disassociation from what is pleasant is suffering. Not to get what one wants is suffering. In short, the five factors[1] of individuality are suffering" (Keown 1996, 46).

A patient presents to a medical provider. She is not feeling well, but her condition does not seem to be a physical ailment. Something is off. She has a generalized feeling of dissatisfaction, dread, dis-ease. The doctor determines that her condition is dukkha. Remembering that single word translations of dukkha such as suffering, stress, and anguish are incomplete and that the Buddha chose to use the metaphor of something being off, he delineated three types of dukkha: *dukkha-dukkha* (physical pain), *viparinama dukkha* (vicissitudes of life), and *sankhara dukkha* (from self or mind, i.e., constructed distress; Peacock 2008). The latter dukkhas are pervasive, subtle, and to a large extent, self-inflicted but dukkha-dukkha is inescapable for corporeal beings, subject to the laws of physics and destined to age, desiccate, fall ill, and die. The cow swishes its tails to swat away flies—dukkha-dukkha—demonstrating unconditioned reactivity with no underlying sense of self and presumably no capacity thereof. Yet the other types of dukkha can seemingly only happen to a self. Dukkha is ever present when things are going well: "the faint, quivering unease that accompanies happiness" (Batchelor 2015, 179) or what might be considered a "background radiation" (Kozak 2018b) that is present with all experience, whether pleasant, unpleasant, or neutral. Like everything else positive experiences would not last. The source of this radiation is the impermanent, precarious, and contingent nature of existence.

"Impermanence" as the single word translation of anicca does not really capture the full range of that concept either. Yes, things are always changing, but that is not necessarily problematic because we are quite adaptive. It is the precariousness of things that is disquieting; we want—crave—a greater sense of stability. If we are really paying attention, we realize how vulnerable we are[2]. At any moment, an illness may strike a loved one; an accident may occur; or a nuclear warhead may explode. We just do not know and we cannot count on things being stable (unless we self-deceive—moha). I think reasonable people can accept that we cannot always get instant gratification and that pleasure would not last even though we pursue it relentlessly. The real problem is that the *very* conditions that give rise to pleasure may disappear at any moment with or without warning. We all stand on the edge of a precipice. We may not fall off of that ledge for a long time, but eventually we will *and* we know that we will (Yalom 1980). The Brahmanic Absolute is birthless and deathless and unified in its perfection. This contingent world of samsara might seem like an inferior version that we need to subdue and transcend. But the Buddha would have none of that. Perfection could be found right in the midst of imperfections, contingencies, and tragedies—"the traumas of everyday life" (Epstein 2013)—provided we can *accept* them. To move from denial to acceptance requires adjusting the perceptual biases that are built into us by evolution and the subsequent conditionings of culture.

The Buddha made it plain that dukkha-dukkha is unavoidable: birth, aging, sickness, and death are unconstructed and happen to all living things. Viparinama-dukkha and sankhara-dukkha require our clinging, craving involvement: wanting things we want, not wanting things we do not want. In terms of sankhara-dukkha, Peacock explains: "The moment that consciousness imagines that it is other than its actual life processes it become agitated and anguished" (2008, 215). These desires are built on an unconditioned biological matrix—the cow swishing its tail—but for humans there is an at least intermittently conscious agency that is weaving these biological reactions into a narrative of self-identity. There is no way to get around this mix of constructed and unconstructed. The Buddha explained:

> When I was still a bodhisatta, he recalls, it occurred to me: "What is the delight of life? What is the tragedy of life? What is the emancipation of life?" Then, bhikkhus, it occurred to me: "the happiness and joy that arise conditioned by life, that is the delight of life; that life is impermanent, *dukkha* and changing, that is the tragedy of life; the removal and abandonment of grasping for life, that is the emancipation of life." (Batchelor 2012, emphasis original)

The Buddha, here, was not anti-joy as he is sometime characterized. There is plenty of it in life. The problem is that it does not last. It is impermanent as is everything else. Joy stands next to dukkha-dukkha, the tragedy of life. Because delight contains the seeds of its own dissolution, it is accompanied by a dis-ease. Delight is undermined if there is a wish for constancy.

Each of the sense gates has its own relationship with delight and danger. For example, seeing gives rise to joy, but since that joy is fleeting, danger lurks if one becomes attached to what is seen, i.e., identifies with it to the point of contingency. The eye may also see something that it does not like or does not want, and it wants to push it away. This is attachment in the negative with aversion replacing grasping—identification leading to contingency remains. The same consideration that applied to the eye applies to the ear, nose, tongue, body, and mind. If one can relinquish that desired hope of permanence, then attenuation of dukkha is possible. A more non-contingent relationship to experience was expressed in William Blake's poem "Eternity": He who binds himself to joy/Does the winged life destroy/But he who kisses the joy as it flies/Lives in eternity's sunrise (Blake and Kazin 1977, 135). Likewise, it is not hard to imagine Seneca enjoying life's evanescent pleasures precisely because they are impermanent (Burkeman 2013). Taking ownership of any experience is the problem—whatever it might be—because no experience is stable. It is impermanent, fragile, precarious, and unpredictable. That sense of ownership stems, likewise, from a self that wishes to be stable. "Things are unsatisfactory because they are impermanent—hence unstable and unreliable—and they are impermanent because they lack a self-nature which is independent of the universal causal process" (Keown 1996, 51). Joy—even pain—is okay, as long as you "kiss it on the fly." If you bind yourself to it with if–then contingency, painful reactivity will follow.

Recall that dukkha is one of the three hallmarks of existence. The other two are impermanence (anicca) and the not-self (anatman). Another way to think of the three hallmarks of existence is as "universal characteristics of embodied human awareness" (Knickelbine 2013). Each one of the hallmarks gives rise to the other. If we jettison the need for self-nature and fully accept that things are changing, the basis for dissatisfaction dissipates into the ceaseless flow of experience. Easy to conceptualize; almost impossible to pull off. If once can orchestrate this feat of letting go—according to the Buddha and Blake—it will be accompanied by the bliss of "eternity's sunrise."

Defining dukkha as "suffering" makes the Buddha's teaching seem like a pessimistic, nihilistic philosophy. But as the Buddha makes clear in the passage above and elsewhere, while certain aspects of dukkha are uncontrollable, others are not. We are capable of self-inflicting ever more dukkha or taking steps to mitigate its impact—we can work ourselves out of the predicament.

Batchelor encourages us to remain open to "the ambiguity, uncanniness, and ineffability of life as it reveals itself and withdraws from moment to moment. . . . To comprehend *dukkha* is to comprehend life intimately and ironically with all its paradoxes and quirks, its horrors and jokes, its sublimity and banality" (Batchelor 2015, 72–73, emphasis original). Furthermore, "Embracing *dukkha* entails abandoning any ontological commitment to a disembodied self or consciousness that is apart from experience yet magically peers in on it" (Batchelor 2015, 203, emphasis original).

NOTES

1. These are most commonly translated as the five aggregates, or the totality of mental life—form, feeling, perception (or apperception), mental factors, and consciousness. These will be explored in the next section.

2. I am editing these pages during the COVID-19 pandemic of 2020. Now, potential calamity has become actual. We don't need to be keen with our attention. The instability is palpable, rampant, ubiquitous.

Chapter 4

The Second Ennobling Praxis
Getting to the Root of the Problem

The Buddha declared his second proposition: "The Truth of Arising (*Samudaya*): This, O Monks, is the Truth of the arising of Suffering. It is this thirst or craving (*tanha*) which gives rise to rebirth, which is bound up with the passionate delight and which seeks fresh pleasure now here and now there in the form of (1) thirst for sensual pleasure, (2) thirst for existence, and (3) thirst for non-existence" (Keown 1996, 49).

To properly treat this patient, we must understand the nature of her illness. What is causing dukkha? What is the etiology? An unquenchable thirst—*tanha*—appears to be the culprit. Tanha can refer to actual thirst or a metaphorical longing that covers the usual suspects: gluttony, lust, and even pride. Tanha is self-perpetuating, like drinking salt water to quench that unending thirst (Penner 2009). Batchelor (2015), however, translates thana as reactivity.[1] Similarly, Peacock translates tanha as "a compulsion to re-become" (2008, 218). Such compulsive reactivity overlaps with *papanca* or proliferations (Olendzki 2010). These proliferations often take the form of stories—whether whole or fragmented—that circulate in the mind and to which the self identifies, i.e., believes are true or reacts to as if they are true or important. The result is distress.

A colorful example of tanha can be found in the long-running satirical television series, *South Park*. Eric Cartman is an obese nine-year-old boy known for his selfishness, conniving, and poor impulse control. In one episode, Cartman is pacing in front of a game store awaiting the release of a new gaming console. Unfortunately for him—and everyone around him—the console would not be released for another three weeks. Cartman grunts, "Come on. . . . Come on. . . . How much longer . . . ?" He bemoans his fate, "Time is slowing down. It's like waiting for Christmas, times a 1000." In order to relieve his anguish, he hatches a scheme to freeze himself in the Colorado winter only to be thawed when the device is finally available. Thirst suggests something elemental, instinctual, and unconditioned. Craving has its roots in the unconditioned as an emotional metaphor based on the physical impulse of thirst (presumably all creatures have a version of this). Due to the human, language-based, self-referential capacities of the prefrontal cortex in conjunction with operant learning, we can come to have an entire universe of conditioned cravings that have nothing to do with survival or propagation of the species. In the privileged, modern context where day-to-day existence does not have life and death consequences, the tanha metaphor is aimed toward things that have no existential value—that pair of shoes, a vacation, a romantic attraction, esteem from everyone that we meet, etc.

Not all desires are counterproductive, some are wholesome, such as the desire to awaken and transcend reactivity (*chanda*). "Let the passions be subdued, as a straw hut is trampled by an elephant. Know all that he who would seek to flee from his passions in the sanctuary of a hermitage would live in error; he must fight them under the open sky, armed with healthy realities" (Percheron 1960, 175). This is the Buddha at his contradictory best: what was his project if not putting people into the protection of hermitage—monkhood. But there is a way out this apparent hypocrisy—one can live in the world with "healthy realities" such as those laid out in the fourth of the ennobling praxes below. The quest for awakening itself can be readily corrupted by greed, aversion, and self-identification if the practitioner is not mindful of how effort is being made or if it is otherwise conducted without wisdom. Wisdom, in conjunction with mindfulness, can lead to a thoroughgoing reorientation to the power of pleasure, opting out, as it were, from evolution's prime strategy to trick us into pursuing things that will ultimately be unsatisfactory yet further the organism's survival chances. Awakening is a different kind of pleasure because it does not involve the self-making activity of a presumed essential self. What the Buddha did under the fig tree appeared to be a successful hack into evolution's operating system that retained joy, pleasure, and purpose without generating unnecessary dukkha.

Whenever tanha/papanca/reactivity arise, there is a commensurate opportunity for insight to occur. It is difficult to stop the mind's production of stories, thoughts, protean expectations, assumptions, and rules. However, with awareness of the mind's craving tendencies these productions or fabrications do not take full form.[2] They can be averted, deconstructed, and made flimsy with awareness. This is true for Buddhas and non-Buddhas alike (Buddhas are—allegedly—just more efficient at it). We can come to see the undisciplined, run-of-the-mill, mind as humorous, ironic, even absurd in its clamoring, clinging, and cajoling. A simple exercise can illustrate the power of reactivity. Try to sit quietly and observe the thoughts that arise in your mind. Try to characterize these thoughts according to what the mind appears to want. If you are rehearsing a future conversation, what is your mind seeking? Reassurance, certainty? Does it just want stimulation, something to do other than to observe?[3] The mind's activity will reveal *samudaya*, that thirst for basics such as safety, okayness, certainty, distraction, comfort, ease, and entertainment. Remember in the Fire Sermon, the Buddha recognized that sheer contact with the world of sensible objects creates dukkha. These contacts encompass both the conditioned and unconditioned sources of contingency. As a great metaphor-maker, the Buddha created an image to express the power of reactivity—Mara—his bedeviling alter ego and proliferation, desire, and aversion all wrapped up into one.

> But the power of these habits, the power of this conditioning, is also what the Buddha calls the power of Mara, the power of death. It's deadening. Mara is a metaphor of a kind of inner death, this grasping, this clinging, this wanting, this fearing, this desiring. And the Buddha says, there is nothing in this world as powerful as the power of Mara, the armies of Mara. And these are not some abstract mythological thing we read about or see depicted in iconographic representations of the Buddha's conquering Mara, but this is what is happening each time we stop and watch ourselves. We experience the power of Mara. (Batchelor 2009)

The Buddha was not just interested in a diminution of life's problems. He was seeking their total annihilation. Not everyone is the caricature of desire represented by Eric Cartman. However, we otherwise sanguine individuals are vulnerable to circumstances that can conspire at any moment to outstrip our ability to cope—a spouse's betrayal, the death of a child, and financial ruin. But it does not require a catastrophic event. It might be an insult, frustration, or trivial happenstance.

The presence of reactivity implies its absence—an absence the Buddha realized in meditation. From his ability to halt the influence of tanha, the Buddha articulated a hopeful note for working with the mind—it can be done—bringing us to next of the ennobling praxes.

NOTES

1. Traditionally, the arising—samudaya—of tanha is seen as the root cause of dukkha. Batchelor goes to lengths to make the case that arising is the arising of craving from dukkha rather than the other way around. The causal direction between tanha and dukkha is an empirical statement that can be tested through practice. You can see how the subtle (and not so subtle) push and pull against experience gives rise to a sense of something being off. It does not make sense to me that craving arises from dukkha because then we must accept a metaphysical claim about the nature of

the world. The world out there and in here is inconstant and in realizing this "truth" you can then let go because it is futile not to do so. Batchelor focuses on the four signs (i.e., dukkha-dukkha) and not the more psychological aspects (viparinama and sankhara-dukkha). However, the pains of life cannot stop the reaction *arising* to it. Batchelor takes issue with the claim that craving gives rise to suffering because if you extinguish craving/reactivity (which might be possible) suffering will continue because we are embodied beings. I think it would be better to distinguish between pain and suffering. Pain is unavoidable as long as we are alive and have bodies subject to the laws of physics. Suffering is the reaction to pain and arises out of the proliferations and elaborations of the mind. Reduce craving and you reduce those sources of suffering, misery, and anguish—dukkha. The Buddha had pains, presumably, but not suffering. Working toward a relative diminution of reactivity is a good aspiration. We cannot extinguish the existential conditions of life—the big and small ticket items—yet we can diminish our reactivity to them by, for example, making them impersonal. Whether samudaya gives rise to dukkha or the converse, the goal is the same—cessation of that reactivity.

2. In Kozak (2018b), I coined the acronym FEAR: fabrications of expectations, assumptions, and rules.

3. Wilson et al. (2014) found that research subjects would rather self-administer an unpleasant electric shock rather than sit alone with their thoughts.

Chapter 5

The Third Ennobling Praxis
Can the Problem Be Resolved?

The Buddha declared his third proposition: "This, O Monks, is the Truth of Cessation of Suffering. It is the utter cessation of that craving (tanha), the withdrawal from it, the renouncing of it, the rejection of it, liberation from it, non-attachment to it" (Keown 1996, 52).

What is the prognosis for our patient? Can she recover now that she understands what her condition is and what is causing it? The Buddha was sanguine about the prospect. By eschewing fate and embracing self-understanding, change was possible. This patient has within herself the means to address her condition (the details of which, will be covered in the next chapter on the fourth ennobling praxis). For now, the Buddha is only speaking to possibility—human potential. He is saying, to inject a contemporary metaphor, that it is feasible, with sufficient wisdom and ethical living, to hack into our minds' operating system and override reactivity. Batchelor notes that the ceasing (*nirodha*) or, more commonly, nirvana (*nibanna* in Pali) is to be beheld (*sacchikata*). Nirvana is also democratic—not just the reserve of serious Buddhist practitioners but available to anyone when there are moments of cessation. Nirvana is a state that transcends language and the conceptualizing, narrative mind. How then can it be described and taught to others without language? Metaphor is one option. Gombrich elaborates:

> The Buddha had a simple urgent message to convey, and was ingenious in finding ever new terms and analogies by which to convey it. . . . *Nirvana* is part of an extended metaphorical structure which embraces Enlightenment and its opposite. What has to be blown out is the set of three fires: passion (or greed), hatred and delusion. . . . Everything O monks is on fire. . . . It is all our faculties (the five senses plus the mind), their objects and operations and the feelings they give rise to. (Gombrich 1996, 65–66)

Shinzen Young, also sensitive to the constraints of language, talks about his teacher's approach to circumventing these limitations:

> Sasaki Roshi had a very eccentric way of talking. For example, sometimes instead of calling a pine tree by its usual Japanese name: *matsunoki*, he would say *matsunoki toyu hataraki*, which means "the activity called pine tree." He also used phrases like *ningen toyu hataraki*, "the activity called human being," and *kami toyu hataraki*, "the activity called God." This is a very idiosyncratic use of the Japanese language. He talked this way to remind people that all the objects in the world can be experienced as waves of impermanence, not just as concrete, separate things. Because any one thing comes from a relational net that is ultimately connected to everything. (Young 2016, 129, emphases original)

The distinction reflected in Sazaki Roshi's idiosyncratic way of describing pine trees and god can be captured in the simple yet powerful distinction between:

This is happening to me.
This is happening.

There is the *happening* in any given moment that can be just of and by itself without being in reference to or owned by an individual. To take ownership is to suggest a separation between subject and object rather than a continuous phenomenal field that includes both without distinction. Dukkha arises when objects are appropriated and quiets when there is just the flow of experience.

Nirvana is like blowing out a flame. For another metaphor, the conditions that gave rise to it have stopped: "Removing craving and ignorance is like taking away the oxygen and fuel which a flame needs to burn" (Keown 1996, 53). The body is still subject to affliction but not necessarily to reaction—one can be, like the Buddha, more imperturbable. The seeds of reactivity never stop dropping to the ground as long as we are sensory-perceptual creatures with a pulse. What can stop, however, is the ownership, contingency, and proliferation of that built-in reactivity.

Here is a formal definition of the term nirvana: "The word is made up of the prefix *nir* (not) and *vana* (effort of blowing; figuratively, craving); probably the origin was a smith's fire, which goes out or becomes extinguished (*nibbayati*) if no longer blown on by the bellows" (Nanamoli Thera 1995). The lay understanding of nirvana conjures up images of bliss—a transcendent ecstasy that cannot be captured by words. As just described, he Buddha recognized that words were insufficient so relied on metaphor. Yet, while bliss (*nirvrti* in Sanskrit or *nibbuti* in Pali) might be part of the nirvana experience, they are distinct concepts such that one can experience bliss with or without nirvana (it is a safe bet that if you are experiencing nirvana, you will be experiencing bliss).[1] Nirvana is expressed in negative language what it is *not* rather than what it *is*.

Thanissaro Bhikkhu provides another metaphorical nuance: "*Upadana*, or clinging, also refers to the sustenance a fire takes from its fuel. *Khandha* means not only one of the five 'heaps' [the five aggregates] that define all conditioned experience, but also the trunk of a tree. Just as fire goes out when it stops clinging and taking sustenance from wood, so the mind is freed when it stops clinging to the khandhas. So the image underlying nirva na is one of freedom" (Thanissaro "The Image of Nirvana").

Thanissaro warns that "The fabrications of language cannot properly be used to describe anything outside of the realm of fabrication" (Thanissaro 1999, 9). Thus, one needs metaphors and ample synonyms: "The unfabricated, the unbent, the effluent-less, the true, the beyond, the subtle, the very-hard-to-see, the ageless, permanence, the undecaying, the surface-less, non-objectification, peace, the deathless, the exquisite, bliss, rest, the ending of craving, the amazing, the astounding, the secure, security, the unafflicted, dispassion, purity, release, the attachment-free, the island, shelter, harbor, refuge, the ultimate" (Thanissaro 1999, 17–18).

Through fire metaphors, nirvana can be seen as a non-mystical but extraordinary state, one not for the faint of heart. When reactivity subsides, then all the guideposts to reality-as-usual are set aside. This can be a disorienting feeling of groundlessness as the familiar markers of thought, feeling, and behavior fall away and a new way of perceiving takes over. Little wonder that it is very hard to stay in this state—the mind's greed can grab hold of it, try to make it last and by doing so make it dissipate; as well, reactivity may take the form of terror as if falling into a rabbit hole of the unknown. When nirvana is experienced, the parts of the brain responsible for self-identity are likely inhibited, giving rise to a more sensory, less-languaged sense of being-in-the-world.

Shinzen Young (2016) points out that nirvana has the dual meaning of cessation and "satisfaction" in the sense of quenching a thirst—in other words, resolving or relieving tanha.[2] Paradoxically, tanha cannot be satisfied by drinking more (desire) or repudiating drinking (aversion) but only in removing reactivity. When the fires burn out they—seemingly—become cold ashes. Seemingly, because the Buddha felt that embers always remained.[3]

Batchelor recasts the Buddha's famous phrase: "I teach suffering (*dukkha*) and the end of suffering (*dukkha*)" replacing the latter suffering with reactivity (Batchelor 2015, 169). Sunakkhatta criticizes the Buddha by saying:

> The recluse Gotama does not have any superhuman states, any distinction in knowledge and vision worthy of the noble ones. The recluse Gotama teaches

a Dhamma *(merely) hammered out by reasoning*, following his own line of inquiry as it occurs to him, and when he teaches the Dhamma to anyone, it leads him when he practices it to the complete destruction of suffering. . . . The Buddha responds (referring to himself in the third person): Thinking to discredit the Tathagata, he actually praises him. (Thera and Bodhi 1994, emphasis added)

Well said, Sunakkhata, you have capsulized the premise of this book: The Buddha was a psychologist, hammering out reasoning in the service of peaceful well-being. Nirvana is not, as it is often portrayed, a final resting place, irrevocable once attained.[4] Instead, nirvana can be seen representing human possibility and arises in accordance with the ratio of reactivity to non-reactivity.

ENLIGHTENMENT AS WELLBEING: METAPHYSICAL ASSUMPTION OR NATURAL FINDING

Is nirvana—awakening—the ultimate expression of wellbeing or is wellbeing a side effect of this profound psychological state? The medical model of the four ennobling praxes suggests the former and I also think that the latter is the case as well—awakening may be natural in the same sense that hypnotic states are natural or that sleep is natural—or any other biological function. Awakening may conduce wellbeing, but it may be more fruitful to think about it as transcending wellbeing. By equating awakening with wellbeing—even if it is *supreme* wellness, it is in the same category with physical fitness, being in love, etc. And to say that awakening is *natural* is not quite right, either. It is not the natural inclination of the human mind—it must be forced, coerced, cajoled, trained, disciplined. It is so awkward that *unnatural* might be a better adjective. Evolution does not care about ultimate wellbeing, a species can propagate itself with only a modicum of wellbeing—just enough to get the job done. The natural *is* unnatural until it becomes the most natural thing in the world.[5] To be natural, it is as if the human mind had this occult way of being that could only be experienced by knowing the secret combination to its safe. Mindfulness meditation was part of the Buddha's hidden code "turn the tumbler left to the number . . . two turns to the right."

NOTES

1. "Nibbana can be seen not as the attainment of a quasi 'mystical' state, but the quelling of behavior patterns based on greed, aversion, and confusion" (Peacock 2014, 16).

2. In his meditation instructions, Shinzen points out that the meditator can attend to the "gone" aspects of phenomenological experience—the vanishings, the

disappearances—and that these can be as interesting as arisings. In a sense, by fully attending to a *gone*, it is a moment of nirvana—he calls these "gone goodies."

3. Unless ultimate nirvana is achieved: "Monks, there are these two forms of the nibbana property. Which two? The nibbana property with fuel remaining, and the nibbana property with no fuel remaining. And which is the nibbana property with fuel remaining? There is the case where a monk is an arahant whose effluents have ended, who has reached fulfillment, finished the task, laid down the burden, attained the true goal, destroyed the fetter of becoming, and is released through right gnosis. His five [sense] faculties still remain and, owing to their being intact, he experiences the pleasing & the displeasing, and is sensitive to pleasure & pain. His ending of passion, aversion, & delusion is termed the nibbana property with fuel remaining. And which is the nibbana property with no fuel remaining? There is the case where a monk is an arahant . . . released through right gnosis. For him, all that is sensed, being unrelished, will grow cold right here. This is termed the nibbana property with no fuel remaining" (Thanissaro 1999).

4. There are many statements throughout the discourses where the Buddha claims to have gone beyond reactivity—this is what *thatagahta* means: one who has gone thus. He has mastered, without exception, reactivity such that no sense contact gives rise to a conditioned experience. Is this possible? Is it useful to conceptualize the Buddha in this way. Has not he re-introduced a sense of absolute and overlaid a permanent state on the otherwise impermanent nature of reality? Perhaps these absolutes are later additions—part of the Buddha's superhuman hagiography? But more realistically, "Mara has a barbed hook, like a fisherman—and every now and again, however much practice we have done, we get hooked, we get snagged and off we go" (Batchelor 2009).

5. Shinzen Young believes that enlightenment is a natural process, i.e., it is an inherent capacity of the neural beings that we are. Like the Buddha, he elucidates this point through metaphor: "Creating a house of cards is difficult because one has to go against entropy to do that. Eliminating a house of cards is simple; just remove any one of the base cards and the house of cards spontaneously tumbles. That's because the tumbling of the house of cards flows with entropy. Natural events tend to flow with entropy. If enlightenment is natural, it's reasonable to assume that it flows with entropy. It's more like collapsing a house of cards, less like having to build one" (Young 2016, 222). Collapsing the house of cards, the human animal loses its animality—no longer driven by acquisitive impulses, no longer self-preoccupied, no longer fearful. The hypervigilance that had gone into protectiveness can now flower into generosity, kindness, compassion, and even joy.

Chapter 6

The Fourth Ennobling Praxis
Resolving the Problem

The Buddha declared his fourth proposition: "The Truth of the Path: This, O Monks, is the Truth of the Path (Magga) which leads to the cessation of suffering. It is this Noble Eightfold Path, which consists of (1) Right View, (2) Right Resolve, (3) Right Speech, (4), Right Action, (5) Right Livelihood, (6) Right Effort, (7) Right Mindfulness, (8) Right Meditation" (Keown 1996, 54).

For our patient to be cured, she must follow a treatment plan; she must take her medicine as prescribed. This therapeutic is provided by the fourth ennobling praxis: "The Eightfold[1] Path is thus a path of self-transformation: an intellectual, emotional, and moral restructuring in which a person is reoriented from selfish, limited objectives towards a horizon of possibilities and opportunities for fulfillment" (Keown 1996, 56). Three categories comprise the path: wisdom (*prajna*), morality/ethics (*sila*), and meditation (*samahdi*). Each category supports and is necessary for the other like a three-legged stool. The Eightfold Path can be viewed synergistically with each component interacting with every other; they are not discreet and independent (Batchelor 2015).

The eight items of the fourth ennobling praxis are all preceded with the term *samma*—traditionally translated as "right." Analayo (2018a) suggests that "toward one point" or "connected in one" might be more accurate translations. "True" can also work in the sense that a wheel that is true is not bent, which works nicely with the broken axle or bad wheel of the Buddha's dukkha metaphor. While preferable to "right," "true" has epistemological connotations that might be distracting. Batchelor translates samma as "complete," which has fewer moral implications. The Pali Text Society's Pali-English dictionary defines samma as "harmony or completeness." *Sammata*, which is derived from samma, can refer to "correctness" or "rightness." This is, perhaps, the source of the confusion. Whatever the preferred term, each of these eight elements requires mastery. Perhaps, then, "integral" might be preferable since "right" connotes right and wrong, whereas integral has a more pragmatic feel. Similarly, I prefer a sense of "wholeheartedness" toward each of them, which seems consistent with Batchelor's "complete."

For the Buddha, there was skillfulness or unskillfulness and instances of the latter were occasions for self-improvement rather than condemnation: "For he who acknowledges his transgression as such and confesses it for the betterment in the future will grow in the noble (*ariyan*) discipline" (Batchelor 2015, 227). The response to unskillfulness is not shaming oneself, penitence, or other deprivation but, rather, learning, accommodation, and betterment in the context of commitment to the path.

In short, 1) wisdom entails understanding the three marks of existence—dukkha, impermanence, and not self (view) and 2) a commitment to working on integrating that intellectual understanding so that it is experiential (resolve). To be resolved requires not only cultivating clear understanding of how things works but dedicating oneself to behaving in a conducive manner (speech, action, livelihood) and devoting some of those behaviors to systematic and disciplined introspective study of oneself (effort, mindfulness, concentration). Wisdom facilitates ethics because one *knows* that acting unskillfully is futile. Ethics facilitates meditation where, of course, mindfulness is central. There are many fine sources that delineate these eight further (e.g., Goldstein 2016), so I will not treat them here in depth. However, given mindfulness's centrality to the Buddha's teaching and the contemporary landscape, this chapter will focus on the mindfulness aspect of the eightfold path.[2]

INTEGRAL MINDFULNESS

Mindfulness is a term that has been appropriated variously. It can be: A personality trait, a state of mind, cognitive flexibility, a beautiful mental factor, a meditation practice, or a thoroughgoing way of being. Jon Kabat-Zinn defined mindfulness as "paying attention in a particular way: on purpose, in the present moment and nonjudgmentally" (Kabat-Zinn 1990). Bhikkhu Annalayo refines this standard popular definition to: "a receptive and widely open mental attitude that is aware of the whole situation without any pressing need to interfere or react to it" (2018a, 36). Analayo hits on the key feature omitted by Kabat-Zinn: Context. I would revise Kabat-Zinn's definition as follows: "Sati is a way of paying attention that is aware of context—the present moment embedded in all contexts of being with awareness of the implications of all mental events and actions—and equanimous to be understood as non-reactive, non-self-reifying."

Reading the research literature, one must be alert to which mindfulness is being discussed. Mindfulness as a dispositional factor has been measured by self-report instruments (Brown and Ryan 2003). Mindfulness was also the term that social psychologist Ellen Langer affixed to her concept of cognitive flexibility (Langer 2014a, b). Her conceptualization of mindfulness does not require meditation. Mindfulness is also the prevailing translation of the Pali word *sati* and represents mindfulness as taught in the Buddhist traditions[3] (Wilson 2014). "Mindfulness" is simply the winning candidate of translations of the term *sati*. It beat out other terms like "recollecting" or "remembering" and emphasizes a heedful aspect. Peacock (2014) suggests "present moment recollection" as a more accurate definition than the ubiquitous "present moment awareness." Mindfulness takes on a different definition in the ancient Buddhist manuals of psychology known as the *Abhidhamma*.[4] Abhidhamma mindfulness is a "beautiful" mental factor that has nineteen component pieces (Olendzki 2010). Two of the features worth noting *hiri* and *ottapa* relate to heedfulness. Hiri is a sense of conscientiousness: what effect will my actions have on myself and others? Hiri is not just concern but skillful discernment of the potential of any considered action. I could be mindful of the question—*is this a good thing?*—but without *hiri* that concern would not have much teeth. Hiri is fueled by ottappa—the revulsion that comes from seeing someone (including oneself) act in a way that generates harmfulness, a kind of moral sensitivity (Amaro 2018). Heidegger employed mindfulness in his philosophical formulation of Care. Heidegger's term *Bessinung* can be translated into English as something similar to mindfulness—"a stance of quiet abstinence, an outlook seeking to recover its bearings through reticence and letting-be" (Dallmayr 2104, ix)—and is relevant to the use of mindfulness within the mindfulness movement to the extent that trivial or selfish mindfulness are limitations of its transformative potential (Dallmayr 2014).

Mindfulness is distinct from concentration, where concentration goes beyond garden variety focus and refers to the *jhanas*—states of meditative absorption. Conducive efforts require a quantity of energy applied to practice—whether mindfulness, concentration, or both and the quality of that energy—skillful effort—guards against bringing a new set of attachments, cravings, or aversions to meditation.[5]

To learn more about mindfulness one consults the Anapanasati Sutta or the discourse on "Mindfulness of Breathing":

> Now how is mindfulness of in-&-out breathing developed & pursued so as to be of great fruit, of great benefit? There is the case where a monk, having gone to the wilderness, to the shade of a tree, or to an empty building, sits down folding his legs crosswise, holding his body erect, and setting mindfulness to the fore. Always mindful, he breathes in; mindful he breathes out. Breathing in

long, he discerns, "I am breathing in long"; or breathing out long, he discerns, "I am breathing out long." Or breathing in short, he discerns, "I am breathing in short"; or breathing out short, he discerns, "I am breathing out short." He trains himself, "I will breathe in sensitive to the entire body." He trains himself, "I will breathe out sensitive to the entire body." He trains himself, "I will breathe in calming bodily fabrication." He trains himself, "I will breathe out calming bodily fabrication." (Thanissaro 2006)

Sati (mindfulness) is to be unremitting, constant, urgent, just as breathing itself is unremitting, constant, and urgent. The Buddha urged his followers to breathe and notice. Pay attention: if the breath is short or long rather than *make* the breath short or long. There is no agenda for any particular outcome and without an agenda, contingency is impossible. However, the breath presents itself—long or short—that is what is attended to. The breath, of course, is situated in the entire body. The Anapanasati Sutta goes on to delineate mindfulness to the jhanic states such as rapture and pleasure. After this, the Anapanasati Sutta goes onto describe the Four Frames of References (also translated as the Four Foundations of Mindfulness[6]). The first frame is breathing and bodily awareness: "On that occasion the monk remains focused on the *body* in & of itself—ardent, alert, & mindful—putting aside greed & distress with reference to the world" (Thanissaro 2006, emphasis original). The second frame is focused on feelings: pleasant, unpleasant, neutral. The third turns to the mind itself, and the fourth delves into mental qualities such as inconstancy, dispassion, cessation, and relinquishment. The Satipatthana Sutta or the "Way of Mindfulness" provides context for mindfulness's potential:

> Then the Blessed One addressed the bhikkhus as follows: "This is the only way, O bhikkhus, for the purification of beings, for the overcoming of sorrow and lamentation, for the destruction of suffering and grief, for reaching the right path, for the attainment of Nibbana, namely, the Four Arousings of Mindfulness." (Soma Thera 1998)

Not only sitting and breathing but in all the physical orientations:

> And further, O bhikkhus, when he is going, a bhikkhu understands: "I am going"; when he is standing, he understands: "I am standing"; when he is sitting, he understands: "I am sitting"; when he is lying down, he understands: "I am lying down"; or just as his body is disposed so he understands it. (Soma Thera 1998)

This mindful body, unlike the body during the Buddha's ascetic phase is not to be denied, suppressed, or vanquished. Instead, it is embraced with full attention in all its exquisite detail, a never-ending, never-the-same, bubbling phenomenological stream. All the activities of daily living are included: eating, drinking, urinating, defecating, sleeping, and waking.[7]

The Buddha gets very detailed in the ten cemetery meditations below. And while this may seem like a rejection of the body, it is meant, perhaps, as a cautionary tale against attaching to a body that is so prone to decay.

> And further, O bhikkhus, if a bhikkhu, in whatever way, sees a body dead, one, two, or three days: swollen, blue and festering, thrown into the charnel ground, he thinks of his own body thus: "This body of mine too is of the same nature as that body, is going to be like that body and has not got past the condition of becoming like that body" . . . eaten by crows, hawks, vultures, dogs, jackals or by different kinds of worms . . . reduced to a skeleton together with (some) flesh and blood held in by the tendons . . . reduced to a blood-besmeared skeleton without flesh but held in by the tendons . . . reduced to a skeleton held in by the tendons but without flesh and not besmeared with blood . . . reduced to bones gone loose, scattered in all directions—a bone of the hand, a bone of the foot, a shin bone, a thigh bone, the pelvis, spine and skull, each in a different place . . . reduced to bones, white in color like a conch . . . reduced to bones more than a year old, heaped together . . . reduced to bones gone rotten and become dust. (Soma Thera 1998)

These explicit existential contemplations are, again, likely not meant to be morbid but to make this body seem less glamorous—unable to be a source of sustainable happiness since—long before death—it is already in a state of flux, change, and decay.[8]

The path to nirvana is meditation or *bhavana*. "The aim of *bhavana*, however is to achieve mindfulness[9]—a state of focused wakefulness that is receptive to whatever is arising in the individual's psycho-physical continuum. This becomes a way of training that allows the individual to enjoy the senses without being caught in the threefold desire of greed, aversion and delusion" (Peacock 2008, 222).

These mindfulness practices lead to an "Assurance of Attainment." The Buddha starts by saying that seven years of practice will lead to a great attainment but then he revises down considerably: "O bhikkhus, let alone half-a-month. Should any person maintain these Four Arousings of Mindfulness in this manner for a week, then by him one of two fruitions is proper to be expected: Knowledge here and now" (Soma Thera 1999). The traditional ten-day or weeklong vipassana retreat format seems to follow from this declaration. If someone spends a week working with mindfulness—in all aspects of their existence—then they can expect insight—*knowledge here and now*. The retreat format mirrors what the monks in the Buddha's day would have experienced—a protected context for practice. This knowledge includes awareness of dukkha, the futility of contingency, and the inessential and impermanent nature of self. There are no explicit ethical admonitions in these instructions, but if hatred and greed are non-conducive to mindfulness, if they are inefficient as means to generate peacefulness, then they are to be—in general—avoided. The mindful person, then, looks like a virtuous person. The goodness, though, is grounded in wisdom—insight—into the subjectivity (dukkha), objectivity (anicca), and nature of self (anatman). This mindful person is ethical because they are not taken in by the—empty—promises of desire and aversion and not confused about who they are and how things work.

REFLECTIONS ON THE FOURFOLD TEACHING IN CONTEXT

The culmination of the fourfold tasks is to move from a reactive automaton to a responsive agent—from the conditioned to the unconditioned.[10] This is the attainment of skillfulness. The Buddha asks: "And what, *bhikkhus*, is the unconditioned? An ending of desire, an ending of hatred, and an ending of delusion; this is the unconditioned. And what, *bhikkhus*, is the path leading to the unconditioned? Mindfulness directed at the body: this is called the path leading to the unconditioned" (Bodhi 2003, 1372). The familiar fires are extinguished by mindfulness.

The Buddha's unconditioned is not the Brahman's unconditioned for which the atman seeks to join achieving *mukti* (liberation). It is a move away from the conditioned basis of being a biopsychosocial organism, subject to the laws of conditioning; it is an absence of contingency, reactivity. The unconditioned is not some absolute truth, not some spiritual transcendence but a work around of the dictates of DNA. Awakening can be seen as the Buddha's mastery of the four ennobling praxis that gives rise to a different image than what is typically described as enlightenment:

> Rather than describing his experience beneath the tree at Uruvela as a transcendent insight into ultimate truth or the deathless. . . . Awakening is not a singular insight into the absolute, comparable to the transcendent experiences reported by mystics of theistic traditions, but a complex sequence of interrelated achievements gained through reconfiguring one's core relationship with *dukkha*, arising, ceasing and the path. (Batchelor 2012, 99)

To navigate the four ennobling praxes requires first a recognition that something is off that must give rise to a motivation to take action, and then those actions, rooted in mindfulness, must be successful. This is a substantial accomplishment.

In fully knowing birth, sickness, aging and death one comes to understand the inevitably transient, tragic, and impersonal nature of human existence. Over time this erodes the underlying rationale of craving: namely, that this world exists for my personal gratification and, if I play my cards right by getting everything I want and getting rid of everything I hate, then I will find the lasting happiness I long for. (Batchelor 2012, 100)

To fully embrace dukkha through the four ennobling praxes does not increase dukkha, but paradoxically enhances the sense of astonishment at being alive.

NOTES

1. The Buddha chose eight elements to this path and this may have as much to do with a wheel having eight spokes as it does that there are eight distinct features. It seems that the ethics category could be collapsed into a single entry "behavior" since speech is an action; one's work comprises actions; so everything would fall under "action" of behavior. With this logic, there would only be six factors on the path, perhaps not as auspicious a number or perhaps the Buddha wanted to differentiate speech behavior from other types of behavior and generic actions from the particular actions people make in their work.

2. "Thus for the Tathagata—who no longer needs to impose notions of subject or object on experience, and can regard sights, sounds, feelings, & thoughts purely in & of themselves—views are not necessarily true or false, but can simply serve as phenomena to be experienced. With no notion of subject, there is no grounds for 'I know, I see'; with no notion of object, no grounds for 'That's just how it is.' . . . Thus the practice of right mindfulness does not repress undesirable mental qualities—i.e., it does not deny their presence. Rather, it notices them as they occur so that the phenomenon of their occurrence can be understood. Once they are understood for what they are as phenomena, they lose their power and can be abandoned" (Thanissaro 1999, 76, 80).

3. Mindfulness is common element to all Buddhist traditions (e.g., *shamatha* in Tibetan Buddhism, *shikantaza* in Zen). *Sati* of the Sathipathana Sutta is the Buddha's take on mindfulness of breathing and the Four Foundations of Mindfulness (e.g., Rosenberg 2004).

4. *Abhidhamma* is one of the three books of the Pali Canon. It is a posthumous compilation of the psychological elements of the Buddha's teachings (as presented in the *suttas*, the first book of the canon). The goal of the Abhidhamma is to provide a topography of mental experience as investigated through meditative discipline. Despite having been criticized for re-introducing essentialism, its conceptualization of mindfulness sees mindfulness as a constellation of different components. In the Abhidhamma it's a specific dhamma—mental quality—and also an aggregate quality, comprised of multiple components. It is used interchangeably to mean concentration (present moment attention), wisdom (insight into the three marks of existence, Vipassana), or shamatha—calming meditation.

5. "The idea that you've had deep spiritual enlightenments is probably one of the biggest problems of all. Because then you can have this illusion that you're somehow immune. No one is immune. Not even the Buddha" (Batchelor 2009).

6. Brazier (2018) alerts us that attention is only a subset of mindfulness—at least as traditionally conceived. She claims that the Four Foundations of Mindfulness do not produce mindfulness because mindfulness is already required in order to practice them. She characterizes mindfulness of the mindfulness movement—utilitarian mindfulness. She points out that *prajna* has the same cognate as the greek *diagnosis*. And certainly to be wise is to be able to diagnosis the human condition (the first of the ennobling praxes). "Mindfulness in its original sense refers to what the mind is full of, or permeated by, and, therefore, what kind of influence lies beneath or behind the states that then come to the conscious mind, the attraction that we have to the things that we subsequently pay attention to" (Brazier 2018, 51).

7. At the same time and almost in contradiction to embracing the body, the body appears to be repudiated: "And further, O bhikkhus, a bhikkhu reflects on just this body hemmed by the skin and full of manifold impurity from the soles up, and from the top of the hair down, thinking thus: There are in this body hair of the head, hair of the body, nails, teeth, skin, flesh, fibrous threads (veins, nerves, sinews, tendons), bones, marrow, kidneys, heart, liver, pleura, spleen, lungs, contents of stomach, intestines, mesentery, feces, bile, phlegm, pus, blood, sweat, solid fat, tars, fat dissolved, saliva, mucus, synovic fluid, urine" (Soma Thera 1998).

8. The Satipatthana goes on to describe the other frames of reference: feeling, mind (consciousness), and mental formations (mental objects), then the five hindrances to practice: sensuality, anger (aversion), sloth and topper, agitation and worry, and doubt. The five aggregates of clinging are reviewed: form, feeling, perception, mental formations, consciousness; the six internal and external sense bases; the five senses plus the mind; and for good measure, the Seven Factors of Awakening; and not to forget, the Four Noble Truths.

9. The man before he become the Buddha—an awakened one—must have been a bodhisattva, an aspiring Buddha (Analayo, 2018). He was not unfamiliar with mindfulness prior to his awakening, but it may not have been fully fleshed out as it came to be later known in the Four Foundations of Mindfulness.

10. "And, monks, as long as this—my three-round, twelve-permutation knowledge & vision concerning these Four Noble Truths as they have come to be—was not pure, I did not claim to have directly awakened to the right self-awakening unexcelled in the cosmos with its deities, Maras, & Brahmas, with its contemplatives & brahmans, its royalty & commonfolk. But as soon as this—my three-round, twelve-permutation knowledge & vision concerning these Four Noble Truths as they have come to be— was truly pure, then I did claim to have directly awakened to the right self-awakening unexcelled in the cosmos with its deities, Maras & Brahmas, with its contemplatives & brahmans, its royalty & commonfolk. Knowledge & vision arose in me: "Unprovoked is my release. This is the last birth. There is now no further becoming" (Thanissaro 1993).

Part III

MIND ON FIRE

THE BUDDHA'S PSYCHOLOGICAL MAP

The psychological Buddha—the proponent of an impermanent view of self—"Bhikkhu, there is no form . . . no feeling . . . no perception . . . no volitional formation . . . no consciousness that is permanent, stable, external, not subject to change and that will remain the same just like eternity itself" (Goldstein 2016, 196)—relied upon the image of fire: it was his most compelling metaphor, forming the cornerstone of his therapeutic praxis. Part I attempted to reclaim him from the Buddhist religions and cast his project further into a psychological light. Part II covered his most famous teaching, popularly known as the Four Noble Truths and recast them as a grouping of ennobling praxes. The Buddha's therapeutic—targeted to the constraints of evolution—is readily naturalized, even falsifiable—distinguishing it from faith-based religions—some of which bear his name. Part III explores his mind model of the five aggregates noting how each domain of mind has an upside (adaptation), a downside (limitation), and a praxis-based solution to remediate the effects of this limitation.

MIND ON FIRE

As the third ennobling praxis made colorfully evident, the Buddha's fire metaphor was central to his psychological project. The entire mind is afire and in this part, it is to each of these fiery mind components that attention will turn. Since everything is on fire and this fire is fueled by metaphorical combustible materials, the fire can be extinguished if one follows the Buddha's curriculum that consists of no longer putting things such as twigs, branches, and logs into that fire. The mind burns because there is an evolutionary property—timber, if you will—for each aggregate that cares only for our capacity to reproduce, not to experience enduring happiness, not to mention, has no regard for the profound psychological release of nirvana. The pressures of evolution provide an explanation for how the mind works that the Buddha surmised but could not have articulated. Each of the mind's five aggregates has a function that provides an adaptive advantage to the organism and also a liability that someone seeking to overcome dukkha and awaken to the further reaches of human potential must navigate. It is to these evolutionary sticking points—if you will—that the Buddha's teachings are aimed, providing an antidote to each of the five liabilities for these otherwise adaptive—from a survival and replication standpoint—functions.

The Buddha's message: being a human being is a hot mess—a conflagration—and without conscientiousness and practice-driven wisdom, there is no chance for cooling. The five fire sites of the mind converge to persist a sense of self that is reified—believed to be essential—and subject to stress. While the Buddha delineated a path beyond dukkha, those very metaphorical fires he pointed to in the Fire Sermon are the obstacles along that path. Findings from neuroscience, the cognitive science of language, and evolutionary psychology can explain these impediments to awakening and provide clues to their resolution—giving a twenty-first century practitioner an advantage over the Buddha's followers. Here is a naturalized dharma, one the Buddha hinted at with his prescient insight, now potentially confirmable—seemingly confirmed. Robert Wright claims that "Buddhism is True" (Wright 2017). A more accurate but wordy title to his book might have been "why the words attributed to the Buddha have true implications" (since Wright catalogues the Buddha's teachings not the sectarian practices of Buddhism). It's remarkable to find that Buddha's psychological claims correspond neatly with evolutionary psychology as Wright documents.

The Buddha attempted to reverse engineer the mind's computational modules[1] without knowing that he was doing so. He proceeded empirically from his own experience—building upon different yogic strategies for psychological transformation. To the extent that we can understand the forces—like desire—that impinge upon us from evolution, the better we can learn to work with our minds. Desire is an evolutionary given and, in conjunction with moha—ignorance—gives rise to contingency: the desperate feeling that pleasures must be satisfied and pains avoided in order for this self—*me*—to be okay. An illusion of self—the chief component of moha—is instrumental to evolution getting what it wants. It is as if we are in our own version of *The Matrix*. Instead of being connected to machines harvesting our bioelectric energy for sentient machines, evolution tricks us into pursuing pleasure—assiduously, relentlessly, compulsively. The Buddha knew that desire could not be eliminated entirely. What he did not know is that it is in our DNA. While he believed the arising of desire cannot be extinguished, contingencies stemming from desire can be—Mara does not have to be in charge. The Buddha's yogic predecessors and contemporaries tried to crush yearning of any kind through mortification of the flesh. Modern day descendants of these intrepid *saddhus* still engage in theatrics such as holding an arm above the head for, let us say, seven years or strapping heavy weights to a flaccid penis and holding them there (Hartsuiker 1993). And while these severe ascetic practices tamped down lust, maybe even temporarily eliminating it, they did little or nothing to address contingency. Anti-desire retains as much attachment as rampant desire. The Buddha advocated a Middle Way: somewhere between indulgence and deprivation.

Recalling from the Preface that the Buddha's project could be captured in the hashtag: #resistevolution—each act of resistance diminishes the power of contingency. One's sense of well-being is no longer dependent on the satisfaction of desires, no longer frustrated by the presence of pain, misfortune, or other unwanted things, and no longer confused about the nature of self. Contingency can no longer issue from a self that is no longer reified, no longer a noun, no longer an essential soul.

As addressed in part II, the Buddha's recommended path consisted of three types of activity: wisdom, ethics, and meditation. Addressing the five blazing aggregates through the lens of evolution leads to additional insights. Understanding the aggregates from the perspective of evolution—how we are tricked into feeling and thinking in particular ways—can enhance efforts made in meditation. As well, their comprehension provides a rationale for ethical action, especially in the form of practices specifically designed to counteract the deleterious effects of the fires.

THE FIVE FIRE SITES (AGGREGATES): FEATURES, FUNCTIONS, ADAPTATIONS, LIABILITIES, AND ANTIDOTES

It is well known that the Buddha divided every sentient being into five sets of components: "Khandha: Aggregate; physical and mental phenomena as they are directly experienced: *rupa*—physical form; *vedana*—feelings of pleasure, pain, or neither pleasure nor pain; *sanna*—perception, mental label; *sankhara*—fabrication, thought construct; and *vinnana*—sensory consciousness, the act of taking note of sense data and ideas as they occur" (Thanissaro 2010). These "exist not as adamantine essences but as dynamic processes. These processes are not random but causally determined"[2] (Gombrich 1996, 4, 6). Thanissaro elaborates: One of the new concepts most central to his teaching was that of the khandhas, usually translated into English as "aggregates." Prior to the Buddha, the Pali word khandha had very ordinary meanings: A khandha could be a pile, a bundle, a heap, a mass. It could also be the trunk of a tree (2010).

The choice of an "ordinary" term for his major psychological concept is, likely, no accident. The prescient metaphor maker, the Buddha got a lot of mileage out of these piles of wood. The aggregates are the totality of subjective experience—what is happening in our experience in any given moment. At first it seems like it is "me" at the center of this subjectivity—an enduring, essential self. But upon further investigation this self cannot be found anywhere—at least not in the aggregates and—according to the Buddha—there is nothing other than the aggregates: "See everything with perfect wisdom. This is not mine, not I, not myself" (Goldstein 2016, 175). The aggregates are not neutral—they all give rise to clinging and through that process, dukkha. Clinging is nearly synonymous with my preferred term of contingency and the five could be renamed the *aggregates of contingency*. Thanissaro continues: "In his first sermon, though, the Buddha gave it a new, psychological meaning, introducing the term 'clinging-khandhas' to summarize his analysis of the truth of stress and suffering" (Thanissaro 2010). Not only do we experience form, feeling, perception, fabrications, and consciousness, we identify with these experiences—fashion a self out of them that needs its experiences to go a certain way in order to feel okay. The clinging-contingent qualifier to the aggregates highlights how self-reification becomes the root cause of dukkha. Recall what the Buddha said in the first of the ennobling praxes: "In short, the five aggregates of clinging are dukkha" (Goldstein 2016, 172). All these are not self:

> Even so, monks, whatever is not yours: Let go of it. Your letting go of it will be for your long-term happiness & benefit. And what is not yours? Form is not yours.... Feeling is not yours.... Perception... Fabrications... Consciousness is not yours. Let go of it. Your letting go of it will be for your long-term happiness & benefit. Thus, monks, any form whatsoever that is past, future, or present; internal or external; blatant or subtle; common or sublime; far or near: every form is to be seen as it has come to be with right discernment as: "This is not mine. This is not my self. This is not what I am." (Thanissaro 1999, 63)

Each of the five features has a distinct function that provides an adaptive advantage. Adaptation notwithstanding, each aggregate has a liability. The Buddha's praxis can be viewed as a solution aimed at the limitations of each aggregate (see table III.1). The five aggregates—those blazing masses of fuel—represent, perhaps the totality of what it is to be a person. As the Buddha painstakingly pointed out that "self" would not be found in any of the aggregates—individually or collectively. For example, self is not the body because the body is not, altogether, under the mind's control and changes

Table III.1 The Five Aggregates: Features, Functions, Adaptations, Liabilities, and Solutions

Mind Feature	Function	Adaptation	Liability	Solution
Form: Neuroanatomy	Learning depends on physical connections	Infinite flexibility	Slow to change	Practice with patience and persistence
Perception	Categorization/labeling	Efficiency/safety/survival	Rigidity, disconnection	Cognitive flexibility: emphasize novelty, mindfulness
Feeling	Pleasant/unpleasant/neutral	Threats and opportunities	Attachment/avoidance	Taking interest, equanimity, containment
Fabrication	Narrative identity	Imagination	Taking things personally; sense of essential self	Thoughts are objects, skepticism, extrication from stories; see self as constructed rather than essential
Consciousness	Mobility, responsiveness, problem solving	Automaticity through unconsciousness	Overestimate free will; assumption of essential self	Humility, appreciation

over time, while self seems to remain constant (although, we will learn that that sense of constancy is mostly illusory). Thanissaro attempts to clarify: "it [the Pali Canon] never quotes him [the Buddha] as trying to define what a person is at all. Instead, it quotes him as saying that to define yourself in any way is to limit yourself, and that the question, "What am I?" is best ignored" (2010). To put out the fire in each location requires a distinct attitude and action. The rupa (form) fire is fueled by the very architecture of the brain and requires the attitude of patience to overcome and necessitates a long-term commitment to and *persistence* with meditation practice (aka effort from the eight of the fourth ennobling praxis). The sanna (perception) fire requires cognitive flexibility (mindfulness) and is addressed, among other things, through deliberately looking for novelty in sameness (Langer 2014a, b), that is finding *distinctions*. The vedana (feeling) fire requires containment and the practice of the phenomenological embodied *investigation* (mindfulness, concentration, meditation). Sankahara (mental formations/conditionings) requires skepticism and the practice of *extrication* from contingency along with equanimity—the capacity to be engaged without reactivity. And finally, vinnana (consciousness) requires humility and the practice of *appreciation*—of the brain's complexity, of the predominance of unconsciousness, of not being in charge. The Buddha cited intellectual understanding as the starting point of wisdom. Patience, flexibility, containment, skepticism, and humility are the by-products of such understanding. But intellect alone is not sufficient. Similar to the ennobling praxes, there are therapeutic actions aimed at the fires: persistence with practice itself along with noticing distinctions, investigation, extrication, and appreciation. It is to each of these burning aggregates that I will turn to briefly now, followed by in-depth treatments in the following chapters.

FORM (RUPA)

The Buddha explicates the first aggregate: "And why do you call it 'form' *[rupa]*? Because it is afflicted *[ruppati]*, thus it is called 'form.' Afflicted with what? With cold & heat & hunger & thirst, with the touch of flies, mosquitoes, wind, sun, & reptiles. Because it is afflicted, it is called form" (Thanissaro 2010). Rupa—*form*—the materiality of being, the tissue, sinew, and matter of the body, the subject of neuroanatomy, subject to the laws of physics, and shaped by evolution. The function of form is the care and feeding of the organism: appetitive instincts, thermo-regulative mechanisms, social-developmental tendencies. The very structure of the brain fosters learning: it proceeds by making physical—that is, neural—connections within itself. New connections represent learning. This gives us the adaptation of near infinite flexibility. Its liability is slowness to change—because the new must stem from the known. Despite what New Age motivational speakers claim, we cannot create connections anew from whole cloth. The Buddha knew nothing of neuroscience yet must have appreciated the brain's intransigence as well as its potential. The praxis solution: one must practice meditation, "diligently, ardently, patiently, and persistently" as Meditation pioneer, S. N. Goenka cajoled his students. Such efforts create new neural pathways. According to the Buddha, form comprises the hard "earthy" substances like bone, flesh, and feces; the "liquids" such as blood, phlegm, and bile; the "fire" of warming, fevers, and the heat generated by burning calories; and the "winds" of flatulence and breathing. Form would also include the brain, although little was known of this organ then and the Buddha did not mention it on his list. The Buddha was less concerned with what the forms of the body did than how the forms of the body were subject to craving and aversion. Nonetheless, the form of the brain places special constraints on experience, because form is not conceptual—it is the direct experience of the body's sensate materiality as detailed, for example, in the Four Foundations of Mindfulness (as discussed in Chapter 6). If one is paying close attention to the body, one cannot but help notice that all of its manifestations are constantly changing—a ceaseless flux of sensations, energies, and experiences. Of course, the next aggregate—perception—wants to take these phenomenologically diverse and changing experiences and apply some constancy to them via categorization in the service of prediction, which is the brain's primary function (Seth 2019).

We cannot escape our embodiment. The Buddha tried. He spent six years practicing harsh ascetics in the forests of what is now northern India. The Buddha and his self-mortifying cadre ate a grain of rice each day, slept under trees, and endeavored to vanquish the body with the strength of their minds. He could pull off this mind-over-matter trick for discrete periods of time, but afterward the body remained a problem—it hungered, it thirsted, it ached, it craved pleasure, relief, and excitement. Embodiment was affliction—dukkha—and he could not ultimately control it, at least not in persistent fashion. Even if he could have vanquished form, the other aggregates presents their own challenges.

PERCEPTION (SANNA)

The Buddha explicates the perception aggregate: "And why do you call it 'perception'? Because it perceives, thus it is called 'perception.' What does it perceive? It perceives blue, it perceives yellow, it perceives red, it perceives white. Because it perceives, it is called perception" (Thanissaro 2010). Perception (sometimes translated as apperception) is the categorizing function. It is usually presented as the third of the five aggregates, but I find it more useful to present it before rather than after the feeling aggregate (i.e., how do we know what to feel until we know what we perceive?). Its purpose is the identification of phenomenon. However, these perceptions should not be construed as the way things *really* are: "Perception is never a direct window onto an objective reality. All our perceptions are active constructions, brain-based best guesses at the nature of a world that is forever obscured behind a sensory veil" (Seth 2019, 42). Perception allows organisms to move through the world efficiently and safely by creating shortcuts—only things that are novel need to be scrutinized carefully; familiar things can be quickly put into categories and the precious resource of attention can be placed elsewhere—looking for more novel experiences. Perception's goal is efficiency. It tends to lump similar things together into categories—which is good for expedience but not so great for accuracy.[3] Categorical concepts facilitate a sense of place and ownership (Goldstein 2016). Many of our categories are arbitrary: for example that the earth is oriented from north to south instead of south to north—there is no right-side up in the vastness of space. Pablo Neruda noted the limitations of place and ownership in his poem "Too Many Names" when he said he did not know what they were talking about when people referred to Venezuelas, Paraguays, and Chiles. These are just lines on a map; they do not exist in nature. His awareness lies with the underlying earth, which he knows does not actually have a name other than the arbitrary, political ones that humans have furnished (Mitchell 1997). Invariably, naming something gives rise to a sense of ownership and something owned must be protected (insert the history of human warfare). Past, present, and future are also mental categories.

FEELING (VEDANA)

The Buddha explicates the feeling aggregate: "And why do you call it 'feeling'? Because it feels, thus it is called 'feeling.' What does it feel? It feels pleasure, it feels pain, it feels neither-pleasure-nor-pain. Because it feels, it is called feeling" (Thanissaro 2010). Vedana is the valence[4] of pleasure/pain: pleasant feelings invite approach, unpleasant feelings encourage retreat, and neutral feelings sanction ignoring. This rubric is fundamental to living beings and can be found in life as simple as the amoeba. Feeling is evolution's bulwark: by pursing pleasure creatures feed themselves and engage with sex, thus surviving and replicating; by finding fear and pain aversive, creatures are motivated to avoid the potentially dangerous situations that give rise to these feelings, thus aiding survival and the opportunity for replication. There is no need to moralize vedana; if you have a brain or even the most rudimentary nervous system, then you will have feeling. It is what is done with those feelings that matters. By approaching things that are pleasant and avoiding things that are painful, organisms—on balance—survive and pass their genes to another generation. It is a strategy that has worked for billions of years and works best when survival is acutely on the line. For present-day human beings that live collectively and without immediate threat from predators, starvation, lack of shelter, or social strife, it can become a very limiting process. Feeling fuels conditioning, reactivity, and contingency. Liking propels us toward; disliking repels us away—we are always in its clutches.

FABRICATION (SANKHARA)

The Buddha explicates the fourth aggregate:

> And why do you call them "fabrications"? Because they fabricate fabricated things, thus they are called "fabrications." What do they fabricate into a fabricated thing? For the sake of form-ness, they fabricate form as a fabricated thing. For the sake of feeling-ness, they fabricate feeling as a fabricated thing. For the sake of perception-hood. . . . For the sake of fabrication-hood. . . . For the sake of consciousness-hood, they fabricate consciousness as a fabricated thing. Because they fabricate fabricated things, they are called fabrications. (Thanissaro 2010)

Sankhara is variously translated as formations (Goldstein 2016), determinations (Nanamoli Thera 1995), volitions (Gombrich 2009), and as above, fabrications (Thannisaro 2010). It is the cognizing functions of mind that include volition, intention,[5] and application of attention. It also involves discrimination, judgment, and evaluation. Intentions can be directed at any of the five senses and also to "ideas" that comprise any kind of mental experience (e.g., imagination, memory, cognition, and affects more specific than pleasure and pain). Fabrications are the narrative details of individuals—the focal points for cognitive–behavioral, psychoanalytic, existential, and humanistic psychotherapies—and the social psychology of individual and group minds. "Of the five khandhas, fabrication is the most complex. Passages in the canon define it as intention, but it includes a wide variety of activities, such as attention, evaluation, and all the active processes of the mind. It is also the most fundamental khandha, for its primary activity is to take the potential for the experience of form, feeling, etc.—coming from past actions—and turn it into the actual experience of those things in the present moment" (Thanissaro 2002).

I like Thanissaro's choice of "fabrication" as the translation of sankhara because it captures the implication that mind produces—manufactures—a sense of self that retains ownership of what is perceived and felt. This notion of fabrication also implies the alternate meaning of fabrication: to make something up with an intention to deceive. The mind both manufactures thoughts (and thus self) and these products, if you will, are inherently distorted, rarely true to form and thus not beneficial, giving rise to the sense of dukkha. That is, they are that way without the mind training provided in the ennobling praxes. Contact with phenomenon gives rise to clinging that gives rise to the one who "owns" or "possesses" the experience. This possessive owner is the essential self—that entity the Buddha claimed did not exist. The Buddha admonished: "an uninstructed run-of-the-mill person regards form as: 'This is mine, this is my self, this is what I am." He regards feeling ... perception ... fabrications ... consciousness as: "This is mine, this is my self, this is what I am" (Thanissaro 1998b). Self is thus, a "constructed" self—fabricated from the constituents of experience and a narrative mind bent—courtesy of evolution—on proprietorship, control, and gratification. To see self and suffering as "manufactured" or "constructed" or "fabricated" is to see the possibility of its opposite. Construction is an elective, if habitual, process. We are fabricated fabricators, but we can do better (the Buddha might have said). The individual committed to the Buddha's psychology can *learn* to not fabricate—as much.

CONSCIOUSNESS (VINNANA)

The Buddha explicates the final aggregate: "And why do you call it 'consciousness'? Because it cognizes, thus it is called 'consciousness.' What does it cognize? It cognizes what is sour, bitter, pungent, sweet, alkaline, non-alkaline, salty, & unsalty. Because it cognizes, it is called consciousness" (Thanissaro 2010). Conscious is awareness of the five senses and their objects plus another sense for "mind" or "intellect." Consciousness is not human self-awareness or even sentience but the simple act of being conscious of something—it is more psychophysics of sensory perception: eye, ear, nose, tongue, skin making contact with sources of light, sound, aroma, taste, and touch and awareness of what the mind thinks.[6]

The Buddha noted, in mechanistic fashion, that "Without a condition there is no origination of consciousness" (Goldstein 2016, 189). This is not the Brahman's absolute consciousness: *satchitananda* (translated from the Sanskrit as being-consciousness-bliss) but only the single mind moments (citta) that follow each other, again in mechanical succession. For the Buddha, there is no substrate to consciousness, no underlying permanence as the Brahmans believed.

THE AGGREGATES IN ACTION

A brief walkthrough of the aggregates in action will conclude this introduction: Let us say there is a person—me—the human being who believes himself to be Arnold Kozak. I am conscious (although conscious experience represents only a tiny fraction of mental experience). I walk into a room to give a lecture, one that I have never been in before, and therefore see things—tables, chairs, light fixtures—that I have never seen before. Nonetheless, I recognize the things in the room because there are mental categories for chairs, desks, and other furniture in my brain. The more prototypic the objects in the room, the more rapidly I will be able to identify them. Each perception is accompanied by a feeling tone: pleasant, unpleasant, neutral. What comes first? If these are a linear process it would seem that perception would have to come first because how do I know what to feel before I know what it is that I am seeing or what it might be? However, this sequence only works for conscious perceptions. But the sequence is not entirely linear because feeling tone can bias what gets paid attention to—what I become conscious of and how that perception is framed. If I am fearful, sticks on the ground might be perceived as snakes. If I am not apprehensive, they are more likely just to be sticks, and just as likely ignored. Any hope for pure objectivity in perception must be abandoned—I can only sense what my sensory organs including the brain can process[7]; it is not reality that I see, only the particular human version. No perception occurs in a vacuum. By the time we become adults, categories have been become deeply engrained. It is through prior learning that everything—including feeling—is perceived.

Olendzki describes the process in more technical fashion:

> It was understood that the mind is naturally beset with a distorted view of reality, in so far as meaning is constructed internally from the importation and interpretation of a vast array of data. . . . As consciousness cognizes a sensory or mental object, perception interprets it, feeling assigns a corresponding hedonic valence to it, and volitional formation responds emotionally to it based upon existing behavioral traits and learned response. Since all this happens again and again in moments of cognition that arise and pass away in rapid succession, it is customary and adaptive for the mind to conjure up and project onto experience such things as object constancy, narrative cohesion, and a more or less coherent sense of personal identity. (Olendzki 2016, 64)

While the Buddha did not address unconscious processing, we can assume that the process works similarly—prior learning biases current perception, feelings and perceptions interact to create the moment. But there is another layer (actually multi-layers). It is not just the perceptual category of chair that guides the experience of the moment; it is my history with chairs—all the stories, consciously accessible or not—that make up "chair." Of course, I am not just perceiving the objects in the room, I am imagining myself in the scene and all the implications that ensue. The color of the chairs will make an impression—a color I find ugly will give rise to a sense of mild disgust and an elitist aesthetic thought about how widespread bad taste is. Most likely, the color will be neutral, not noticed. In addition to perceiving the room, I bring in my context—my emotional landscape of the moment. Will this lecture go okay? Am I prepared enough? How will people perceive me? These thoughts stem from sankhara—my collected mental fabrications, formations, conditions of the moment, which of course includes a lifetime of memory, learning, and beliefs. Perhaps I am not even paying conscious attention, or not that much, to what is happening in the room because I am preoccupied with something that occurred on the way to this room, perhaps some bad traffic or a near collision on the drive in. Or, perhaps, my preoccupation has a future time-stamp on it, and I am worried about something that needs my attention after the lecture. The sankhara aggregate is largely responsible for the experience of myself in any given moment because it is the only aggregate that has personal information. The other four are generic, shared by most creatures. Since sankhara is where intentions/volitions/judgments reside, it has to be the target for intervention if the patterns of experience are to change.

My consciousness will only ever be intermittent. It is not clear what details will rotate into awareness—perhaps a face in the audience, perhaps awareness of my own obsessive thinking, the tone of my voice, the use of filler words, or the need to clear my throat. Nevertheless, I will experience my consciousness, much like my sense of self, as a seemingly continuous phenomenon. Like my self, this continuity is an illusion—I am stringing together moments of consciousness into an apparent unified cloth, my brain filling in the gaps to create the illusion of uninterruptedness. The five aggregates converge to create my experience, moment-by-moment as I move through the world. Without exception, the particulars of each aggregate arise involuntarily based on previous experience. I am causally conditioned to experience what I experience. However, the wild card of mindfulness permits me to intervene with the unfolding of events. Instead of believing the thoughts that enter my mind, I note them as mental objects, I shift attention to my breathing, soothing myself in the process. By grounding my attention in the aggregate of form, consciousness becomes more robust. While my feelings and perceptions seek to manipulate my actions, meta-awareness allows me to by-pass their influence.[8]

NOTES

1. Mind modules are covered in the chapter on mental fabrications. Obviously, not all the modules are going to be relevant. It is not necessary to know that vision modules assume that lighting is relatively constant. However, it is useful to know that vision is not given but constructed by the brain.

2. Gombrich indicates that this mind model is not confined to humans, although humans have obstacles—language principal among them—that other animals do not.

3. Things that are not solid are seen as solid. On one level, the brick is solid—it has mass; it can be an effective projectile to throw through a window. At a deeper level, the brick, as with even the densest material, is mostly space. This illusion is not particularly problematic unless the self is considered to be like a solid object.

4. Specific and variegated emotions are found in the fourth aggregate—fabrications.

5. Goldstein (2016) presents sankhara from an Abhidharma perspective: as either universal, occasional, unwholesome, and beautiful mental factors. Volition/intention (*cetana*): "It is common to every moment of consciousness, and its function is to organize, gather, and direct all the other mental factors for a particular end" (Goldstein 2016, 186). An unaddressed question is who or what does the intentioning?

6. The mind is a computational system that integrates the millions of bits of, for instance, visual information that is available in each second and make coherent images out of it. These images are not simply the impressions of light energy as they register on the retina. The brain processes that information, transforms it, and the mind sees. Vision—the sense that gets its own chapter in most psychology 101 texts—is through and through a psychological process not simply mechanical engineering. The taken for granted acts of seeing, walking, and moving our hands nevertheless are engineering marvels—nearly impossible to replicate in machine form. The constructive process continues as the sensory organs select and process information. As much of 90 percent of vision is processed in the brain (Lakoff and Johnson, 1999).

7. We can only see light between 430 and 770 Hz, only hear sounds between 20 and 20,000 Hz (the possible range exceeds 100 kHz) frequencies, and within this narrow band of electromagnetic radiation, things are still not given. The brain continues to process.

8. By considering the five aggregates, we hope to be able to accomplish the following Buddha's counsel: "And how is non-agitation caused by lack of clinging/sustenance? There is the case of an instructed noble disciple . . . who does not assume form to be the self, or the self as possessing form, or form as in the self, or the self as in form. His form changes & is unstable, but consciousness does not for that reason alter in accordance with the change in form. His mind is not consumed with any concomitant agitation born from such a change. Because his awareness is not consumed, he does not feel fearful, threatened, or solicitous. It is thus, friends, that non-agitation is caused by lack of clinging/sustenance. [Similarly with feeling, perception, fabrications & consciousness]" (Thanissaro 1999, 91).

Chapter 7

Form

Brain Architecture and the Neuroplastic Forest of Self

OVERVIEW

Everything that we do is encoded in the brain, from instincts to new learning and each datum requires a physical connection of some sort. Whenever something new is encountered, it is interpreted through what is already represented in the brain (Ascoli 2015). This strategy makes the brain infinitely flexible and also very slow to change. It is also a metaphoric process: the known is always the basis for the unknown. If one wishes to change the structure of this brain in an enduring way, one must practice the wished for change with patience and persistence. Because of this, awakening is difficult—despite all the stories of monks instantaneously becoming enlightened while listening to the Buddha's lectures; awakening requires arduous work—stories of Chinese peasants becoming enlightened by watching a leaf fall notwithstanding. The brain must be changed, bit-by-bit, connection-by-connection, electrical field-by-electrical field.

FORM IS NOT SELF

Can the self be found in form?

> Thus I heard. On one occasion the Blessed One was living at Benares, in the Deer Park at Isipatana. There he addressed the bhikkhus of the group of five: "Bhikkhus."—"Venerable sir," they replied. The Blessed One said this: "Bhikkhus, form is not-self. Were form self, then this form would not lead to affliction, and one could have it of form: Let my form be thus, let my form be not thus." And since form is not-self, so it leads to affliction, and none can have

it of form: "Let my form be thus, let my form be not thus." (Ñanamoli Thera 1995)

The Buddha had no way of knowing how the brain worked, yet his insights accord with the emerging neuroscientific picture of the brain (e.g., Hanson 2020). The brain is not capable of experiencing something completely new and will always use acquired knowledge—e.g., categories—to interpret new experiences. Heuristic though they may be, categories does not exist in nature. Underlying the category-impulse is hardware—anatomic constraints of brain architecture. By considering form we can: 1) appreciate the staggering complexity of the brain and 2) explore how the brain's architecture and function constrain learning through the metaphorical process of using the familiar to apprehend the unfamiliar.

THE BEAUTIFUL BRAIN: TREES OF THE BRAIN, ROOTS OF THE MIND

Santiago Ramón y Cajal was the first to articulate the discrete forms of the brain and their electrical functions. He drew the brain and its components extensively and accurately, documenting the beauty of this most complicated of organs (Cajal 2017). Nothing in the known universe is more complex than the brain. This three-pound mass of gelatinous substance is home to 70 to 100 billion neurons, on the high end of that estimate roughly the number of stars that populate the Milky Way galaxy. Each of these neurons can make anywhere between 1 and 100,000 connections (averaging 50,000), resulting in about 1 quadrillion synapses. Put another way, if you had a penny for every synapse your wealth would equal the entire GDP for the world. If your job was to count your own neurons as a full time job, after a 50-year career you would have covered 3 percent. In any moment, each of these connections can be in any one of ten different electrical states. These electrical states determine the action of the neuron—whether it gets excited and fires or whether it becomes inhibited and does not fire. These "decisions" to go or not to go are a calculus of tens of thousands of interconnected electrical inputs (Ascoli 2015). The complexity of the brain's hardware is even more impressive when you consider the quantity of length. Ascoli explains:

> Axonal branches constitute more than 95% of all the wiring in the brain . . . the overall branching length of a typical axon sums up to a yard or more! . . . To appreciate how stunning this measure is, consider the total length of all axons in a human brain: about 50 million miles. This is more than twice the length of all paved roads of the entire world! If you don't find that impressive enough,

try this: if you were to unfold all the axonal wiring of a single human brain and wrapped it around the equator, you would circle the Earth more than 200 times before running out; it would take ten years for a Boeing 747 to fly that distance continuously, without accounting for take-off, landing or refueling. To put it another way, the axons of a single human brain could go all the way to the moon, and back one hundred times. Stitching together the axons of an average married couple, one could reach all the way to the Sun. (2015, 50–53)

Ascoli suggests that we can understand the intricate branching of the neurons by looking at the branching of trees—thus a "neurobotanical world completely filled with trees" (2015, vii). As metaphors go, this one is useful but not complete—the trees show branching but not the interconnections between neurons. Still the images of trees are heuristic and map closely to the actual structure of neurons. Neurons that fire together wire together is a now famous axiom and simplification of Donald Hebb's observation: "When an axon of cell A is near enough to excite B and repeatedly or persistently takes part in firing it, some growth process or metabolic change takes place in one or both cells such that A's efficacy, as one of the cells firing B, is increased" (Hebb cited in Ascoli 2015, 45).

The brain has two fundamental properties: stability and plasticity (Ascoli 2015). Not every experience results in plastic changes in the brain—we forget most of what we experience and most of what we experience never registers with consciousness. Ascoli asks why is it that we remember certain things but not others; why we selectively attend to some things rather than other things? The answer to these questions has to do with how useful or predictive the experience is. Context is central to the way the brain functions and leads to this bold claim: *We cannot experience the world de novo. It is always experienced in the* context *of what has already been learned.*

Ascoli's theory has three principles. The first principle asserts that *mental states correspond to patterns of spikes in the nervous system.* This is a basic assumption, unproblematic to most neuroscientists, and it consequently requires rejecting any form of idealism—mind independent of body.[1] Information is distributed over groups of neurons, not single ones (based on current data). Contrary to popular representations such as the films *Eternal Sunshine of the Spotless Mind*, and the Pixar movie *Inside Out*, perceptions and memories are not to be found in specific neurons or regions in the brain. Instead, mental states such as memories or affects would be found distributed as ensembles across brain regions. Coming to understand how these ensembles function is a significant task. The brain also encodes in parallel to create resilience through redundancy. The brain is robust because if one encoding is damaged, the redundant encodings can take over. These alternative ensembles will not be as efficient (at least at first) as the primary one but will still work.

A conscious moment equals 50 milliseconds and is comprised of up to twenty-five neuronal spikes. In any given moment, one pattern of spiking is experienced. The *connectome* is the collected synaptic connections for an individual. In a sense, this *connectome* is identity—everything that is known, everything that can be experienced. While we study the brain with a relatively few distinct anatomical regions (e.g., prefrontal cortex, occipital region, parietal lobes, etc), there are actually hundreds of distinct functional areas. If the *connectome* is the map of all synaptic connection, the *projectome* encompasses patterns of connectivity across different areas of the brain. It is still a crude representation, dashing hopes of mapping subjectivity—even *projectomes* would not be adequate enough to represent the mental states that might accompany even a single word. While all this synaptic connectivity must capture a person's storehouse of knowledge, the exact specifics are not yet known, such as which firing patterns are significant. Even if this assertion that *connectivity equals knowledge* is correct, it is still not known what mental patterns map onto which synaptic activity—only that it appears to map in some way as yet unknown to us and probably unknowable given how relatively coarse the imaging technology currently is (Ascoli 2015).

Ascoli's second principle: *Learning, meant as the acquisition of the potential to instantiate a previously unknown mental state, corresponds to the change of connections in circuits of neurons.* Again, this principle may seem obvious yet is of crucial importance. Without circuit changes nothing happens. We are not fixed entities—provided with a packet of knowledge at the outset and never changing, as might be a robot given a preset amount of information and programming. Presumably, creating or modifying circuits is what is happening when we experience and remember something new—even memories of factual events are not completely static. The brain is constantly changing and constantly in flux, e.g., there are billions of spikes moving through the brain in each moment and each of these spikes gives rise to tens of thousands of additional electrical events. This forest of electrical activity is the totality of our subjective experience as well as unconscious experience and the regulation of the body. Ascoli explains—without any reference to Buddhism—the neuronal underpinning of anicca or impermanence:

> As trains of spikes travel down the axons and dendrites integrate synaptic information, billions of new synapses are formed, billions are wiped out, and the strength of billions of other existing synapses adjust up or down. Therefore, the relationship between structure and activity in the brain is fundamentally one of *reciprocal* cause and effect. The connectivity of the network along with all synaptic weight determines what patterns of activity can be instantiated and which among those are selected any time. Conversely, the continuous flow of

activity steadily sculpts and resculpts the connectome and its synaptic weights from before birth to death. (Ascoli 2015, 86–87, emphasis original)

The relationship between structure and activity determine the probability of experiencing something as well as the capacity to experience it. We can already see the Buddha's idea of dependent origination playing out here. Previous activity gives rise to the possibility and probably of subsequent activity. We are never starting from zero. This principle is also the rationale for mindfulness practice because what we do influences—through reciprocal cause and effect—future possibilities and probabilities. The "neural patterns in cell assemblies" may resemble what the ancient Buddhist psychologists meant by moments of consciousness (cetana). The brain abides in probabilities. Nothing is fixed from the outset. As experience unfolds, it changes the probabilities of what might come next. For example, if a conscious thought facilitates doing something wholesome, then the likelihood of other wholesome events is increased. Each moment is shaped by past moments and the particular configuration of any given moment will shape future moments.

Ascoli's third principle asserts that axonal-dendritic *overlaps* are the neural correlate of the capability of learning, but we do not learn everything that could be learned. We only learn a tiny fraction of what is possible. This is adaptive because we would otherwise be overloaded.[2] Despite all this changing activity, memory and a sense of identity persist. Our brains achieve both stability and plasticity despite its incredible complexity (Ascoli 2015). The fire together—wire together finding makes us associative creatures. There must be firing together *and* a sharing of the same physical space in the brain somewhere amidst the thousands of trillions of connections. It would not do for parallel firing in different parts of the brain that are not proximal through axonal-dendritic connections. As mentioned above, a one-to-one correspondence cannot be found between single neurons and mental states such as thoughts. Instead each experience is represented by "'cell assemblies' consisting of complex activation patterns of a substantial number of neurons" (Ascoli 2015, 100).

Ebbinghaus famously and painstakingly demonstrated that re-learning something occurs more rapidly than learning it in the first place. In other words, "Learning is gated by background information" (Ascoli 2015, 101). For the brain, this is an efficient computational mechanism. As synaptic connectivity slowly changes itself, the knowledge base changes and this process is occurring in every single moment of existence. The extant connectivity collection in any given moment will constrain what synapses are likely to be affected next by new experience.

Neurons change slowly but inexorably in response to experience. Mostly we are stable, but there is some wiggling going on somewhere. Given enough time, these minute changes can result in a "comprehensive reorganization of the network" (Ascoli 2015, 116)—the Buddha's awakening might be considered such a process. Change is possible *and* slow to occur. This explains why 1) so much practice is necessary, 2) why practice is hard, and 3) why it takes so long to make small changes in patterns of reactivity. Ascoli likens these changes to the movements of glaciers—slow yet inexorable—therefore work *diligently, ardently, patiently, and persistently*. Repetition is required as Thoreau—similar to Goenka—admonished, "A single footstep will not make a path on the Earth, so a single thought will not make a pathway in the mind. To make a new physical path we walk again and again. To make a deep mental path, we must think over and over the kind of thought we wish to dominate our lives." Ascoli emphasizes: "Each of us learns only those aspects of experience that are somehow *compatible with our existing knowledge*. If on the surface the third principle appears to curb our potential as thinking machines, it in fact endows each individual with an inimitable cognitive identity" (2015, 182, emphasis added). Ascoli's third principle explains the metaphoric basis of cognition and perhaps why metaphor is so crucial in the development of concepts (Lakoff and Johnson 1980, 1987, 1999). It is in the architecture of the brain: *the known is the basis for apprehending the unknown.* Therefore, we can *only* learn or know on the basis of what is already known. Thus, any time that something new is encountered, it is apprehended with and filtered by our existing connectome. These connections become the metaphors for understanding what comes next. We are contextual creatures—always. Past information that is encoded into the brain directs our cognitive life. Here again, this principle appears to be support for the Buddha's insight of dependent origination or this–that causality. The unfolding of experience is filtered through the metaphorical matrix of the known, remembered, or otherwise encoded experience. Despite this, we are not slaves to our previous conditioning because we can intervene in the process—within manufacturer's constraints, e.g., the proximity principle. The connectome is the foundation for sankhara. These mental formations or fabrications are the repository of past experience and the matrix or top-down filter for experience in the present. What arises in any given moment is conditioned by events in the past as they collide with events in the present. Again, if we were omniscient, we could trace all the causal linkages and interactions and create a map for how any particular moment arose. Since we are not we must be content with something more modest. As we meet this conditioned moment with some degree of awareness, we change the trajectory of future conditioning. This does not mean we necessarily have free will because that sense of agency—that believes itself to have free will—is also conditioned. What cannot be denied is there are multiple courses of action in any given moment, each with a different legacy of consequences.

NOTES

1. An essentialist view of self violates the principle of neural cognitive correlation (NCC). NCC is criticized for a materialistic reduction of the subjective self (e.g., Gyatso 2006), but new imaging techniques, such as fMRI, allow (if primitive) methodology for investigating the subjectivity of experience without resorting to an essentialist idealism (e.g., Brewer 2011).

2. People with the highly distressing condition, known as hyperthymesia, do not forget most of the details that normal people forget.

Chapter 8

Perception

Categorization

OVERVIEW

The perception aggregate of mind helps us to process complex and vast quantities of information to efficiently navigate toward adaptive ends. It works closely with the aggregate of feeling to identify percepts that have functional utility. The drawbacks of categorical efficiency are bias, rigidity, and inaccurate perceptions—although these are not necessarily problematic where evolution is concerned as long as those strategies lead to useful behaviors. Percepts with subtle distinctions are lumped together in the same category,[1] reducing varied textures to homogenized groupings. Taken to a greater level of complexity, collections of disparate experience are lumped into the unified category of self. The principle error that the Buddha identified was the category of I, me, mine—unique phenomenological moments of experience are gathered together into a fabricated self-concept. To transcend categorical perception requires cognitive flexibility and a commitment to make distinctions in the moment as per Shunryu Suzuki's famous adage: "The beginner's mind knows many possibilities, the expert mind few" (Suzuki 1982, 147).

PERCEPTION IS NOT SELF

Can the self be found in perception?

> "Bhikkhus, how do you conceive it: is perception permanent or impermanent?"—"Impermanent, venerable Sir."—"Now is what is impermanent painful or pleasant?"—"Painful, venerable Sir."—"Now is what is impermanent, what is

painful since subject to change, fit to be regarded thus: 'This is mine, this is I, this is my self?'"—"No, venerable sir." (Nanamoli Thera 1995)

Dan Siegel defines the mind as "an embodied and relational processes that regulates the flow of energy and information" (Siegel and Siegel 2014, 24). To make sense of this flow, we must be able to recognize meaningful patterns. This is the function of categorization. But all sense-making is interpretive: "Some researchers suggest that there is even a specific brain module, called the 'interpreter,' that is tasked with sifting out patterns from the slurry of information continuously flowing through our skulls" (Geary 2011, 33). What we know of the world is not the world in and of itself. Our experience is always an interpretation of the world "out there."[2] Since perceptions are constructed by the brain, they can be thought of as "controlled hallucinations" (Seth 2019, 47).

Pinker guides us through a moment of mental process:

> First, we are aware, to varying degrees, of a rich field of sensation: the colors and shapes of the world in front of us, the sounds and smells we are bathed in, the pressures and aches of our skin, bone, and muscles. Second, portions of this information can fall under the spotlight of attention, get rotated into and out of short-term memory, and feed our deliberative cogitation. Third, sensations and thoughts come with an emotional flavoring: pleasant or unpleasant, interesting or repellent, exciting or soothing. Finally, an executive, the "I," appears to make choices and pull the levers of behavior. (1997, 139)

Categorization happens in the second step as the raw energy and information of the senses gets processed by attention. Whatever we pay attention to will have upstream consequences for cognition: the known and the basis for the new. We are very good at pattern recognition (thanks to, among other things, von Economo cells): "Pattern recognition is the most primitive form of analogical reasoning, part of the neural circuitry for metaphor" (Geary 2011, 35). As already mentioned, our ability to employ categories makes us very efficient at acting-in-the-world but poor phenomenologists. There is a trade-off between accuracy and utility, and utility trumps precision. In any given moment, rather than appreciating the unique presence of these freshly perceived objects—as might have been the case with my never seen before chairs—as scintillating masses of color and form (however, I might have seen them that way if I had disrupted my usual perceptual processes with LSD, psilocybin, DMT, mescaline, or other hallucinogen), we just sit in those chairs, perhaps without any conscious consideration at all. The world was more phenomenologically fresh when we were children, but we have lost that capacity. Indeed: "Young children are such prolific metaphor producers because their pattern recognition circuits, not yet confined by conventional categorizations, are working full blast" (Geary 2011, 155). Siegel explains how learning creates categories and that these categories begin to filter subsequent cognition. The older we get, the more we learn, and the more structures we have.

> In many ways such learning oppresses our raw sensory experience by muddying the waters of clear perceptions with prior expectation. As we grow into adulthood, it is very likely that these accumulated layers of perceptual models and conceptual categories constrict subjective time and deaden our feelings of being alive. Without the intentional effort to awaken, life speeds by. We habituate to experience perceiving through the filter of the past and not orienting ourselves to novel distinctions of the present. (Siegel 2007, 105)

The brain searches for likenesses first. To find novel distinctions requires deliberate effort and setting aside the tendency to mindlessly search for likeness, sameness, and routine (i.e., Langer's concept of mindfulness). Every datum that is encountered could be—in principle—assessed on its own merits and with curiosity.

Our categories attempt to impose order on the chaos that is the phenomenal world and through our cognitive processes we come to see the world as humans think that it is. One fall-out of this otherwise adaptive process is that sometimes patterns are seen when none are actually there. For example, we tend to attribute agency to objects that are in motion. Objects that move tend to be seen as alive, so when we see an object move—even one that is inanimate—we attribute agency to it. This was demonstrated in the classic Heider experiment where subjects watched an animated movie of geometric shapes moving in random patterns (Heider and Simmel, 1944). Subjects could readily recount stories—creating a narrative out of the movement. The ability to see agency in movement likely stems from the causal operator (Newberg 2001)—a mind function that tends to link together proximal events as causally related. It is adaptive to make a causal link between, for example, eating a particular fungus and getting violently ill—learning—because it will spare the organism caloric costs in the future.[3]

DECONSTRUCTING CATEGORIES THROUGH PRESENT MOMENT AWARENESS

As the previous chapter on form argued, categorization is not an elective habit; it is constrained by the hardware of the brain. What we learn is limited by what we already know. We cannot—even if we wanted to—experience the world de novo. This is not how our brains work (Ascoli 2015). Furthermore,

"We cannot, as some meditative traditions suggest, 'get beyond' our categories and have a purely uncategorized and unconceptualized experience. Neural beings cannot do that" (Lakoff and Johnson 1999, 19). Was the Buddha exempt, somehow special? (e.g., Wilber 2007). While the Buddha may have approached that limit, he likely did not reach it entirely, given the hardwired constraints of form and perception. As discussed, categories are patterns—trading expedience for accuracy and specificity. This was useful for our hunter–gatherer ancestors who struggled for survival, but now many of us have the luxury to enjoy the world without constant threat and with abundance of food and other resources. The specificity of the world can make life richer. Over-efficient categorization cuts off creative process, richness, and a more accurate view of the world. "Art removes objects from the automatism of perception.... The technique of art is to make objects 'unfamiliar'" (Victor Shklovksky cited Geary 2011, 200). Likewise, Henry Moore said, "If I set out to sculpt a standing man and it becomes a lying woman, I know I am making art" (cited in Kozak 2015c). Creative flexibility comes from suspending the categorical habit. This type of awareness demonstrates a commitment to moment-to-moment perception and the energies that flow from it rather than a enslavement to preconceived ideas.

The benefit of fresh perception was touched on in the film, *My Dinner with Andre*. During the dialog between theater director Andre Gregory and playwright and actor Wallace Shawn, Wally says: "Why do we require a trip to Mount Everest in order to perceive one moment of reality? Is Mount Everest more real than New York? Isn't New York real? I think, if you could become fully aware of what existed in the cigar store next to this restaurant, I think it would just blow your brains out!" To "blow our minds," we must recognize how perception automatically operates through category and metaphor and bring awareness to these processes and make the effort to transcend these categories to the extent that we neurally can. In a sense, we are attempting to shift the ratio of automatic to deliberate category formation. As Ascoli would predict, Lakoff and Johnson point out: "A small percentage of our categories have been formed by conscious acts of categorization, but most are formed automatically and unconsciously as a result of functioning in the world. Though we learn new categories regularly, we cannot make massive changes in our category systems through conscious acts of recategorization" (1999, 18). But with mindfulness, we can make small, incremental ones.

T. S. Eliot in his poem, "The Cocktail Party," reminds us that we are always meeting a stranger, even when that person is known to us. The sense of familiarity is facilitated by categorization. Eliot recognizes that our normal everyday perception of each other is a desiccated process, bereft of the richness of the actual encounter that is taking place. Instead, we are remembering that person—fitting the experience of the moment into a memory, that is, in a sense, a constructed category. What gets missed are the changes that have occurred, however subtle, since that category was formed. The process of reacting to the remembered person instead of the actual person is a social convention, a convenience born of laziness, conditioning, and fear of intimacy, perhaps. But in reality, the encounter is always between two strangers. Much the same, whenever we encounter ourselves we are also encountering a stranger, but we react to ourselves with the remembered categories of the essential self.

Batchelor argues that the contemplative experience is aesthetic, not strictly a cognitive–behavioral–affective affair. If this is true, then every moment of existence could be a creative act, not merely derivative and subordinated to existing knowledge. The fact that most moments of a life are not aesthetic, creative acts—in the sense of being original—demonstrates, once again, the deadening power of categories. I agree with Batchelor that the artist and the meditator aim for that kind of startling yet hard won freshness. Such perception requires both effort and letting go in almost the same moment. The effort is like straining to keep an aperture of attention open long enough that thoughts to do not close prematurely. The letting go is like Rilke's protagonist in "The Swan" who falls into the water and everything that used to confirm and burden this awkward bird on solid ground is now lost in weightless free fall into graceful navigation of water. To continue the aperture image, the arms work to hold open a space into which the body allows itself to fall through, letting gravity pull attention into an uncertain and, perhaps, terrifying abyss. Yet, at the very same time, that chasm has a familiar quality to it, almost as if it were the home one has been estranged from, one we have been exiled from by excessive thinking. The essential self's wish for safety makes this falling seem terrible. The realization that there is no such thing as constancy can make this free fall wonderful, enlivening, and confirming. That confirmation is a paradox: by recognizing that no solid ground exists, one is grounded all the same. It is only by embracing impermanence that any semblance of stability is preserved. In a sense, it is only through becoming psychologically homeless that one returns from exile.

E. H. Gombrich (not be confused with Buddhist scholar Richard Gombrich) said, "It takes an artist to make us attend to the message of reality" (cited in Batchelor 2017, 224). A clever demonstration of originality is no guarantee of that truth. For both the meditator and the artist, the relinquishment of pre-existing knowledge goes hand-in-hand with a renunciation of self-centeredness. Jenny Boully speaks to a parallel between poetry and what otherwise, in a Buddhist rather than literary context, might be called nirvana: "Poetry is an instant. It is an instant in which transcendence is achieved, where a miracle occurs, and knowledge, experience, and memory are obliterated and transformed into awe. The instant passes quickly, so quickly, and then you are just your regular self again" (2018, 45). Both the artist and the meditator can succumb to the tendency to say, "Look at me! See how clever I am." In meditation, self-aggrandizing always seems to occur in those moments when primordial—before language—perception opens up and awareness falls through the aperture—"It's happening!—only to find itself being named and attention yanked back into the personified, languaged, and already characterized identity.

NOTES

1. Ronald Reagan is infamous for having said: "If you've seen one redwood tree, you've seen them all." What he actually said was: "I think, too, that we've got to recognize that where the preservation of a natural resource like the redwoods is concerned, that there is a common sense limit. I mean, if you've looked at a hundred thousand acres or so of trees—you know, a tree is a tree, how many more do you need to look at?" The actual quote reflects a similar logic as the paraphrase—to be perceptually expedient, why bother?

2. *"Out there"* is, of course, also itself a metaphorical concept. We make distinctions between subjective and objective, inside and outside, yet in reality we are in a process of exchange even at the non-quantum level.

3. The same tendency can make people think that their prayers have been answered—"I asked God for this to happen and it happened so God must have been listening to me"—or to think that the Universe is a sentient and responsive agent and that thoughts can manifest what they think about (e.g., Byrne 2006). It seems that much of the memetic power (Blackmore 1999) of religions stems from erroneous causal attribution to randomly occurring events (e.g., Dawkins 2008). Science has fostered a great advance of humanity by providing a methodology that circumvents the causal operator and our penchant for finding patterns where none exist. Unfortunately, individual psychology and even scientists themselves are still very much vulnerable to these kinds of associations (Kozak 2017).

Chapter 9

Feeling

Pain and Pleasure Drive Evolution's Primary Agendas (and Give Rise to a Sense of the One Having Pleasure and Pain)

OVERVIEW

Feeling is evolution's most cunning tool: "The things that become objects of desire are the kinds of things that led, on average, to enhanced odds of survival and reproduction in the environment in which we evolved: water, food safety, sex, status, mastery over the environment, and the wellbeing of children, friends, and kin" (Pinker 1997, 143). Evolution pursues its primary agendas of survival and reproduction by manipulating creatures with pleasure and pain. Human animals—even with our sophisticated cortical development—are not exempt. Evolution has tricked us here in grand fashion. For example, through its henchman dopamine, it makes the pursuit of pleasure more pleasant than the actual having of pleasure, thus keeping creatures on a hedonic treadmill. Every experience has a feeling tone—pleasant, unpleasant, or neutral—that serves the purpose of evaluation: what should be done about what is happening now; should I approach, avoid, or ignore? Pleasant feelings naturally gives rise to liking and approach; unpleasant feelings to disliking and avoidance. Through the one who likes and dislikes a process of attachment occurs. Not only does one want the desired object or experience, one must have it or a sense of desperation otherwise prevails—if only momentarily and if only subtly, but often enduringly and not so subtly.

FEELING IS NOT SELF

Can the self be found in feeling?

"Bhikkhus, how do you conceive it: is feeling permanent or impermanent?"—"Impermanent, venerable Sir."—"Now is what is impermanent painful or pleasant?"—"Painful, venerable Sir."—"Now is what is impermanent, what is painful since subject to change, fit to be regarded thus: 'This is mine, this is I, this is my self?'"—"No, venerable sir." (Nanamoli Thera 1995)

The Buddha clarifies the dangers of feeling:

For all delights in sensuality are burning & boiling,
aggravated, aglow . . . A blazing grass firebrand,
held in the hand:
Those who let go
do not get burned.
Sensuality is like a firebrand. It burns
those who do not let go. (Thanissaro 1999, 44)

It is easy to see how a sense of self with both its generic—evolutionary—and unique—personal identity—preferences drives the unfolding configurations of desire. The self is, in one sense, a map of everything that is liked and disliked, the loved and reviled, the important and irrelevant. Out of this matrix of liking and disliking and along with the form and perception aggregates comes a sense of a self that is somehow different than the experiences being had. Instead of just experiencing, this self *owns* the experience, has a vested interest in it. The antidote to feeling's liability is be curious about what is felt—even the unpleasant can be fascinating. Such interest-driven curiosity is a liberating alternative to the vested interests of contingency where pleasure and pain no longer determine one's sense of well-being in any given moment. In cases without survival implications, awakened individuals—or individuals who wish to awaken—can choose to override the impulses of feeling (participating in civilized society makes similar demands). These people do not have to be pushed and pulled by these forces. Without self-ownership, even the extremes of ecstasy and torture can enjoy an equivalence. To #resistevolution requires much work. Interest leads to investigation, which helps with containment: the impulse to act out the demands of pleasures and pains is reduced or eliminated. Eventually, with continued practice, the force in which conditioned impulses arise can diminish.

NATURAL DESIRE: MASTER MANIPULATOR

If we look at the three fires from an evolutionary standpoint, we can appreciate that they are natural rather than evil: "Our entire notion of good and bad, our whole landscape of feelings—fear, lust, love, and the many other feelings, salient and subtle, that inform our everyday thoughts and perceptions—are products of the particular evolutionary history of our species"[1] (Wright 2017, 237). Greed, desire, and passion are the fires of pleasure that facilitate survival through eating and, when the organism reaches sexual maturity, the delights of sex facilitate replication. In the legacy environment of our ancestors, the fire of hatred, aversion, anger, and other so-called destructive emotions[2] (Goleman 2014) enabled social status negotiation, rivalry management, and general survival against threats from the environments, including other people. The fire of moha—delusion, confusion, and self-deception—is the byproduct of otherwise beneficial adaptations but leads to the situation where feelings are untrustworthy: "Our feelings are in some sense or another dubious guides to reality" (Wright 2017, 233) because they only serve evolution's agendas. According to Wright and common sense, false perceptions can be adaptive: "Natural selection doesn't 'want' us to be happy, after all; it just 'wants' us to be productive, in its narrow sense of *productive*. And the way to make us productive is to make the anticipation of pleasure very strong but the pleasure itself not very long-lasting" (Wright 2017, 8, emphasis original). If pleasures were more than fleeting, if having was more enjoyable then pursuing, then we would be too complacent. If we did not fool ourselves about how empty pleasures can be, we would be much less motivated to chase them—anticipation is always more reinforcing[3] than the actual experience. "Part of *Tanha's* job description is to never be satisfied" (Wright 2017, 214, emphasis original). Restless seekers of renewed pleasures means brisk business for survival and replication. Schopenhauer, not unfamiliar with Eastern systems of thought, recognized this human foible:

> In the first place a man never is happy but spends his whole life in striving after something which he thinks will make him so; he seldom attains his goals and, when he does it is only to be disappointed: he is mostly shipwrecked in the end, and comes into harbor with masts and riggings gone. And then it is all one whether he has been happy or miserable; for his life was never anything more than a present moment, always vanishing; and now it is over. (Yalom 2009, 234–35)

Feelings[4] have worked well for organisms throughout the history of life; the amoebae encounters a noxious substance and retreats. Jumping ahead a few eons, they worked well for our hunter–gatherer ancestors living in small groups of no more than 150 members. However, in the complexity of today's world, the "truth value" of feeling is misleading:

> Indeed, for ninety-nine percent of human existence, people lived as foragers in small nomadic bands. Our brains are adapted to that long vanished way of life,

not to brand-new agricultural and industrial civilizations. They are not wired to cope with anonymous crowds, schooling, written language, government, police, courts, armies, modern medicine, formal social institutions, high technology, and other newcomers to the human experience. (Pinker 1999, 42)

How then can we navigate through the noise that feelings provide? The Buddha recommended a middle path between the extremes of indulging feelings on the one hand and trying to extinguish them on the other: "It is wrong, certainly, to give oneself riotously to the pleasures of the body. But it is no better to deny the body those satisfactions that its needs demand" (Percheron 1960, 222).

SENSUALITY AND RENUNCIATION: THE CHALLENGE OF PERMISSIBLE PLEASURES

For the Buddha, sensuality sounds burdensome to deadly proportions:

> Furthermore, it is with sensuality for the reason, sensuality for the source . . . that (men), taking swords & shields and buckling on bows & quivers, charge slippery bastions while arrows & spears are flying and swords are flashing; and there they are splashed with boiling cow dung and crushed under heavy weights, and their heads are cut off by swords, so that they incur death or deadly pain. Now this drawback too in the case of sensuality, this mass of stress [dukkha] visible here & now, has sensuality for its reason, sensuality for its source, sensuality for its cause, the reason being simply sensuality. (Thanissaro 1999, 43)

The Buddha distinguished between pleasures that were unwholesome—typically, carnal ones—and wholesome pleasure—the joy that comes from absorptive meditation. On sensual pleasures:

But if this pleasure fades away,
  The person with this desire,
  —Who gives birth to this desire—
  Is pained as if pierced by an arrow.
  (Fronsdal 2016, 42, from the Kama Sutta, The Discourse on Desire)

This verse contains a key observation and a critical proposition. There is no question that pleasures are ephemeral and unsatisfactory—evolution's empty hedonic treadmill, as it were. Yet, cannot one—especially with insight—mitigate the pain of its passing? Does all desire require self-fabrication?[5] If one knows intellectually and experientially that any given phenomenon is impermanent, then cannot it be enjoyed while it is present in all its fleetingness and then not mourned or clung to when it changes? In principle, the answer to that question must be yes, yet the Buddha contends that it cannot not. Surely, for the enlightened person, such relinquishing must be possible but he thought this problem was so pernicious that even serious practitioners should limit their exposures to pleasure (especially for the male monks, those provided by women). Was this proscription a symptom of the Buddha's avoidant personality? There are the "healthy realities" associated with awakening, and if this is the case then it must be possible—in principle—to take a salubrious approach to any desire, whether related to awakening or not.[6] Impermanence is not the entirety of the issue—if pleasure was permanent, dissatisfaction would surely follow in the cloud dust of boredom.

The Buddha's recommendation: be independent (*viveka*) from sensuality, especially sex. That sounds like abstinence, and it is what he required of his monastics. But what if he meant—instead avoiding sex—not to have greed and craving, not to be contingent—the perception that without the desired object, the self is incomplete, deficient, abnormal. Why not view copulation with the same dispassionate interest as urinating or defecating—a biological function of the body? Such an approach to the senses *is* possible but, alas, exceedingly difficult. The more intense the sensuality—as in sex—the more likely the temptation to succumb to contingency, however subtle. The Buddha may have had his own reasons for embracing celibacy—as discussed elsewhere—his avoidant attachment style, potential homosexuality, the impracticality of supporting a large community of aspirants *with* families. Perhaps, the Buddha's decision to avoid sex was utilitarian because it maximized benefit for the majority—if one hundred monks were tempted, a handful could remain non-contingent while the rest would fail.[7] Thus, the Buddha hedged his bets. Renunciation as a policy is ambiguous. It could mean giving up behavior, although one can still crave with the mind. The Buddha would include such mental behavior in what is to be renounced. Or, perhaps what is renounced is a contingent state of mind, rather than giving up any particular behaviors.

Since engaging sensuality without attachment is difficult to pull off, it is more expedient to avoid contact altogether rather than to try to engage with it and, likely, fail. Because of this difficulty, the Buddha's approach seems like an absolute kind purity that dictates renunciation of all sensuality: "A thought of sensuality arose in me. I understood this: 'This thought of sensuality has arisen in me. It leads to affliction for oneself, it leads to affliction for others, it leads to affliction for both, it destroys wisdom, leads to distress, and does not conduce to Nirvana'" (Stanley, Purser, Singh 2018, 35).

The Buddha's bias is apparent in the Discourse to Tissa Metteya, part of the *Book of Eights*. He starts by cautioning against "addiction" to sex or reckless sex after a period of solitude, and from this extreme, he recommends giving sex up altogether. Missing seems to be the middle ground—ironic for the founder of the Middle Way. Later in the poem, addiction is substituted with "attachment." It is not clear if these are meant as synonyms, for addiction might be a more severe form of attachment. Because of its propensity for creating attachment, sex is dangerous in the Buddha's mind, and he counsel's against it, advising his followers: "become firm in the single life" (Fronsdal 2016, 69). Can there be sex without self-making? [The Buddha said,]

seeing craving, aversion, and lust
> I have no desire for sex.
> What is this, full of urine and excrement,
> [that] I don't want to touch even with my foot?

. . .

It is by letting go, not grasping, and not being
> dependent.

That they, the peaceful, do not huger for becoming. (Fronsdal 2016, 77)

By renouncing the fire of desire, the Buddha appears to succumb to the fire of aversion when he repudiates the sexual object. Here again, it is possible to imagine sexual contact that does not involve grasping and does not, thereby, contribute to self-making and does not require aversion. In the "Discourse on Breaking Apart" the Buddha provides this line: "They see seclusion in the midst of sense contacts" (Fronsdal 2016, 84) that suggests the very possibility I am highlighting. But the Buddha did not trust himself or his renunciants—sex was prohibited.

Lust, hatred, or whatever feeling does not matter *if* the observing mind can withhold making the phenomenon a condition of well-being—this is the feat of non-contingency. I feel the fire of lust, let's say. I may be able to act on that lust—a willing sexual partner is available—or I may not be able to act on it. Whether I indulge the feeling or not, I can know that it is a passing phenomenon—it does not have to define me. It does not have to become a cornerstone of my identity, i.e., it does not matter, does not mean anything—I can take it or leave it. I do not have to feel shame about its arising, and I do not have to feel frustrated if its expression is "frustrated"—because I also know that even if this lust is "satisfied" that satisfaction will be short-lived; I know the feeling would not last, no feelings do. How much dukkha will be generated if I can adopt this attitude?

The problem with pleasure is not impermanence per se. Yes, it is true that the most beautiful person is just skin over fat and bones and guts and bile—"full of urine and excrement" as the Buddha was wont to point out. So what? It is still pleasing to look at, pleasing to touch. What difference does it make that the beauty is only skin deep—that skin is an amazing organ! The issue seems to stem from wishing that the impermanent would somehow be permanent. This is how dukkha is traditionally rendered. But I think we need the additional caveat of contingency. If I can enjoy beauty, fleeting as it is, without making my wellbeing *contingent* on it lasting, then everything is okay—I am not generating excessive dukkha. But we *do* make ourselves contingent, if not consciously, then unconsciously, if not obviously, then subtly. I, too, am skin over fat and bones and guts and bile; I, too, will deteriorate over time; I, too, am impermanent. No *thing* can provide enduring satisfaction—no thought, sense pleasure, or action—except, perhaps, the integral actions detailed in the eightfold path.

Recognizing the power of the mind's three fires—the temptations, illusions, and distortions of Mara—the Buddha created an insulated monastic community. Monks were allowed few personal possessions and could not use money. They had to beg for their food and thus ate only once per day. It is not clear if the Buddha was an anti-hedonist or an anti-materialist. He was a pragmatist and knew that living in the world without these protections would make the monks' work that much harder. For instance, the Buddha said, "There are few people in the world who, when they obtain great wealth, do not become intoxicated and careless, give in to greed for sensual pleasure, and mistreat others" (Bodhi 2003). It takes integrity to transcend the lure of the fires as the Buddha points out in this passage: "When an inferior man gains abundant wealth, he does not make himself, his family, his slaves, his servants, or employees happy. The wealth not being used properly, goes to waste, not to utilization" (Bodhi 2003). With or without success, then, material existence is fraught. The man who works hard and does not achieve wealth: "sorrows, grieves, & laments, beats his breast, becomes distraught: 'My work is in vain, my efforts are fruitless!' If he were to achieve this prized wealth, dukkha would come from trying to protect it: 'How will neither kings nor thieves make off with my property, nor fire burn it, nor water sweep it away, nor hateful heirs make off with it?'" (Thanissaro 1999, 46).

One more point on contingency: *All truth is relative.* If this statement is true, then it is no longer relative—it becomes an absolute. If this conundrum happened on an episode of *Star Trek,* smoke would start coming out of the computer. Any notion of absolutes, must be approached cautiously but not absolutely (nor relativistically). Was the Buddha proscriptive about sensuality? This certainly sounds like it: "In the same way, monks, there are some contemplatives & brahmans who hold to a doctrine, a view like this: 'There is no harm in sensuality.' Thus they meet with their downfall through sensuality. They consort with women wanderers who wear their hair coiled and long" (Thanissaro 1999, 52). Was the Buddha being absolute? From his statements, it certainly sounds like it. But what if this statement were qualified—*unchecked* sensuality is destructive rather than sensuality per se.

One not enflamed with forms
—seeing a form with mindfulness firm—
knows with mind unenflamed
and doesn't remain fastened there.
The touch of a woman stays in a man's mind and consumes it. [only if he clings]
(Thanissaro 1999, 48)

By bringing awareness to the sensual thought, the Buddha is checking it, qualifying it, transforming it. Checked sensuality: one can take it or leave it. Renunciation would favor leaving it, but why? Why shouldn't both options be equally plausible? "In other words, neither the senses nor their objects are fetters for the mind. Beautiful sights, sounds, & so forth, do not entrap it, nor do the senses themselves. Instead, it is trapped by the act of desire & passion based on such things" (Thanissaro 1999, 47). Not everyone can be a monk or a nun; non-contingency, then, is the path to permissible pleasures. I have focused here extensively on the pleasurable side of feelings; the same arguments can be made for the painful side: contingency is not necessary, if difficult to achieve.

Mindfulness is a key process for investigating the feelings that drive desire and aversion. By apprehending what is happening in the body with precision, calmness, and interest, contingency can be addressed—and overcome. Mindful awareness puts one in direct contact with the ebbing and flowing of sensations and their attendant energies—whether pleasant or unpleasant—and mitigates the sense of ownership and thereby contingency. Without identification, dukkha is reduced, the fires are not proliferated.

NOTES

1. "Pleasure and pains must have been evolved as the subjective accompaniment of processes which are respectively beneficial or injurious to the organism, and so evolved for the purpose or to the end that the organism should seek the one and shun the other" (Darwin, *Origin of the Species,* cited in Wright 2017, 29).

2. Feelings like anger were appropriate in intimate hunter–gatherer situations. Resources were commodities that needed to be protected, and social status meant access to resources. It is rare nowadays in the privileged world that anger is either necessary for survival or resource protection, so it is rarely appropriate. It is a vestige that now only furthers contingency.

3. Take, for example, this neuroscientific mindfulness study's findings: "stronger activity of the putamen and caudate during a resting state following mindfulness training and lower activation in the caudate nucleus during reward anticipation in experienced meditators.... These studies might indicate altered self-regulation in the motivational realm, with possibly reduced susceptibility to incentives and enhanced reward-related activity during rest" (Tang, Holzel, and Posner 2015, 219) See also Kirk et al. (2014), Tang et al. (2009).

4. In the absence of unlimited time and experimental conditions, the affective system creates proxies for evolutionary selection. Few decisions can be made on the basis of pure logic—the information required to make a decision is incomplete and inconclusive. One decision precludes another: Whom should I vote for? Where should I go to college? Should I stay in this relationship? What do I want to order from this menu for dinner? When we cannot make purely logical choices, which is just about every choice of consequence we make, then we must rely on feelings that function as *affective heuristics* (Brown and Kozak 1998). On balance, feelings will guide us toward adaptive decisions as they did for our ancestors when these systems were evolving. To understand affective heuristics, it is necessary to differentiate affects (i.e., feelings) from emotions that are complex adaptations that include feelings but also behavior, e.g., facial expressions, physiological arousal. Feelings correspond more closely to what we understand as gut feelings—bottom-up sources of embodied information (e.g., Gladwell 2005). Take for example the simple fact that emotional outbursts decrease as children age and gain the cognitive and motor skills to get their needs met. Emotions arise when coping fails—even for positive emotion—and serve the function of restoring equilibration. Feelings function as proxies for adaption, they are evolution's foot soldiers.

5. Montaigne warned: "Since what is present fails to gratify us, we hanker after future things of which we know nothing. It is not that what is present is unable to gratify us but we grasp it in a sick and uncontrolled way" (cited in Batchelor 2020, 60).

6. It is also the case that animals can experience pleasures and pain without—apparently—language-based self-making capacities. Craving and clinging, though, do seem to require self-making. But animals (including human animals) are still always subject to dukkha-dukkha. Every organic being is bound by the laws of physics, aging, illness, and death.

7. Celibacy was a utilitarian short-cut and one that would be subverted centuries later by Vajrayana monks in Tibet practicing yogic tantras, some of which involved sexual contact that sometimes became abusive (Finnigan and Hogendoorn 2019).

Chapter 10

Mental Fabrication and the Modular Self

OVERVIEW

However sankhara is translated—fabrications, mental formations, formations, determinations, volitions, intentions—it corresponds with the narrative functions of mind: storytelling, the activity of the default mode network (DMN[1])—and is most closely associated with personal identity—that storied sense of being a person with a name, history, and anticipated future. The adaptive advantage of this capacity for internal narration is imagination—anticipating and remembering things that are not currently present. The downside is the tendency to identify with the mind's contents—reifying them into a self. If feeling is the fuel that drives this reified self, then sankhara is its particulars. The power of narratizing fabrications requires metacognitive skepticism and a commitment to extricate attention from any given story into the phenomenology of the present moment, releasing identification with the essential, objectified self.[2] The stories we tell about ourselves are constraining and costly at times as the photographer Richard Avedon's work highlighted: "As an artist, Avedon told the truth about lies, and why we need them or metaphors to survive, and how people fit into their self-mythologizing like body bags, and die in them if they're not careful" (Als 2017). To #resistevolution for this aggregate we must understand how we are constructed through language—we are narrative creatures, storytelling animals (Gotschall 2012) as if our world is made of stories (Loy 2010).

FABRICATIONS ARE NOT SELF

Can the self be found in fabrications?

> "Bhikkhus, how do you conceive it: is determination [formations, fabrications, conditionings] permanent or impermanent?"—"Impermanent, venerable Sir."—"Now is what is impermanent painful or pleasant?"—"Painful, venerable Sir."—"Now is what is impermanent, what is painful since subject to change, fit to be regarded thus: 'This is mine, this is I, this is my self?'" (Nanamoli Thera 1995)

Wittgenstein famously said in his *Tractatus Logico-Philosophicus* that: "The sense of a separate self is only a shadow cast by grammar" according with the Buddha's view. Just as the brain is a prediction machine utilizing controlled hallucinations (Seth 2019), the essential self is likewise a controlled hallucination.

The brain appears to be comprised of computational modules[3] that serve adaptive functions, i.e., expertise in solving problems that would have benefited the reproductive fitness of our hunter–gatherer ancestors. "The mind . . . is not a single organ but a system of organs, which we can think of as psychological faculties or mental modules" (Pinker 1997, 27). These modules will not necessarily be in discrete brain regions but more in ensembles across the connectome.

The brain is not, contrary to popular opinion, a "general problem-solver." All complex systems have functional specialization. The human brain is no exception, although this remains controversial (Kurzban 2010). Kurzban notes that functional specialization is fully accepted in other domains such as physiology, so why not psychology? The reason appears to be because we are not yet ready to give up our cherished notions of self—that general problem solver. Modules operate unconsciously, for the most part, and some modules are hidden. Others, even while hidden can still communicate erroneous information to other modules to get them to do their particular function. Given that modules are independent, the demands of the environment can put modules into conflict. We are, thus, contradictory, we are hypocritical (Kurzban 2010).

Cognitive and neuroscientists have not been able to locate a general self within the brain. When it comes to self, modularity applies as well. Minsky noted a "society of agents" (Minsky 1988), and Daniel Dennet (1991) cautioned against finding some kind of president in the Oval Office of the mind. Kenrick and Griskevicius have identified seven different modules or sub-selves each that serve an adaptive evolutionary fitness function that include "1) evading physical harm, 2) avoiding disease, 3) making friends, 4) gaining status, 5) attracting a mate, 6), keeping that mate, and 7) caring for family"

(2013, 30). There is no master self that considers the input from each of these subselves. Instead, "although it feels as if there is just one single self inside your head, at a deeper evolutionary level, you have a multiplicity of selves. . . . Each of these selves is like a little dictator who completely changes your priorities and preferences when he or she takes charge" (Kenrick and Griskevicius 2013, 24).

Pinker warns that the specialized, modularity of mind should not be taken to mean there is no hierarchical structure whatsoever:

> But the theory [society of mind] can be taken too far it outlaws any system in the brain charged with giving the reins or the floor to one of the agents at a time. The agents of the brain might very well be organized hierarchically into nested subroutines. . . . It would not be ghost in the machine, just another set of if-then rules or a neural network that shunts control to the loudest, fastest, or strongest agent one level down. (1997, 144)

The self falsely gives the sense of central control, but there is no all-knowing homunculus, no miniature self pulling the levers of control like the Wizard of Oz: "Pay no attention to the man behind the curtain!" In the self's case, Toto pulls the curtain back to reveal an empty space. But empty is not quite right—even though there is no central agent who reviews streams of information, evaluates the most appropriate course of action, and then selects, there are competing, overlapping modules, each with its own programmed agenda, seeking to get its particular need met—perhaps more a buzzing melee of competing little wizards. Gazzaniga clarifies: "While hierarchical processing takes place within the modules, it is looking like there is no hierarchy among the models. All these modules are not reporting to a department head—it is free-for-all, self-organizing system" (Micheal Gazzaniga cited in Wright 2017, 88–89). But how do decisions get made? This remains unknown. With conscious selection, it is as if that choice must be justified as rational, coherent, ineluctable. But this is more post-hoc reasoning than anything else: *I did it so I must have chosen to do it.* "They [Tooby and Cosmides] concluded that what emotions[4] do—what emotions are *for*—is to activate and coordinate the modular functions that are, in Darwinian terms, appropriate for the moment" (Wright 2017, 96, emphasis orginal). It seems as though I am thinking my thoughts but modules generate thinking-based mind activity. It seems as though consciousness is the source of thinking but rather than producing thoughts its function may be more to receive thoughts that arise elsewhere—outside of consciousness (Wright 2017).[5]

To whatever degree there is a hierarchy, there still is no master, omniscient, agentic self in this description in the way that we typically construe self. It recognizes that some rules are considered more important than others, and it would not be surprising if these rules corresponded with features of personality, axiology, and life context. Unlike Gazzaniga, Pinker is saying that choices are not a free-for-all. Clearly, there are functions of will as many cases of brain damage will attest. However, volition is closer to an algorithm than an autonomous psychological agent deciding freely—something must "choose" between the demands of competing modules. The lack of a president or CEO in charge of the mind is similar to the position the Buddha put forth, "Unlike a king who issues commands to his subjects that he can expect to be obeyed, we find ourselves powerless over our own sensorium—a situation at odds with the deeply rooted intuition that we are in charge of what is going on" (Batchelor 2015, 64). While there may be hierarchical rules at play, there is no sense of a "me," no "person" in charge. A master rule is not the same as a CEO in charge. It is more a gatekeeper than an agent endowed with free will.

Kurzban has argued that rather than a CEO in charge, consciousness is more of a press secretary who, in post-hoc fashion, makes sense of the decisions that were just made. As with any good press secretary, spin is put on events and it's even capable of confabulation to explain the facts of what just happened. From this perspective, the conscious narrative self is not controlling decision making but is more engaged in self-promoting bias (Kurzban 2010).

In a now classic review, Nisbett and Wilson explore the claim that "we may have no direct access to higher order mental processes such as those involved in evaluation, judgment, problem solving, and the initiation of behavior" (1977, 232). Furthermore, "The accuracy of subjective reports is so poor as to suggest that any introspective access that may exist is not sufficient to produce generally correct or reliable reports" (1977, 233). People do not use introspective awareness when reporting on mental experience but rather rely on a priori causal theories. Sometimes, these are incidentally correct, but most often they are not. In this review article, Nesbitt and Wilson report on an experiment they conducted that presented four identical pair of nylon stockings to consumers. The subjects had preferences based on position, i.e., the stockings on the right were preferred 4:1 over the stockings on the left. When queried about their preference, no subject mentioned the position of the object as influencing their decision (Nesbitt and Wilson 1977).

The press secretary metaphor shows how the module for language and self-perception interprets the flow of information into a coherent narrative, even if some or all of it is confabulated (some modules are not in contact with the modules that talk and self-represent). A president makes decisions; a press secretary makes sense of the decision that was made by some invisible calculus (based on program weights, algorithms, mental formations, the exigencies of the moment). From the perspective of the untrained eye, the pronouncements of the president and the press secretary may seem to be identical;

however, their differing attributive causes have profound consequences for the natures of selves.

The modular theory of mind provides two fundamental insights: 1) there is no "me" that owns experience and 2) "I" don't run the show. Thus, we have a self that is: 1) informed by unconscious functions, 2) often confabulatory, and 3) non-centralized. The Buddha would not have known anything about functional specialization, natural selection, or evolutionary psychology. He did, however, have the correct insight that there is no president or in his parlance, "king" running the show. A centralized self was not to be found by way of an eternal soul—atman—nor was it to be found in the rudimentary functional specializations he outlined for the mind: form, perception, feeling, fabrications, or consciousness.

METAPHORICAL IMPLICATIONS

Reified selves are metaphorical: *self-as-thing*; their essence is the real and true self and with this realness comes the capacity for a false self that shrouds the true self. Lakoff and Johnson explain: "The Subject is the locus of consciousness, subjective experience, reason, will, and our 'essence,' everything that makes us who we uniquely are. There is at least one Self and possibly more. The Selves consist of everything else about us—our bodies, our social roles, our histories, and so on" (1999, 268). While the notion of multiple selves is consistent with the modular theory of mind (e.g., Pinker 1997, Kurzban 2010), it is the *essence* of the self that is problematic. Lakoff and Johnson continue: "In the metaphor, there are two Selves. One Self (the 'real,' or 'true,' Self) is compatible with one's Essence and is always conceptualized as a person. The second Self (not the 'real,' or 'true,' Self) is incompatible with one's Essence and is conceptualized as either a person or a container that the first Self hides inside of" (1999, 282). That essential self is seen as real, immutable, and true, whereas the inauthentic self is experienced as an aberration or at least an obfuscation of that real self. With these assumptions in place, we can get metaphorical constructions as follows. Self-Discrepancy Case 1: The Inner self Self 1 (Real Self) is hidden inside Self 2 (Outer Self). The Real Self is fragile, shy, or awful.

> Her sophistication is a façade. You've never seen what he's really like on the inside. He is afraid to reveal his inner self. She's sweet on the outside and mean on the inside. The iron hand in the velvet glove. His petty self came out. He won't reveal himself to strangers. She rarely shows her real self. Whenever anyone challenges him, he retreats into himself. He retreats into his shell to protect himself. (Lakoff and Johnson 1999, 283, emphases original)

Self-Discrepancy Case 2: The External Real Self (Real Me): Self 2 is hidden inside Self 1.

> I'm not myself today. That wasn't the real me yesterday. That wasn't my real self talking. (Lakoff and Johnson 1999, 283, emphases original)

Self-Discrepancy Case 3: The True Self: Self 2 is in search of Self 1:

> He found himself in writing. I'm trying to get in touch with myself. She went to India to look for her true self, but all she came back with was a pair of sandals. He's still searching for his true self. (Lakoff and Johnson 1999, 284, emphases original)

All three cases assume an essential self that is either bad, misrepresented, or waiting to be revealed. It is hard to think of selfhood outside of these terms. These assumptions, though, are not benign. As just explored, the essential self, while ringing subjectively true has no objective reality. Some self-deception is necessary (e.g., Kurzban 2010). However, the cognitive error of reifying this wraith-like, essential self has consequences: dukkha, principle among them. The essential self is the one who can own, identify with, and proliferate moment-to-moment experience into anguish, misery, dissatisfaction, and despair.

SELF AND NOT SELF FROM THE MODULAR PERSPECTIVE

The Buddha declared *anatman*—that means the negation of *atta* (Pali), of atman—literally "not atman." He was redirecting attention from the eternal atman—what might otherwise be known as soul in the West—and rejecting—or noting in a more matter of fact manner—that there was no essence to the more mundane sense of one's self—the everyday folk psychological sense of *me,* a person who endures through time, who has a name, a story, a future, present, and past. He did not claim there was no self, only that self-as-regarded for the run-of-the-mill person, was mistaken. *The self you think you are is an illusion,* he might have said. It prefigures the title of Bruce Hood's 2012 book, *The Self Illusion.* Two thousand five hundred years ago, the Buddha asked his followers to consider the self as an illusion, self is not what we think it is—we see it as being more substantial and in control than it actually is. Whatever we experience as self arises out of the activity of the aggregates, nothing more. What the Buddha could not have told his faithful followers is how evolutionary psychology provides us with an illusory self to further its own ends. He could not quite clarify that in addition to this essential self, there are other things designed[6] into us by evolution that made sense in early hunter–gatherer small, close-knit communities that were problematic in the Iron Age on the Gangetic plain: the so-called destructive emotions of painful self-consciousness, shame, anger, etc.

THE SELF IS NOT IN CONTROL

If I reflect on myself, I feel as though I am in charge of my experience. I am the CEO, the president, or the prime minister of my being; I am the king! I make decisions, exercise free will, and can claim a continuity with my younger self and feel confident—short of a cerebrovascular accident or other traumatic brain injury—that I'll maintain a connection to my future self. However, patients with brain damage provide clues to the intact-brain dependency of self. Split-brain patients lose communication between the hemispheres of their brains and the language dominant left-hemisphere will readily confabulate a story when the right hemisphere does something it didn't have access to (e.g., Gazzaniga and Sperry 1967). Accuracy takes a backseat to some sense of soundness. In terms of natural selection coherent stories make sense (Wright 2017) because impression management is an important social demand. "It is possible to argue that the primary evolutionary function of the self is to be the organ of impression management, rather than, as our folk psychology would have it, a decision-maker" (Jeremy Barkow cited in Wright 2017, 86).

A powerful blow to the sense that the self-agent is in control comes from experiments about initiating an action. Prior to deciding to initiate an action, the brain area that readies the body for action has already activated. The declaration of intention is after the fact, even though it feels as if the subject has authorized the action. If the self-agent were really in control, intention would precede brain activation, not vice versa (see Libet 1985; Matsuhashi et al. 2008).

THE SELF IS BIASED

Without a need for accuracy, we are free to engage in self-serving bias (e.g. Hoorens 1993). As anyone who listened to *A Prairie Home Companion* knows, Garrison Keillor celebrated this bias when he said: "Welcome to Lake Wobegon, where all the women are strong, all the men good looking, and all the children are above average." A sense of specialness stems from the selfish gene. This, of course, is an illusion if not delusion—moha. Everyone cannot really be special. From morality to driving skills and even when it comes to being non-self-biased, the majority of us believe ourselves to be above average.[7]

At a certain development age—around four years—children acquire the capacity to attribute essences to things, including themselves as their own essential self starts to emerge. A lot of science fiction is predicated upon an essential self. Take for example Doctor McCoy holding Spock's Katra at the end of *Star Trek II: The Wrath of Kahn* and its return to Spock in *Star Trek III: The Search for Spock*. For yet another instance, consider the scenario in the *Star Trek Next Generation* episode from Season Two: "The Schizoid Man," where a cyberneticist transfers his consciousness and personality to an unwitting Data. It is also the sinister underlying theme of HBO's *Westworld*, where humans are secretly surveilled and recorded so that their minds can be installed into immortal android versions of themselves. Of course, this transfer of mind can only happen if there is non-material energy and information that can exist separate from the body or at least the body with which it was originally associated. Medical science provides its own examples of seeming non-materiality. Capgras delusion is diagnosed when a person is convinced that someone close to them, like a spouse or a parent—is an imposter. They recognize the external features of this person yet believe them to be an exact fake. Such a belief relies upon the assumption of an essential self. These patients have a lesion in or near the fusiform gyrus—a brain area responsible for facial recognition[8]—that connects visual and affective parts of the brain like the amygdala. The patient thinks their relative is an imposter because they cannot feel what they are supposed to feel when they see this person. Without the usual feelings their perception rings false (Ramachandran and Blakeslee 2009). Here we can see that feeling serves as more than just an affective heuristic, it animates, enlivens, and gives things their sense of reality. "That's the way perception of essence works; it smuggles judgments into our mind by cloaking them in feelings that are themselves so subtle, or at least so routine, as to often escape conscious recognition" (Wright 2017, 238). Mirror misidentification disorder is another example, where ones reflection rings false. Less clinically significant, most people experience temporary states of depersonalization from time to time, where they do not feel like themselves or derealization where their surroundings seem alien.

If a Rembrandt is revealed to be a forgery, the owner—no matter how faithful a reproduction—is going to feel that her $33.2 million was not well spent. The painting's "essence" is not in the image it presents and the feelings it inspires but the *belief* about its authenticity—the real painting is infused, infected, inured with Rembrandt's essence; the facsimile is not. Likewise, my self must have an authentic essence that—like the painting—has a material basis. But this materiality is more facsimile than authenticity. In just one year, 98 percent of the atoms of "my" body change as I live in exchange with the environment around me. Give it some more time and there is hardly any material that is "me" now that was "me" five years ago.[9] Am I now a forgery—of my former self? The Buddha somehow knew that self was in a ceaseless flux of change. Perhaps it was the energetic effervescence he experienced during meditation that suggested an underlying atomic changeover. The Buddha did not know about atoms, per se, but he must have had some sense that material was built of constituent parts that were somehow more a dance of energy than fixed entities.

Moving away from an essential notion of self might move us closer to a sense of interconnectedness. The essential self stands apart—is separate—but the nonessential self participates. As Carl Safina pointed out, this self, while having some validity, is not autonomous: "We are in constant interaction with the natural world when we breathe, drink water, and eat the foods that sustain us. We are self-in-exchange then and inextricably connected to the world around us—proximal and remote" (WBUR 2011).

GETTING BEYOND ESSENTIALISM

The universally experienced essential self (e.g., Bloom 2011) helps evolution to get what it needs. Other than getting genes into the next generation, though, essentialism causes inter- and intra-personal problems. Robert Wright, also the author of *The Moral Animal* bemoans: "I consider tribalism the biggest problem of our time" (Wright 2017, 18)—friends have good essences, enemies bad. If the violence of tribalism was not enough, then dukkha can fill the gap: only a reified, essential self can experience the psychological forms of dukkha: "The [essential] self is revealed as a secondary, almost parasitic, epiphenomenon to the human psychophysical system, bringing with it all manner of difficult and suffering" (Olendzki 2016, 124). Overcoming the instinctual tendency to attribute essence including to *our* selves, is, perhaps, the most challenging task of #resistevolution and yields the biggest payoff: freedom. Mindfulness plays a key role in this process: "In principle , you can describe much of mindfulness meditation this way—as depriving modules of the positive reinforcement that has given them power" (Wright 2017, 139).

Where does this sense of essence come from? David Hinton suspects that it emerges from a metaphoric process:

> In the process of metaphoric transference through which consciousness has given form to itself. I suspect our immediate perceptual experience of sky as living absence created the fundamental structure of consciousness as an opening. Our immediate experience of earth as a constant physical and visual presence

must have created in consciousness the sense of something solid and enduring underlying experience, and that ground must have become the primal sense of a stable and enduring identity. (Hinton 2012, 143)

This essential self has two major liabilities that give rise to a persistent, pervasive, and often profound sense of dis-ease as it attempts to be-in-the-world. Namely, these are *ownership* and *identification*. Once the self is reified, it can take ownership of experiences. Passing phenomenological experiences *belong* to this abstract entity, and just like material possessions, these must be safeguarded, insured, shown-off—they remain vulnerable to any and all losses. When the self is reified, it will *identify* with the experiences in the sense that they are "happening to me" rather than being experienced as the passing phenomenological experiences they are. Ownership and identification giving rise to contingencies are the root sources of the psychological forms of dukkha. According to the Buddha, the self is a view, perspective, or attitude applied to the ongoing stream of experience that emerges, in part, from the aggregate of perception—sanna—the categorization instinct: Each moment of perception is a discreet event yet is experienced subjectively as a continuity.

Again, the Buddha's denial of an essential self did not mean that selves did not exist or that whatever selves were, they were automatons. He recognized that agency was lawful, just as everything else in experience was. That is, the sense of agency arose out of conditioned experience just like everything else. Intentions can help to hack the system, but there is no freestanding volition within the system. The Buddha said: "These feelings, these perceptions, these dispositions, these [moments of] consciousness—are not yours" (Olendzki 2016, 114). Ownership is a metaphorical projection from the material world, misappropriated to experience.

Self—the fabricated fabricator—is synthesized by the faculties of mind. From this perspective, it is not the self that gives rise to desire but the other way around. It is through the mechanism of desire that self emerges as the Buddha succinctly states: "Only when there is what belongs to a self is there a self" (Olendzki 2016, 120).

Sankhara operating through modularity, provides narrative identity as well as the benefits and liabilities of imaginative capacity. With the ability to narrate one's experience comes the liability of taking things personally and imagining an essential self that requires protection, glorification, and gratification. The Buddha's—correct—insight regarding the absence of a centralized self provides the justification for being skeptical of self-referential activity. Instead of believing the stories of this presumed essential self, one can be skeptical; instead of feeling compelled to act on behalf of this illusory self, one can be circumspect and not act out whatever actions are being dictated (unless those actions are deemed to be skillful). The narrative mind produces thoughts—mental objects—that, like feelings, can be dubious guides to reality. When stories grip the mind, mindful awareness can help one to extricate from whatever pressing drama is occurring to the experience of the present moment with its action and accompanying sensations.

NOTES

1. DMN thinking is self-referential, including others as they impinge on self, along a time continuum—recollecting past and anticipating future (e.g., Brewer et al. 2011).

2. As Dan Siegel conjectured: "With the acquisition of a stabilized and refined focus on the mind itself, previously undifferentiated pathways of firing become detectable and then accessible to modification. It is in this way that we can use the focus of the mind to change the function and ultimately the structure of the brain" (Siegel 2007b, 260).

3. Pinker (1997) claims that thinking is computation but that the computer is not the best metaphor for the mind. Computers compute in ways different than human minds. The mind is modular, but these modules are not geographically discreet in the brain. Genes create the modules, and the genetic basis of the mind does not invalidate the role of learning.

4. Brown and Kozak (1998) take the field of psychology to task for its imprecision with the terms emotions, feelings, and affects and argue for functional distinctions. Feelings would be a better term here.

5. This idea of consciousness receiving thoughts echos Julian Jaynes controversial theory of the bicameral mind where the Ancient Greek gods were hallucinated voices (Jaynes 1976).

6. At the risk of sounding teleological, we can say that evolution "designed" us in certain ways to solve certain problems, and this is a shorthand for the process of natural selection. Genes "wish" to replicate themselves, and this agenda will drive our thoughts, emotions, and behaviors. There is, of course, no teleology—mutations might lead to advantages, which lead to enhanced replication. When unexpected variations lead to a procreative advantage, they persist. Those that do not fade out. Thus, we have inherited the genome that produced the successful adaptation of our ancestors. "The mind is a system of organs of computation, designed by natural selection to solve the kinds of problems our ancestors faced in their foraging way of life, in particular, understanding and outmaneuvering objects, animals, plants, and other people" (Pinker, 1997, 21).

7. The driving study is particularly telling (Svenson 1981). A majority of people think they are above-average, even expert drivers, even when they have been in at-fault accidents. I do not think I am an above-average driver. I have been in a lot of accidents, all of them my fault. Perhaps it is because I am a psychologist and have studied bias that I can self-correct my own. Or perhaps it is that I have been meditating for all these decades and can see through my need to delude myself. Perhaps it is both? When I get behind the wheel, though, I feel like Rain Man—*I'm a very good*

driver—even though objectively, I am not. If I did not believe that I was, perhaps I would never drive again, so the biasing self-delusion makes life in the country feasible.

8. I must have a very robust fusiform gyrus because I see faces everywhere and quite readily—in any patterned surface. I am also pretty good at remembering faces. If my fusiform gyrus got damaged, perhaps I would have a severe case of Capgras Syndrome.

9. More colorfully, Richard Dawkins exclaims: "Think of an experience from your childhood. Something you remember clearly, something you can see, feel, maybe even smell, as if you were really there. After all, you really were there at the time, weren't you? How else would you remember it? But here is the bombshell: you *weren't* there. Not a single atom that is in your body today was there when that event took place" (Dawkins 2008, 371).

Chapter 11

Consciousness

Apparently Ubiquitous, Certainly Overestimated

OVERVIEW

Consciousness[1] is the fifth of the Buddha's aggregates. The Buddha could not appreciate just how much of mental life is unconscious and selective. For instance, while there may be 11,000,000 bits of information available to our senses in any given moment, we are only consciously aware of sixteen of these (Nørretranders 1999), a ratio of 687,500 to 1! And whether we are consciously aware of that information or not, whatever comes in from the outside to get processed by the brain is greatly reduced—about 100 to 1 for visual information. Julian Jaynes warned that consciousness tends to overestimate itself:

> Consciousness is a much smaller part of our mental life than we are conscious of, because we cannot be conscious of what we are not conscious of. How simple that is to say; how difficult to appreciate! It is like asking a flashlight in a dark room to search around for something that does not have any light shining upon it. The flashlight, since there is light whatever direction it turns would have to conclude that there is light everywhere. And so consciousness can seem to pervade all mentality when actually it does not. (Jaynes 1976, 23)

The adaptive advantage of unconscious processing is the capacity to handle vast amounts of information in automatic fashion, while the conscious agent—the subjectively perceived essential self—can attend to a small subset of information while unconscious processing continues in the background. The liabilities stemming from consciousness are: 1) its apparent flashlight ubiquity—singular—unified, robust, seems consistent with the presence of the essential self (while fabrications are responsible for providing its contents) and 2) the tendency to overestimate consciousness contributes to the sense of specialness one—and presumably all of humanity—has.

Julian Jaynes provides further clarification on the "constructed" nature of consciousness and how it might not be free of contamination or contribution from other mental aggregates:

> Subjective conscious mind is an analog (like a map) of what is called the real world. It is built up with a vocabulary or lexical field whose terms are all metaphors or analogs of behavior in the physical world. Its reality is of the same order as mathematics. It allows us to shortcut behavioral processes and arrive at more adequate decisions. Like mathematics, it is an operator rather than a thing or repository. And it is intimately bound up with volition and decision. (1976, 55)

Here, the subjective awareness of consciousness cannot be separated from fabrications, just as it is difficult to segregate perceptions from feelings—*how do I know how to feel unless I know what I'm perceiving?* (And in reverse fashion, the prevailing feeling tone in any moment will bias what conscious attention perceives).

Appreciation for the magnitude of unconscious processing along with humility in the face of its limitations is an appropriate antidote. One can—using the Buddha's methods that expand consciousness—cultivate new forms of awareness. This does not give us unfettered free-will, but does allow us to participate in the mechanistic forces that impinge upon us in every moment. To deal with consciousness beneficially one engages in "participatory determinism" (Kozak 2018b).

CONSCIOUSNESS IS NOT SELF AND THE POSSIBILITY OF PARTICIPATORY DETERMINISM

Can the self be found in consciousness?

> "Bhikkhus, how do you conceive it: is consciousness permanent or impermanent?"—"Impermanent, venerable Sir."—"Now is what is impermanent painful or pleasant?"—"Painful, venerable Sir."—"Now is what is impermanent, what is painful since subject to change, fit to be regarded thus: 'This is mine, this is I, this is my self?'"—"No, venerable sir." (Nanamoli Thera 1995)

Volition is traditionally included in the aggregate of mental fabrication. Of the aggregates, consciousness seems to be the least fleshed out and the least useful until it turns itself back towards fabrications. In this case, there is the opportunity to become conscious of the mind's processes themselves as it volitions, intends, reacts, or does anything that it does. I will, then, include the concept of participatory determinism in this chapter, instead of the previous. As Spinoza suggests: "Men are mistaken in thinking themselves free; their opinion is made up of consciousness of their own actions, and ignorance of the causes by which they are determined" (cited in Hood 2012, 122). Consciousness, then, does not grant free-will but is more of a post-hoc awareness. As just discussed in the previous chapter, the essential self believes itself to be fully in charge. And while the chapter on form considered how difficult change is, change *does* sometimes occur and consciousness can play a role. "The intentions of one moment alter one's dispositions, out of which the next moment's intentions will be molded. This allows for radical though incremental, transformation of character, brought about by moment after moment of healthy rather than unhealthy action" (Olendzki 2016, 116). Awareness, while seemingly immaterial, is a natural function and should be treated as such. There is no need to add anything, as the Buddha urged: "It is in this fathom-long carcass, with its perceptions and thoughts, that the world arises and passes away" (Olendzki 2016, 118). Mindfulness[2] practice seeks to increase the pipe of consciousness somewhat beyond the sixteen bits otherwise available. While not rising to the level of free-will, it can lead to what I call *participatory determinism.* Mindfulness highlights how lacking in control we actually are. Each time attention turns in on itself to contemplate its options, think about the implications of its actions or potential actions, these actions become the seeds for future mindful actions; likewise the more we just go along with the flow—conditioned by the three fires—the stronger that flow gets. The *apparent* free-will moments of choosing one thing over another are efficacious (as is everything the mind does). Apparent free-will will give rise to more apparent free-will. In Kozak (2018b), I summarized participatory determinism with the axiom: *We are not to blame and we are responsible.* Whatever happens in any given moment is the causal consequence of all preceding moments, so we cannot be blamed for whatever happens—because it had to happen that way. However, with mindfulness, I can take responsibility for what has just happened. I can understand how my indulgence in desire, anger, or whatever contributed to that previous moment and make an apparent free-will decision to not allow myself to be pushed around by contingencies. Here and again, my free-will invocation of mindfulness is only apparent because there were actions I have taken or that have happened to me[3] in the past that have made mindfulness an option. An apparent action of free-will would, according to this view, be determined by past actions—ones that have somehow favored a conscious action—little bits of mindfulness that snowball into a decision. I can know I am making a decision, decide between various options and have reasons for doing so; I can read my affective heuristics that have become sharper, clearer due to meditation practice. But ultimately, the volitional lever I pull had to be pulled—if I were omniscient and could trace every casual linkage, I would know why it had to be so and why it *has* to be so in every moment of existence.

There is no experience of a world out there that is not constructed, influenced by individual perception. It is human arrogance to assume that the world is the way it is. It is only that way to us, as beings with the psychophysical capacities that we have. Beyond these generic limitations, there is each individual's psychology—based on temperament, personality, and a lifetime of learning. "Rather than being the starting point of experience, the essential agent needed to *have* experience. Self is regarded as the end product of an elaborate process of assimilating data, constructing meaning, and building a world of local experience" (Olendzki 2016, 118, emphasis original). If the mind is a self-organizing system, participatory determinism explains how a sense of conscious agency can be more or less involved in the ongoing flow of experience. I can be a fully functioning member of society—work a job, raise a family, consume goods—without much in the way of consciousness—automatic pilot guides the way. Mindfulness practice makes us better participants in the process as conscious efforts guide the causal flow of predetermined factors, nudging ourselves into something that looks more and more like free-will. "The conscious you [the apparent essential, centrally controlled self] isn't choosing modules so much as being commandeered by modules that have prevailed over competing modules" (Wright 2017, 109). To the extent that we participate in determinism is to the extent that we are less pushed around or hijacked by competing modules. An acquisitive impulse that, without mindfulness, feels otherwise compelling can be observed arising in awareness as it attempts to push behavior—without needing to act on that impulse. In other words, the craving for something can be seen as empty of necessity—I will be fine without it. In that moment, contingency is severed, freedom increases.

DAMPENING EMOTIONS

Perception of an essential self aggravates emotional reactivity—as if there was a *thing* to protect.

Perception of a non-essential self attenuates reactivity—there is no *thing* there to protect, just a succession of different energy and information patterns. Insight can lead to reduced reactivity—less emotional disturbance. But it also may work the other way around: "Dampening of feelings *is* the clarity of vision, so finely intertwined with perception—in particular, with the perception of essence" (Wright 2017, 165). To become less volatile, it is as if we see through the ruse of evolution's ploy.

Like all the aggregates consciousness is impermanent and not self. It is helpful to be mindful of the language we use to describe consciousness. If "I" am doing the seeing, hearing, feeling, smelling, or tasting there is a sense of ownership. By eliminating the sense of ownership, consciousness becomes more animal-like, less filtered by narrative identity, and thus more direct, clear, and robust.

Consciousness appears integral to awakening as Thanissaro Bhikkhu illuminates:

> Consciousness without surface is thus the awareness of Awakening. And the freedom of this awareness carries over even when the awakened person returns to ordinary consciousness. As the Buddha said of himself: "Freed, dissociated, & released from form, the Tathagata dwells with unrestricted awareness. Freed, dissociated, & released from feeling . . . perception . . . fabrications . . . consciousness . . . birth . . . aging . . . death . . . suffering & stress . . . defilement, the Tathagata dwells with unrestricted awareness." (Thanissaro 2002)

Appreciation seems a necessary virtue because it recognizes that most of mental life is unconscious. Humility is another critical value because it acknowledges that since consciousness is a precious resource it should be directed toward beneficial ends, like the aspiration for awakening.

NOTES

1. The Buddha's consciousness, unlike the Brahmanic atman, is conditioned—linked to what it is seen (a perceptible object), limited by what it can see (the limits of human vision), and dependent on the presence of light (or any of the other senses) and attention. Colorfully, "dead molecules erupt into flavors of bitterness or sweetness, electromagnetic frequencies bursts with color, hapless air pressure waves become the laughter of children, and the impact of a passing molecule fills a conscious mind with the aroma of roses on a warm summer afternoon" (Victor S. Johnson, cited in Goldstein 2061, 190).

2. One might wonder what the difference between the aggregate of consciousness and the factor of awakening mindfulness. When mindfulness is presented as present-moment attention or bare awareness it certainly seems to be the same as consciousness—a mirror to whatever is happening. However, as discussed above in the Introduction, mindfulness traditionally includes an aspect of memory and conscientiousness that is not found in simple monitoring of the present. Still, the more mindful we are the more conscious of phenomenon we will be, perhaps increasing the pipe beyond the usual eleven bits per second.

3. For example, I was wandering the narrow streets of Bodhgaya when I saw a retreat schedule on the iron gate at a vipassana meditation center. I counted the number of hours to be spent on the mediation cushion—some thirteen hours each day—and said to myself "sounds like fun." Little did I know how difficult it would be when I did my first retreat four years later. Not fun, but one of the most significant experiences of my life.

Conclusion

RECAPTURING THE PRIMORDIAL MOMENT FROM THE METAPHORICAL SELF

Nietzsche observed how our minds make sense of experience by collapsing phenomenologically dissimilar (or similar but inexact) things into comprehensible and usable categories—an essentially metaphoric process, because the familiar becomes the basis for the unfamiliar. In the following quote, he is not talking about the poet's arsenal of images but rather the deeper sense of how the mind proceeds through experience:

> Let us give special consideration to the formation of concepts. Every word immediately becomes a concept, inasmuch as it is not intended to serve as a reminder of the unique and wholly individualized original experiences to which it owes its birth, but must at the same time fit innumerable, more or less similar cases—which means, strictly speaking never equal—in other words, a lot of unequal cases. Every concept originates through our equating what is unequal. No leaf ever wholly equals another, and the concept "leaf" is formed through an arbitrary abstraction from these individual differences, through forgetting the distinctions; and now it gives rise to the idea that in nature there might be something besides the leaves which would be "leaf"—some kind of original form after which all leaves have been woven, marked, copied, colored, curled and painted, but by unskilled hands, so that no copy turned out to be correct, reliable, and faithful image of the original form. (1982, 46)

Nietzsche is talking about more than concepts; he is talking about perception itself. Each leaf that we encounter is a "unique and wholly individualized original experience," yet that uniqueness is overlooked when it gets assigned to the category "leaf." We could replace the language thusly, "*Self* originates through our equating every unequal *self-moment*," and in this way, self is a concept that emerges from the abstraction of unique moments as though there were something in nature called "self"—some prototype that produces through inexact but related replicas. And once this abstract entity is established, it can then begin to own and identify with the experiences it has. Notice how the syntax of the previous sentence implies ownership—the self possess experience. "We project through the process of metaphor one experience of *me* to the next experience of *me*. In this way, a sense of self is perpetuated, but it is a conceptual self and not an experiential one" (Kozak 2011a). Nietzsche cautioned:

> We do not only designate things with [words and concepts] we think originally that through them we grasp the true in things. Through words and concepts, we are continually misled into imagining things as being simpler than they are, separate from one another, indivisible, each existing in and for itself. A philosophical mythology lies concealed in language that breaks out again every moment, however careful one may be otherwise. (1996, 306)

The alternative to this mythology requires an intentional backing away from habitual use of language to categorize unique phenomenological perceptions. Nietzsche pushes the boundaries further, pressing on the question of what truth could possibly be. Like the Buddha, the answer is not some privileged ontological revelation but a practical one situated in the limitations of language:

> What then is truth? A mobile army of metaphors, metonyms, and anthropomorphisms—in short, a sum of human relations, which have been enhanced, transposed, and embellished poetically and rhetorically, and which after long use seem firm, canonical, and obligatory to a people: truths are illusions about which one has forgotten that this is what they are; metaphors which are worn out and without sensuous power; coins which have lost their pictures and now matter only as metal, no longer as coins. (Nietzsche 1982, 46–47)

When we, again, insert "self" into Nietzsche's insight that "truths are illusions about which one has forgotten that this is what they are," we get a self-concept that appears to be a truth simply because its metaphorical origins have been forgotten or, in this case, might never have been known in the first place (Kozak 2011a). Disparate, changing experiences are considered under a single self rubric. These noun selves give rise to properties of constancy, agency, ownership, survival, responsibility, and awareness (Olendzki 2016). This process was also recognized by Geary (2012) when he said, "Metaphors, once forgotten or ignored, are easily mistaken for objective facts" (178). Likewise, if we forget that the self is constructed through metaphor, it is easy to treat it as objective fact. The self is a repository for similar but not identical members—memories, perceptions, desires, etc. Self appears to own the experience because it, like categories, is a superordinate organizer.

Every moment of existence is a configuration of energies and information—unique—if we pay close enough attention. Yet, it is natural—though still lazy—to take short cuts. Perception is *always* interpretive and misses the "compelling uniqueness of the moment"; it compels because of its "radical specificity" (Olendzki 2016, 59). Of the approximate 10 billion moments to be experienced in a lifetime, each radically specific event that we experience is diminished by the category instinct and the bias of previous experience.

Language—especially writing—gives rise to a sense of dualism. Indeed, consciousness as we know it today may have arisen from the creation of writing (Jaynes 1976). At some point in our existence before the advent of language, there was little sense of separation of self from landscape or what Hinton calls the "ontological or existence tissue of the universe" (Hinton 2011, 2016). Paleolithic human before language was not separate from the cosmos—experience was immediate. We, of course, can do things via language and thinking that Paleolithic hunter gatherers could never do. It is a trade-off between science, technology, and civilization versus the immediate, animalistic appreciation of the world. Via meditation, we do not have to choose between one or the other; we can, in a sense, live in both worlds. We can be conversant in both realms and shift the center of identity from story to landscape—into the larger contexts that can make life feel sacred. Moment-to-moment existence can be a conversation between the languaged, conceptualized, metaphoric rendering of the world, and the primal moments that our ancestors likely dwelled within, moving us closer to *presence*:

> There is only Presence, physical material evolving through one form after another, a process in which those forms all grow directly out of one another, not out of some ineffable emptiness. The structures of thought and identity are constructed from that Presence through metaphoric transference; and as identity is the entity that knows and linguistic thought is the medium of knowing, we can only know Presence. Absence lies always outside Presence and those metaphoric structures, so any knowledge of absence is impossible. But it does nevertheless remain available to us. (Hinton 2012, 70)

That sense of Absence—the possibility of nirvana—is informing experience as we move toward it and away from it. Whether its poetry, meditation, wine, or all three—as in the case of the ancient Chinese mystic poets

(Hinton 2010)—we seek to reach that immediacy, to wrest ourselves from language if only for a moment to apprehend a moment before language reifies the self.

There is a brief and illuminating dialog between Huineng who was the sixth patriarch of Ch'an and his student Huariang who had spent the past eight years contemplating the question, "What is this?"

Huineng: What is this?
Huairang: To say it is like something misses the point. (Batchelor 2015, 244)

We are creatures that are "designed" to perceive—to categorize conceptually and to label with language. We do so instinctively and unconsciously. Huairang's response recognizes that to answer the question "What is this?" requires some kind of metaphoric process "to say it is *like* something." Once we name the experience we have moved away from its immediacy. Much of the point of dharma practice as well as ancient Chinese poetry is to recapture or retain that sense of immediacy by invoking the question of "what is this?" that requires paying acute attention, while not lapsing into habitual cognition that abstracts the experience into cognizable elements. For example, similar to the Buddhist approach, the Tao Te Ching reminds: "the named is the mother of ten thousand things/but the unnamed is origin to all heaven and earth" (Hinton 2010, 40). Or consider Li Po's contemplation of the mountain: "Inexhaustible, this mountain and I/gaze at each other, it alone remaining" (Hinton 2010, 187). *What is this?* also presumes—or invites consideration—that each experience is unique before its metaphorical process of comparison.

To become—as the Buddha had—a *thatagata*—one has gone forth or "one who is just so" (Bodhi 2012, 410), one has to be mindful of both words and actions and their consequences. If one is "just so" then nothing is added, i.e., no fuel is put on the fires. When the Buddha refers to the "deathless," it is commonly interpreted to mean that he would not take rebirth. However, if we consider that term metaphorically, it would make more sense as the end of reactivity, the extinction of the fires. Peacock explains:

> Due to the delusion produced by desire, the mind cannot perceive dispassionately. It "measures" or evaluates "things" in terms of good or bad (for me). What causes this, Sariputta asks, and answers: *nimttakarano*—by way of signification—literally "by sign-making." As signs, every percept becomes a signifier. When percepts are seen as they are becoming, and not as signs, they cease to be signifiers of desire. They are empty! As signs, they are full—of desire. Thus, under the power of desire everything becomes a sign; the desire-driven individual experiences everything as signifiers of greed and aversion. (Peacock 2008, 218–19)

The goal for the practitioner is to *attempt* to transcend these signifying language functions. It is an attempt to realize that all such signification is a metaphorical process that invariably results in substituting symbols, words, and concepts for the lived experience that is otherwise available. It requires a process of deconstructing the constructed nature of all experience. The Buddha claimed that all forms are fabricated. The categorizing habit of experience with its concomitant signification leads to ownership and it is such appropriation that is the root source of dukkha: "What the Buddha realised was that we humans could only live non-injurious lives, hurting neither ourselves nor others, nor ourselves and others, if we liberate ourselves from the 'objects' within and without produced by the desire for pleasure, the desire for being and the desire for non-being" (Peacock 2008, 221).

The challenge and opportunity of relinquishing the *self-as-thing* metaphor is to come closer to the lived landscape that the Western transcendental soul has exiled us from. As Hinton reminds us:

> If we could trace consciousness back to its origins in the primeval word-hoard, back beyond the metaphoric constructions of subjectivity with its intentionality and reason, all the way back to some primal self-awareness of the opening of consciousness with all its life and movement, we would no doubt find its empirical origin in a dynamic living sky with its ever-changing breezes and humidity. . . . In the West, this consciousness as living sky-space became, through a process of metaphoric transference, a transcendental spirit exiled from both earth and sky. The archaeology of mind can trace the West's transcendental "spirit" back to the Latin *spiritus,* meaning "air, breath, life, spirit." Here, we are at the transition point where mind creates itself from the empirical by means of metaphors, and if we could follow the trail another step further back into the word-hoard, we would no doubt encounter the empirical; sky itself, prior to any connection with spirit. (2012, 97)

Since we are both constructed and exiled through language, we need a process like mindfulness—be with the breath without adding anything without concept, label, and thinking about—to revoke this exile and return us to an empirical home in the elements: water, sky, earth, and wind (ironically, when we become at home in the natural world we become homeless from the conceptual world). The transcendental spirit was a philosophical turn that removed us further from experience giving rise to a self—like the Brahmanic atman—that is separated from the world. Prior to that, there was just "sky" or just "breathing" without that sense of separation. When the Buddha referred to himself as a tathagata, he was capturing this sense of returning home from language-imposed exile. "So the Buddha is referring to himself as 'the one who is like that.' This is tantamount to saying that there are no words to describe his state; he can only point to it" (Gombrich 2009, 151). Life can, then become more of an unfolding exchange between language and experience, as David Whyte articulates:

> We free ourselves from suffering by *being* fully in the conversation rather than something static *having* a conversation and trying to defend that something at every turn. . . . I must learn to live at a kind of frontier between what I think is me and what think is not me, so that my identity is more of a meeting place; an edge between past and present rather than an island around which the events of life swirl and move on. (Whyte 2009, 300)

To be original in the moment requires relinquishing the known for a stance of uncertainty. This originary moment is impeded at every step by the instinct of categorical perception and a lifetime of established learning. The Buddha showed us that a different way was possible.

Hinton's Presence is undefended because there is no essential self to protect, there are no narratives pressing for validation (e.g., "is it okay?"), manifestation (e.g., "can I make this happen?"), or contingency (e.g. "I need this in order to be okay"). In the absence or emptiness—one can relax into time because the usual markers of remembering past and imagining future or pushing and pulling against the present moment fall away. As language-driven activity falls away, perception emerges as the prevailing mind activity and here categories give way to perceptions that are closer to pure sensation (but of course these perceptions can only approach purity but never reach it). Rilke calls this state the Open and his poem "Eighth Duino Elegy," he laments how difficult it is for humans to experience it. Children have their moments, but they get pulled back—more and more as they mature. Perhaps a person near death can drop the pretense (i.e., defendedness) and experience the Open, and that is a late consolation. A wild animal is the only one who can live in the Open: "and when it moves, it moves already in eternity, like a fountain" (Mitchell 1982).

The experience that Presence or the Open points to is often called one's "true" self. In Zen, it is referred to as one's original face. That truth (that is also loving and tender) might be one's essence[1] (e.g., Brach 2019). To avoid abstractions—and essences—a more descriptive, metaphorical approach might be helpful. The self unadorned by story, unencumbered by defensive reaction is *naked*, stripped of the vestments of narration and self-making. Elevating this nakedness to a special status—whether mystic or transcendent—brings with it the risk of attachment-laced preference or reification or both (spiritual materialisms if you will). Every metaphysical assertion carries the potential of re-introducing the problems that the work of the four ennobling praxes tries to undo. Instead of specialness, nakedness could be seen as ordinariness. After all, we go into and come out of nakedness every day. Likewise, there is the potential to go into and out of the awakened state (Presence, Open) naturally, ordinarily, without recourse to metaphysics, reification, and elitism.[2] To wit, the Buddha's accomplishment is often called enlightenment rather than the more technically correct awakening. Each metaphor has its own entailments (Batchelor 2009). Enlightenment suggests illumination, while awakening points to a natural biological function; one is mystical, one is commonplace—we go to sleep and wake up each day.

The tendency to valorize awakening/enlightenment, again, re-introduces essence and may undermine the efforts that led one toward Presence in the first place. A rendition of the Buddha stripped of hagiography favors the metaphor of awakening over enlightenment for its accessibility and views the Presence of awakening not as the end point but—like sleeping and waking—as cycles of contraction and expansion, approach, and avoidance. If not an endpoint, awakening is a reliable by-product of certain kinds of activity: the cultivation of cognitive-affective fluidity, an intellectual and embodied understanding of the three fires and the three hallmarks with facilitative behavioral support (e.g., meditation and ethics).

This natural, ordinary view of Presence accords with evolution. Presence is an extreme approach state (parasympathetic, vagal) characterized by a neurohormonal elixir of endorphins, oxytocin, and other feel good chemicals. This cocktail mimics the early infant–caregiver attachment state that was—fittingly—prior to categories, language, and the capacity for self-reference. It also—obviously—feels good and Presence can be intensely pleasurable.

Freud maligned the mystic's state as an infantile regression to an oceanic oneness. Intense states of concentration may mimic the infant's merging, yet Presence need not be seen as regressive because adult, autonomous awareness remains while other mature functions—such as narratization—fall away. Also gone is defensiveness, fear (the opposite of the parasympathetic, vagal approach state driven by the sympathetic HPA axis). Presence, then, could be viewed as a form of self-attunement where one provides to oneself what the infant received early on (e.g., Siegel 2007a)—an enveloping sense of euphoric well-being. Unlike the baby's state, Presence is not contingent on the safety and feeding of the adult caregiver. Presence is self-perpetuating.

FINAL CONSIDERATIONS

While the Buddha claimed to have extinguished his fires, most of us will have to be content with tempering them, cooling them to a manageable glow, perhaps even to embers one is not sure have gone out—they are quiet but readily inflamed. Even though Ananda encouraged Vangisa to extinguish his flames, we can understand this to be a relative accomplishment:

Ven. Vangisa:
With sensual lust I burn.
My mind is on fire.
Please, Gotama, out of kindness,
tell me how to put it out.
Ven. Ananda:
From distorted perception
your mind is on fire.
Shun the sign of the beautiful,
accompanied by lust.
See fabrications as other,
as stress,
not as self.
Extinguish your great lust.
Don't keep burning
again & again. (Thanissaro 1999, 49)

To seek total extinction is to invite perfectionism—yet another source of flammable fuel.

The first rescue mission was to free the Buddha from Buddhism. I have sketched a flesh and blood individual—charismatic, yes, prodigious, yes—human, flawed, and influential. But, perhaps, there is further to go, the Buddha might need to be rescued from himself, saved from his own avoidance-driven rhetoric. This freed, psychological Buddha—not afraid of sensuality—is more suitable for the postmodern, twenty-first century, scientific, secular West (or at least the portions of the culture that strive to become that[3]). This Buddha is fully engaged with material existence all the while skillful at not self-fabricating during these experiences. He eats, drinks, socializes, fornicates, and works with an unshakable evenness of mind. Without the burden of an essential self, he is free to be generous, humorous, and gentle. Without an investment in I, me, and mine, he is liquid, light, and loving. He presents a way of being in the world that others can emulate and while most of the time these Buddha-inspired efforts will be failures, trying and failing is better than not trying at all. I argue for a relative model of awakening—not an absolute one.

Era by era, region by region, confabulation by confabulation, the Buddha's hagiography takes him from what might have originally been an anti-essentialist preacher of self-reliance to a luminous, supernatural essentialist. Poisons replace fires. The Buddha glows; a major world religion forms. I have tried to situate the Buddha outside the hagiography—a conjectural project at best—as is any attempt to represent the Buddha as flesh (Lopez 2013). My own self-serving representation is conceit at worst; heuristic, practical, and provocative at best.

This psychological Buddha, in contrast to the Buddha of myth and canon, embraced the following positions: 1) Sensuality, while dangerous is—in principle—manageable; he knew his monks were weak and impressionable, so he made them reject sensuality altogether (he recognized that he was also subject to the temptations of flesh so chose to be avoidant). 2) He could not possibly have known what happens after death, therefore any reference to ultimate nirvana or rebirth are either rhetorical devices or not attributable to what he actually might have said. 3) While the fires can go to embers, there is nothing absolute, extreme, or mystical about his attainment (neural beings cannot go beyond the constraints of the nervous system). 4) An avoidant, renunciant approach worked for him; he never intended it to be universal (or it was just a mistake). 5) Mindfulness—key to his praxis—is not just present-momentism, not just concentration, not just flow; it is a dharma meter: It monitors the three fires and the activity of self-fabrication in any given moment. Mindfulness is clearinghouse for wisdom:

> He still has with regard to the five aggregates for sustenance a slight, lingering residual "I am" conceit, an "I am" desire, an "I am" obsession. But at a later time he keeps focusing on the phenomena of arising & passing away with regard to the five aggregates of sustenance: "Such is form, such its origination, such its disappearance. Such is feeling. . . . Such is perception. . . . Such are fabrications. . . . Such is consciousness, such its origination, such its disappearance." As he keeps focusing on the arising & passing away of these five aggregates for sustenance, the slight, lingering residual "I am" conceit, "I am" desire, "I am" obsession he had with regard to them disappears. (Thanissaro 1999, 87)

I have tried to offer a Buddha that is more fully human, but he might say I am trying to justify my sensual entanglements—amplifying self-fabrication. Scholars and saints may protest that the Buddha presented here is not consistent with his canonical portrayal—that he has been cherry-picked, indeed imagined as a fictional character. Whatever the case, I stand on firm precedent. Wherever the Buddha's teachings went in the world they were entwined with the beliefs, rituals, and customs of the indigenous host culture. My host culture of materiality entwines to make the Buddha-as-psychologist. Rather than get embroiled in authenticity arguments, a better question is: Is this Buddha useful? Do his teachings—pared to psychology—reduce dukkha? Would the world be a better place if everyone practiced the four ennobling praxes? If the answer to these questions is yes, then authenticity is irrelevant (and so are the Buddhist religions).[4]

NOTES

1. Any mention of essence is a dangerous re-purposing of a reified self, not to mention a metaphysical commitment that finds no quarter in the Buddha's not self.

2. The emphasis on lineage in Tibetan Buddhism and dharma transmission in Zen traditions attests to the elitist coopting of what was once—in the Buddha's time—a more democratic process where anyone with willingness had the potential to awaken.

3. While science pervades the cultures of the developed world and provides a background legitimacy for anyone who drives a car, flies in an airplane, or takes antibiotics, there is still a vast majority of people that believe in a creator god. Among those, a substantial minority of them reject evolution and take the creation story of Genesis literally, putting the age of the earth at about 6,000 years. If you replace relativist and creationist, the sentiment is similar: "Show me a cultural relativist at 30,000 feet and I'll show you a hypocrite" (Dawkins 2004, 15).

4. Buddhism of any flavor is not a solution to the world's problems. Political strife prevails in Buddhist countries. The Buddhisms are not immune to dogma, infighting, and hypocrisy. The Buddha's project is an individual solution. Then as now, it was a failure, or partial failure. Individuals cannot tolerate ultimate responsibility, absolute freedom. We seek refuge in rules, rituals, and dogma. The most difficult task is to relinquish essence. While the Buddha rejected essence—soul—the history of Buddhism is nothing other than the re-introduction of essence.

Epilogue

Imagine if the Buddha could be transported through a space–time distortion into the present day to observe everything that is being done in his name. After this glimpse, he returns through this temporal rift and finds himself talking to his trusted cousin and administrative assistant, Ananda.

Ananda: What did you see, my lord?
Buddha: Don't call me lord. We've been over this before.
Ananda: But you are so radiant. May I call you Thataghata, Lion of Shakyas?
Buddha: Buddha will suffice. There is this thing called Buddhism in the year 2021. There's Zen Buddhism, Tibetan Buddhism, Theravadan, and even something called Nicheren where they chant Nam Myoho Renge Kyo in order to receive anything they desire (I don't recall teaching this). They—all these so-called Buddhisms—sport statues of me. Funny that I look Chinese in China, Japanese in Japan, Thai in Thailand, Tibetan in Tibet (or North India for the most part, since they are in exile). This is not what I wanted for the future. I will not name a successor because this will only create a cult of personality. I will urge them to follow the dharma, to be islands unto themselves.
Ananda: People have always loved and needed religion. Is it such a bad thing? The prophecies surrounding your birth predicted that you'd change the world. It appears that you have.
Buddha: Buddhism is thriving but it is a lesser of the major world religions and still predominant only in Asia, although Europe and America seem to have a fetish with it. That it's one of the great world religions is—itself—a problem. I didn't mean for that to happen. Even when my influence was at its apogee, its influence was limited to India, China, Tibet, and Japan. While the dharma is central to all these efforts, I feel like I've failed. I suppose, given that the dharma didn't change the world, that all of the cosmic prophecies in my origin

story—since they didn't come true—must be viewed with circumspection—colorful mythologizing at best and soteriological distraction that undermines my teaching at worst.

Ananda: I see, my lord, I mean your Buddha-ship, I hear how difficult this is for you, but I think I can understand why people have done this. It's hard to take all the responsibility for oneself; it's hard to be an island unto oneself. I try to keep the dharma squarely in my mind and heart, and yet I often long for a bit of ritual, pageantry, mythology.

Buddha: You disappointment me, cousin. There is a New Hope (I got to watch some Star Wars movies when I was projected into the future) and it can be found in the mindfulness movement, insight meditation, and secular Buddhism. They are trying to rescue me from the various Buddhisms. I applaud that effort. My earliest teachings were about the problem with essences and it seems that essences have crept back in. Why can't people live without a soul? (I also learned about genetics when I was in the future, and it turns out that the need for and predilection towards believing in a soul is in our DNA).

Ananda: What are we going to do?

Buddha: Perhaps if we dispense with the notion of rebirth, we can bypass the revival of essentialism. Even if rebirth were true, it's speculative. I don't want people focusing on past and future lives but this life—the consequences of actions here and now.

Ananda: I'm sorry Lord, this will not work, Rebirth is too important, too ubiquitous to get rid of. People will revolt, call you a heretic.

Buddha: I'll split the difference. I'll talk about rebirth and with such exaggeration that people must realize that I'm being symbolic.

Ananda: Perhaps that will work, or they'll think you a saint; they'll tell stories of your countless lives as if you were a god, as if the gods bowed down to you. Furthermore, without fear of rebirth in hell, what's to stop people from perpetrating evil?

Buddha: You know I don't approve of that word. People can still realize the consequences of their action in this very life—*because of this, that!* People will act good because it is beneficial, beautiful, and harmonious and they will avoid "evil" because it—ultimately—does not feel good. It is not beneficial. It is harmful, destructive, ugly.

Ananda: I wish that were always the case, my saintly master—I mean cousin—but you know even your own monks—even our cousin Devadatta cannot help doing harmful things. Think of the elephants he'd sent to murder you, the bandits he commissioned to kill you . . . his evil plotting never ceased!

Buddha: I wish you wouldn't bring that up.

Ananda: Is there any hope for us?

Buddha: Perhaps one day, we'll let go of our attachments to dogma, but probably no. We'll embrace being more self-reliant. We'll be curious instead of facile. Perhaps we won't be so afraid. I'd like my legacy to be: There was someone who knew himself, who lived a good life, who helped others. I'm not that different from anyone else: *Let the psychology and the discipline that I have taught you be your guide. All conditioned things are inconstant. Strive on, untiringly.*

Bibliography

Als, Hilton. "Nothing Personal." *The New Yorker*, November 13, 2017.
Amaro, Ajahn. "Forgiveness: Making Beneficial Judgments in Relation to Self and Others." In *Handbook of Ethical Foundations of Mindfulness,* edited by Steven Stanley, Ronald E. Purser, and Nirbhay M. Singh, 67–84. Springer, 2018.
Analayo, Bhikkhu. "Turning the Wheel of Dharma." In *Handbook of Ethical Foundations of Mindfulness,* edited by Steven Stanley, Ronald E. Purser, and Nirbhay M. Singh, 33–50. Springer, 2018a.
Analayo. *Rebirth in Early Buddhism and Current Research.* Somerville, MA: Wisdom Publications, 2018b.
Arch, Joanna J., and Lauren L. Landy. "Emotional Benefits of Mindfulness." In *Handbook of Mindfulness: Theory, Research, and Practice,* edited by Kirk Warren Brown, J. David Creswell, and Richard M. Ryan, 208–224. New York: Guilford, 2015.
Armstrong, Karen. *Buddha.* New York: Penguin, 2001.
Armstrong, Guy. *Emptiness: A Practical Introduction for Meditators.* Boston, MA: Wisdom Publications, 2017.
Ascoli, Giorgio A. *Trees of the Brain: Roots of the Mind.* New York: Oxford University Press, 2015.
Baer, Ulrich, ed. and trans. *Rainer Maria Rilke: Letters on Life.* New York: Modern Library, 2006.
Batchelor, Stephen. *Buddhism Without Beliefs.* New York: Riverhead, 1997.
Batchelor, Stephen. "Awakening and the Four Noble Truths." Talk given at the Upaya Zen Center, Santa Fe, New Mexico, 2009. https://www.upaya.org/uploads/pdfs/BatchelorAwakeningandtheFourNobleTruths.pdf.
Batchelor, Stephen. *Confessions of a Buddhist Atheist.* New York: Spiegel & Grau, 2011.
Batchelor, Stephen. "A Secular Buddhism." *Journal of Global Buddhism,* 13 (2012): 87–107.

Batchelor, Stephen. *After Buddhism: Rethinking the Dharma for a Secular Age.* New Haven, CT: Yale University Press, 2015a.

Batchelor, Stephen. "The Four Noble Tasks." *The Upaya Zen Center Blog,* February 2, 2015b. https://www.upaya.org/2015/02/stephen-batchelor-four-noble-tasks/.

Batchelor, Stephen. "The Limits of Belief, The Massiveness of the Questions. *On Being,* January 14, 2016. http://www.onbeing.org/program/stephen-batchelor-the-limits-of-belief-the-massiveness-of-the-questions/transcript/8357.

Batchelor, Stephen. *Secular Buddhism: Imagining the Dharma in an Uncertain World.* New Haven, CT: Yale University Press, 2017.

Batchelor, Stephen. *The Art of Solitude: a Meditation on Being Alone with Others in This World.* New Haven, CT: Yale University Press, 2020.

Bernhard, Toni. *How to Wake up: a Buddhist-Inspired Guide to Navigating Joy and Sorrow.* Boston: Wisdom Publications, 2013.

Blackmore, Susan. *The Meme Machine.* New York: Oxford University Press, 1999.

Bloom, Paul. *How Pleasure Works Why We like What We Like.* London: Vintage, 2011.

Blake, William, and Alfred Kazin. *The Portable Blake.* Penguin, 1977.

Bodhi, Bhikkhu. "The Exposition on Burning." SuttaCentral, 2000. https://suttacentral.net/sn35.235/en/bodhi.

Bodhi, Bhikkhu. *The Connected Discourses of the Buddha: A Translation of the Samyutta Nikaya.* Boston, MA: Wisdom, 2003.

Bodhi, Bhikkhu. *The Numerical Discourses of the Buddha: A Translation of the Anguttara Nikaya.* Boston, MA: Wisdom, 2012.

Boully, Jenny, and Jenny Boully. *Betwixt-and-between: Essays on the Writing Life.* Minneapolis, MN: Coffee House Press, 2018.

Bowlby, John. *A Secure Base.* London: Routledge, 2014.

Boyce, Barry, ed. *The Mindfulness Revolution.* Boulder, CO: Shambhala, 2011.

Brach, Tara. *Radical Acceptance: Embracing Your Life with the Heart of a Buddha.* New York: Bantam, 2002.

Brach, Tara. 2012. *Radical Compassion.* New York: Viking.

Brach, Tara. 2019. *True Refuge: Finding Peace and Freedom in Your Own Awakened Heart.* New York: Bantam.

Brasington, Leigh. *Right Concentration: A Practical Guide to the Jhanas.* Boulder, CO: Shambhala. 2015.

Braun, Erik. *Birth of Insight: Meditation, Modern Buddhism, and the Burmese Monk Ledi Sayadaw.* Chicago, IL: University of Chicago Press, 2016.

Brazier, David. "Mindfulness as Ethics Foundation." In *Handbook of Ethical Foundations of Mindfulness,* edited by Steven Stanley, Ronald E. Purser, and Nirbhay M. Singh, 51–66. Springer, 2018.

Brewer, J. A., P. D. Worhunsky, J. R. Gray, Y.-Y. Tang, J. Weber, and H. Kober. "Meditation Experience Is Associated with Differences in Default Mode Network Activity and Connectivity." *Proceedings of the National Academy of Sciences* 108, 50 (2011): 20254–20259. doi:10.1073/pnas.1112029108.

Brown, K. W., and R. M. Ryan. "The Benefits of Being Present: Mindfulness and Its Role in Psychological Well-Being." *Journal of Personality and Social Psychology* 84, 4 (2003): 822–848.

Brown, Terrance and Arnold Kozak. "Emotion and the possibility of Psychologists Entering into heaven. In: M. Mascolo & S. Griffin (eds.), *What develops in Emotional Development?* New York: Plenum Press, 1998.

Burkeman, Oliver. *The Antidote: Happiness for People Who Can't Stand Positive Thinking.* London: Vintage, 2013.

Byrne, Rhonda. *The Secret.* New York: Atria, 2006.

Cajal Santiago Ramón y, Eric A. Newman, Alfonso Araque, Janet M. Dubinsky, Larry W. Swanson, Lyndel King, and Eric Himmel. *The Beautiful Brain: the Drawings of Santiago Ramón y Cajal.* New York: Abrams, 2017.

Carmody, James. 2015. "Reconceptualizing Mindfulness: The Psychological Principles of Attending in Mindfulness Practice and Their Role in Well-Being." In *Handbook of Mindfulness: Theory, Research, and Practice,* edited by Kirk Warren Brown, J. David Creswell, and Richard M. Ryan, 62–80. New York: Guilford.

Cleary, Thomas. *The Flower Ornament Scripture a Translation of the Avatamsaka Sutra.* Shambhala, 1985.

Coleman, James William. *The New Buddhism: the Western Transformation of an Ancient Tradition.* Oxford: Oxford University Press, 2001.

Cooper, Cricket. *Chemo Pilgrim: an 18-Week Journey of Healing and Holiness.* New York: Church Publishing, 2017.

Dallmayr, Fred. 2014. *Mindfulness and Letting be: On Engaged Thinking and Action.* London: Lexington Books.

Dawkins, Richard. *A Devil's Chaplain.* New York: Mariner, 2004.

Dawkins, Richard. *The God Delusion.* New York: Mariner, 2008.

Dennett, D. C. *Consciousness Explained.* Little Brown, 1991.

Diamond, S. L., and Kozak, A. A course on biotechnology and society. *Journal of Chemical Engineering Education,* Spring (1994): 140–144.

Dimidjian, Sona, and Zindel V. Segal. "Prospects for a Clinical Science of Mindfulness-Based Intervention." *American Psychologist,* 70, no. 7 (2015): 593–620. doi:10.1037/a0039589.

Epstein, Mark. *Thoughts Without a Thinker.* New York: Basic Books, 1995.

Epstein, Mark. *The Trauma of Everyday Life.* New York: Penguin, 2013.

Finnigan, Mary, and Rob Hogendoorn. *Sex and Violence in Tibetan Buddhism: the Rise and Fall of Sogyal Rinpoche.* Portland, OR: Jorkvik Press, 2019.

Flanagan, Owen. *The Really Hard Problem: Meaning in a Material World.* Cambridge, MA: MIT Press, 2007.

Flanagan, Owen. *The Bodhisattva's Brain: Buddhism Naturalized.* Cambridge, MA: MIT Press, 2011.

Fronsdal, Gil. *The Dhammapada.* Boulder, CO: Shambhala, 2005.

Fronsdal, Gil. *The Buddha before Buddhism: Wisdom from the Early Teachings.* Boulder, CO: Shambhala, 2016.

Fulton, Paul R. 2008. "Mindfulness as Clinical Training." In *Mindfulness and Psychotherapy,* edited by Christopher K. Germer, Ronald Siegel, and Paul R. Fulton, 55–72.

Gazzaniga, M. S., and R. W. Sperry. "Language After Section of The Cerebral Commissures." *Brain,* 90, no. 1 (1967): 131–148. doi:10.1093/brain/90.1.131.

Geary, James. *I is an Other: The Secret Life of Metaphor and How it Shapes How We See the World.* New York: Harper, 2011.

Germer, Christopher and Ronald Seigel. *Wisdom and Compassion in Psychotherapy.* New York: Guilford, 2014.

Germer, Christopher, Ronald Siegel, and Paul Fulton. *Mindfulness and Psychotherapy* (2nd edition). New York: Guilford, 2016.

Gladwell, Malcolm. *Blink: the Power of Thinking without Thinking.* New York: Little Brown, 2005.

Gleig, Ann. *American Dharma: Buddhism beyond Modernity.* New Haven, CT: Yale University Press, 2019.

Godfrey-Smith, Peter. *Other Minds: the Octopus, the Sea, and the Deep Origins of Consciousness.* New York: Farrar Straus and Giroux, 2017.

Goldstein, Joseph. *Mindfulness: a Practical Guide to Awakening.* Boulder, CO: Sounds True, 2016.

Goleman, Daniel. *Destructive Emotions.* London: Bloomsbury, 2014.

Gombrich, R. F. *How Buddhism Began: The Conditioned Genesis of the Early Teachings.* London: Athlon, 1996.

Gombrich, R. F. *What the Buddha Thought.* London: Equinox, 2009.

Gottschall, Jonathan. *The Storytelling Animal: How Stories Make Us Human.* Boston, MA: Houghton Mifflin Harcourt, 2012.

Gunaratana, Henepola, and Jeanne Malmgren. *Journey to Mindfulness: the Autobiography of Bhante G.* Somerville, MA: Wisdom Publications, 2017.

Gyatso, Tenzin. *The Universe in a Single Atom: the Controversy of Science and Spirituality.* Little, Brown, 2006.

Hanh, Thich Nhat. *The Miracle of Mindfulness!: A Manual of Meditation.* Beacon Press, 1987.

Hanh, Thich Nhat. *Peace Is Every Step.* Bantam Books, 1991.

Hanson, Rick. *Neurodharma.* Harmony Books, 2020.

Hartsuiker, Dolf. *Sadhus: Indias Mystic Holy Men.* Rochester, VT: Inner Traditions International, 1993.

Hayes, Stephen, Victoria Follette, and Marsha Lineman. *Mindfulness and Acceptance.* New York: Guilford, 2011.

Hayes, Stephen, Kirk Strosahl, and Kelly Wilson. *Acceptance and Commitment Therapy.* New York: Guilford, 2016.

Hecker, Hellmuth. *Similes of the Buddha: An Introduction.* Kandy, Sri Lanka: Buddhist Publication Society, 2009.

Heider, Fritz, and Marianne Simmel. "An Experimental Study of Apparent Behavior." *The American Journal of Psychology* 57, no. 2 (1944): 243. doi:10.2307/1416950.

Herreid, C. F., and Kozak A. Using students as critics in faculty development. *Journal on Excellence in College Teaching*, 6 (1995): 17–29.

Heuman, L. Meditation Nation: How convincing is the science driving the popularity of mindfulness meditation? Retrieved January 30, 2016 (2014a, April 25), from http://www.tricycle.com/blog/meditation-nation.

Hinton, David. *Classical Chinese Poetry: an Anthology.* New York: Farrar Straus and Giroux, 2010.

Hinton, David. *Hunger Mountain: A Field Guide to Mind and Landscape*. Boston, MA: Shambhala, 2012.
Hinton, David. *Existence: A Story*. Boulder, CO: Shambhala. 2016.
Hood, Bruce M. *The Self Illusion: How the Social Brain Creates Identity*. Oxford: Oxford University Press, 2013.
Hoorens, Vera. "Self-Enhancement and Superiority Biases in Social Comparison." *European Review of Social Psychology*, 4, no. 1 (1993): 113–139. doi:10.1080/14792779343000040.
Ikkyū, Sarah Messer, and Kidder Smith. *Having Once Paused: Poems of Zen Master Ikkyū (1394-1481)*. Ann Arbor, MI: University of Michigan Press, 2015.
James, William E. *The Varieties of Religious Experience: a Study in Human Nature*. New York: Penguin Classics, 1985.
Jaynes, Julian. *The Origins of Consciousness in the Breakdown of the Bicameral Mind*. Boston, MA: Houghton Mifflin, 1976.
Jennings, Pilar. *Mixing Minds: the Power of Relationship in Psychoanalysis and Buddhism*. Somerville, MA: Wisdom, 2011.
Kabat-Zinn, Jon. "An Outpatient Program in Behavioral Medicine for Chronic Pain Patients Based on the Practice of Mindfulness Meditation: Theoretical Considerations and Preliminary Results." *General Hospital Psychiatry*, 4, no. 1 (1982): 33–47. doi:10.1016/0163-8343(82)90026-3.
Kabat-Zinn, Jon. 1990. *Full Catastrophe Living*. New York: Banatm Doubleday Dell.
Kenrick, Douglas T., and Vladas Griskevicius. *The Rational Animal: How Evolution Made us Smarter Than We Think*. New York: Basic Books, 2013.
Kearny, Patrick and Yoon-Suk Hwang. "Dharma and Diversity." In *Handbook of Ethical Foundations of Mindfulness*, edited by Steven Stanley, Ronald E. Purser, and Nirbhay M. Singh, 285–304. Springer, 2018.
Keown, Damien. *Buddhism*. New York: Oxford, 1996.
Khenpo, Nyoshul, and Surya Das. *Natural Great Perfection: Dzogchen Teachings and Vajra Songs*. Ithaca, NY: Snow Lion Publications, 2008.
King, P. M., and K. S. Kitchener. *Developing Reflective Judgment: Understanding and Promoting Intellectual Growth and Critical Thinking in Adolescents and Adults*. San Francisco, CA: Jossey-Bass Kolts, 1994.
Kirk, Ulrich, et al. "Adaptive Neural Reward Processing during Anticipation and Receipt of Monetary Rewards in Mindfulness Meditators." *Social Cognitive and Affective Neuroscience*, 10, no. 5 (2014): 752–759. doi:10.1093/scan/nsu112.
Knickelbine, Mark. "From Both Sides: Secular Buddhism and the 'McMindfulness' Question." Secular Buddhist Association, August 12, 2013. https://secularbuddhism.org/from-both-sides-secular-buddhism-and-the-mcmindfulness-question/.
Kozak, Arnie. *Wild Chickens and Petty Tyrants: 108 Metaphors for Mindfulness*. Boston, MA: Wisdom, 2009.
Kozak, Arnie. 2011a. "We are Constructed Through Metaphor." *Insight Journal*, August 13 2011 (electronic journal of the Barre Center for Buddhist Studies).
Kozak, Arnie. *The Everything Buddhism Book* (2nd edition). Boston, MA: Adams Media, 2011b.

Kozak, Arnie. *The Everything Essential Buddhism Book.* Boston, MA: Adams Media, 2015a.

Kozak, Arnie. *The Awakened Introvert.* Oakland, CA: New Harbinger, 2015b.

Kozak, Arnie. *Mindfulness A to Z: 108 Insights for Awakening Now.* Boston, MA: Wisdom, 2015c.

Kozak, Arnold. The Epistemic Consequences of Pervasive and Embodied Metaphor. *Theoretical and Philosophical Psychology,* 12 (1992): 137–154.

Kozak, Arnold. "Understanding Pseudoscience Vulnerability Through Epistemological Development, Critical Thinking, and Science Literacy." In *Pseudoscience: The Conspiracy Against |Science,* edited by Allison B. Kaufman and James C. Kaufman, by Arnold Kozak, 223–238. Cambridge, MA: MIT Press, 2018a.

Kozak, Arnie. *Timeless Truths for Modern Mindfulness: a Practical Guide to a More Focused and Quiet Mind.* New York: Skyhorse Publishing, 2018b.

Krägeloh, Christian U. "Mindfulness, Heedfulness, and Ethics." In *Handbook of Ethical Foundations of Mindfulness,* edited by Steven Stanley, Ronald E. Purser, and Nirbhay M. Singh, 85–100. Springer, 2018.

Kurzban, Robert. *Why Everyone (Else) is a Hypocrite: Evolution and the Modular Mind.* Princeton, NJ: Princeton University Press, 2010.

Kusserow, Adrie. "Mismatch in the Modern West." Vox Populi, August 28, 2019. https://voxpopulisphere.com/2019/08/26/adrie-kusserow-mismatch-in-the-modern-west/.

Lakoff, George, and Mark Johnson. *Metaphors We Live By.* Chicago, IL: University of Chicago Press, 1980.

Lakoff, George, and Mark Johnson. *Women, Fire, and Dangerous Things: What Categories Reveal About the Mind.* Chicago, IL: University of Chicago Press, 1987.

Lakoff, George, and Mark Johnson. *Philosophy in the Flesh: The Embodied Mind and Its Challenges to Western Thought.* New York: Basic Books. 1999.

Langer, Ellen. *Mindfulness, 25th Anniversary Edition.* Boston, MA: De Capo, 2014a.

Langer, Ellen. "Mindfulness Forward and Back." In *The Wiley Blackwell Handbook of Mindfulness,* edited by Amanda Ie, Christelle T. Ngnoumen and Ellen J. Langer, 7–20, 2014b. West Sussex, UK: John Wiley & Sons Ltd.

Lindahl, Jared R. "Why Right Mindfulness Might Not Be Right for Mindfulness." *Mindfulness,* 6, no. 1 (2014): 57–62. doi:10.1007/s12671-014-0380-5.

Lopez, Donald S. *Buddhism and Science: a Guide for the Perplexed.* Chicago, IL: University of Chicago Press, 2009.

Lopez, Donald S. *The Scientific Buddha: His Short and Happy Life.* New Haven, CT: Yale University Press, 2012.

Loy, David. *The World Is Made of Stories.* Boston, MA: Wisdom Publications, 2010.

Magid, Barry. *Ordinary Mind: Exploring the Common Ground of Zen and Psychotherapy.* Boston, MA: Wisdom Publications, 2002.

Mikulas, William L. "Buddhist Ethics, Spiritual Practice, and the Three Yanas." In *Handbook of Ethical Foundations of Mindfulness,* edited by Steven Stanley, Ronald E. Purser, and Nirbhay M. Singh, 101–120. Springer, 2018.

Minsky, Marvin Lee. *The Society of Mind.* Touchstone, 1988.

Mitchell, Stephen, ed. and trans. 1982. *The Selected Poetry of Rainer Maria Rilke.* New York: Vintage.

Mitchell, Stephen, trans. 1997. *Full Woman, Fleshly Apple, Hot Moon: Selected Poems of Pablo Neruda.* New York: Harper Collins.

Morone, Natalia E., Charity G. Moore, and Carol M. Greco. "Characteristics of Adults Who Used Mindfulness Meditation: United States, 2012." *The Journal of Alternative and Complementary Medicine* 23, no. 7 (2017): 545–550. doi:10.1089/acm.2016.0099.

Mu Soeng. *The Question of King Ajatasattu: Fractured Narratives of the Samannaphala Sutta.* Barre MA: Barre Center for Buddhist Studies, 2020.

Ñanamoli Thera. "Adittapariyaya Sutta: The Fire Sermon." *Access to Insight (BCBS Edition).* 1993. Accessed June 20, 2020. https://www.accesstoinsight.org/tipitaka/sn/sn35/sn35.028.than.html.

Ñanamoli Thera. "Three Cardinal Discourses of the Buddha." *Access to Insight (BCBS Edition),* 1995. Accessed June 20, 2020. http://www.accesstoinsight.org/lib/authors/nanamoli/wheel017.html.

Ñanamoli Theraand and Bodhi, Bhikkhu "Maha-sihanada Sutta: The Great Discourse on the Lion's Roar." *Access to Insight (BCBS Edition),* 1994. Accessed June 20, 2020. http://www.accesstoinsight.org/tipitaka/mn/mn.012.ntbb.html.

Nesbitt, Richard E., and Wilson. Timothy. "Telling More Than We Can Know: Verbal Reports on Mental Processes." *Psychological Review,* 84, no. 3 (1977): 231–259.

Newberg, Andrew. *Why God Won't Go Away: Brain Science and the Biology of Belief.* New York: Ballantine, 2001.

Nietzsche, Friedrich. On Truth and Lie in the Extra Moral Sense. In *The Portable Nietzsche,* edited by W. Kaufmann (Trans.), 42–47 (original work written 1873). New York: Norton, 1982.

Nietzsche, Friedrich. *Human All Too Human.* New York: Cambridge University Press, 1996.

Nørretranders, Tor. *The User Illusion: Cutting Consciousness down to Size.* London: Penguin, 1999.

Olendzki, Andrew. *Unlimiting Mind: The Radically Experiential Psychology of Buddhism.* Boston, MA: Wisdom, 2010.

Olendzki, Andrew. *Untangling Self.* Boston, MA: Wisdom, 2016.

Orsillo, Susan and Lizabeth Roemer. *The Mindful Way Through Anxiety.* New York: Guilford, 2011.

Park, Jungnok. *How Buddhism acquired a Soul on the Way to China.* Bristol, CT: Equinox, 2012.

Peacock, John. "Suffering in Mind: The Aetiology of Suffering in Early Buddhism." *Contemporary Buddhism,* 9 (2008): 209–226.

Peacock, John. "Buddha the Radical to Creeping Brahmanism." Interview with Secular Buddhist Association, 2012. http://secularbuddhism.org/2012/01/06/episode-98-john-peacock-buddha-the-radical-to-creeping-brahmanism/.

Peacock, John. "Sati or Mindfulness? Bridging the Divide." In *After Mindfulness: New Perspectives on Psychology and Meditation,* edited by Manu Bazzano, 1–22. Basingstoke: Palgrave Macmillan, 2014.

Penner, Hans H. *Rediscovering the Buddha: Legends of the Buddha and Their Interpretation*. New York: Oxford University Press, 2009.
Percheron, Maurice, and Adrienne Foulke. *The Marvelous Life of the Buddha*. New York: St. Martins Press, 1960.
Pinker, Stephen. *How the Mind Works*. New York: Norton, 1997.
Pollan, Michael. *How to Change Your Mind: What the New Science of Psychedelics Teaches Us About Consciousness, Dying, Addiction, Depression, and Trancendence*. New York: Penguin, 2018.
Purser, Ron, and David Loy. "Beyond McMindfulness." *HuffPost*, HuffPost, August 31, 2013. www.huffpost.com/entry/beyond-mcmindfulness_b_3519289.
Purser, Ronald E. *McMindfulness: How Mindfulness Became the New Capitalist Spirituality*. London: Repeater, 2019.
Ramachandran, V. S., and Sandra Blakeslee. *Phantoms in the Brain: Probing the Mysteries of the Human Mind*. New York: Harper Perennial, 2009.
Roemer, Lizabeth and Susan Orsillo. *Mindfulness- and Acceptance-Based Behavioral Therapies in Practice*. New York: Guilford, 2010.
Rosenberg, Larry. *Breath by Breath: The Liberating Practice of Insight Meditation*. Boulder, CO: Shambhala, 2004.
Rosenberg, Larry, and Laura Zimmerman. *Three Steps to Awakening: a Practice for Bringing Mindfulness to Life*. Boston, MA: Shambhala, 2013.
Ryan, Richard M., and C. Scott Rigby. "Did the Buddha Have a Self: No-Self, Self, and Mindfulness." In *Handbook of Mindfulness: Theory, Research, and Practice*, edited by Kirk Warren Brown, J. David Creswell, and Richard M. Ryan, 245–268. New York: Guilford, 2015.
Safina, Carl. *Beyond Words: What Animals Think and Feel*. New York: Picador, 2015.
Safran, Jeremy D. *Psychoanalysis and Buddhism: an Unfolding Dialogue*. Boston, MA: Wisdom Publications, 2005.
Seager, Richard Hughes. 2012. *Buddhism in America*. New York: Columbia University Press.
Segal, Williams, and Teasdale. *Mindfulness-Based Cognitive Therapy for Depression* (2nd edition). New York: Guilford, 2013.
Seth, Anil K. "The Neuroscience of Reality." *Scientific American* (2019): 42–47.
Siegel, Dan. *Mindful Brain*. New York: Norton, 2007a.
Siegel, Daniel J. "Mindfulness Training and Neural Integration: Differentiation of Distinct Streams of Awareness and the Cultivation of Well-Being." *Social Cognitive and Affective Neuroscience*, 2, no. 4 (2007): 259–263. doi:10.1093/scan/nsm034.
Siegel, Dan and Siegel. "Thriving with Uncertainty: Opening the Mind and Cultivating Inner Well-Being Through Contemplative and Creative Mindfulness." In *The Wiley Blackwell Handbook of Mindfulness,* edited by Amanda Ie, Christelle T. Ngnoumen and Ellen J. Langer, 21–46. New York: Wiley Blackwell, 2014.
Soma Thera. "The Way of Mindfulness: The Satipatthana Sutta and Its Commentary," by Soma Thera. *Access to Insight (BCBS Edition)*, 1998, Accessed June 20, 2020. http://www.accesstoinsight.org/lib/authors/soma/wayof.html.

Stanley, Steven, Ronald E. Purser, and Nirbhay M. Singh Singh (eds). *Handbook of Ethical Foundations of Mindfulness*. Springer, 2018.
Strassman, Rick. *DMT: The Spirit Molecule*. Rochester, VT: Park Street Press, 2001.
Suzuki, Shunryu, and Trudy Dixon. *Zen Mind, Beginners Mind*. New York: Weatherhill, 1982.
Tang, Y.-Y., et al. "Central and Autonomic Nervous System Interaction Is Altered by Short-Term Meditation." *Proceedings of the National Academy of Sciences*, 106, no. 22 (2009): 8865–8870. doi:10.1073/pnas.0904031106.
Tang, Yi-Yuan, et al. "The Neuroscience of Mindfulness Meditation." *Nature Reviews Neuroscience*, 16, no. 4 (2015): 213–225. doi:10.1038/nrn3916.
Taylor, Charles. *Sources of the Self: the Making of the Modern Identity*. Harvard University Press, 2012.
Thanissaro, Bhikkhu. "Dhammacakkappavattana Sutta: Setting the Wheel of Dhamma in Motion." *Access to Insight (BCBS Edition)*, 1993. Accessed June 20, 2020. http://www.accesstoinsight.org/tipitaka/sn/sn56/sn56.011.than.html.
Thanissaro, Bhikkhu. "Kalama Sutta: To the Kalamas." *Access to Insight (BCBS Edition)*, 1994. Accessed June 20, 2020. http://www.accesstoinsight.org/tipitaka/an/an03/an03.065.than.html.
Thanissaro, Bhikkhu, ed. and trans. *The Wings to Awakening*. Valley Center, CA: Metta Forest Monastery, 1996.
Thanissaro, Bhikkhu. "Aggi-Vacchagotta Sutta: To Vacchagotta on Fire." *Access to Insight (BCBS Edition)*, 1997. Accessed June 20. http://www.accesstoinsight.org/tipitaka/mn/mn.072.than.html.
Thanissaro, Bhikkhu. "Abhisanda Sutta: Rewards." *Access to Insight (BCBS Edition)*, 1997. Accessed June 20, 2020. http://www.accesstoinsight.org/tipitaka/an/an08/an08.039.than.html.
Thanissaro, Bhikkhu. "Kaccayanagotta Sutta: To Kaccayana Gotta (on Right View)." *Access to Insight (BCBS Edition)*, 1997. Accessed June 20, 2020. http://www.accesstoinsight.org/tipitaka/sn/sn12/sn12.015.than.html.
Thanissaro, Bhikkhu. "Maha-parinibbana Sutta: The Great Discourse on the Total Unbinding." *Access to Insight (BCBS Edition)*, 1998. Accessed June 20, 2020. http://www.accesstoinsight.org/tipitaka/dn/dn.16.5-6.than.html.
Thanissaro, Bhikkhu. "Gaddula Sutta: The Leash (2)." *Access to Insight (BCBS Edition)*, 1998b. Accessed June 20, 2020. http://www.accesstoinsight.org/tipitaka/sn/sn22/sn22.100.than.html.
Thanissaro, Bhikkhu. "Uppadana Sutta: Clinging." *Access to Insight (BCBS Edition)*, 1998c. Accessed June 20, 2020. https://www.accesstoinsight.org/tipitaka/sn/sn12/sn12.052.than.html.
Thanissaro Bhikkhu. "Mind Like Fire Unbound: An Image in the Early Buddhist Discourses." *Access to Insight (BCBS Edition)*, Fourth Edition, 1999. Accessed May 22, 2020. https://accesstoinsight.org/lib/authors/thanissaro/likefire/index.html.
Thanissaro, Bhikkhu. "Five Piles of Bricks."*Access to Insight (BCBS Edition)*, 2002. Accessed June 20, 2020. https://www.accesstoinsight.org/lib/authors/thanissaro/khandha.html.

Thanissaro, Bhikkhu. "Reconciliation, Right & Wrong." *Access to Insight (BCBS Edition)*, 2004. Accessed June 20, 2020. http://www.accesstoinsight.org/lib/authors/thanissaro/reconciliation.html.

Thanissaro, Bhikkhu. "Anuradha Sutta: To Anuradha." *Access to Insight (BCBS Edition)*, 2004. Accessed June 20, 2020. http://www.accesstoinsight.org/tipitaka/sn/sn22/sn22.086.than.html.

Thanissaro, Bhikkhu. "Sivaka Sutta: To Sivaka." *Access to Insight (BCBS Edition)*, 2005a. Accessed June 20, 2020. http://www.accesstoinsight.org/tipitaka/sn/sn36/sn36.021.than.html.

Thanissaro, Bhikkhu. "Dona Sutta: With Dona." *Access to Insight (BCBS Edition)*, 2005b. Accessed June 20, 2020. http://www.accesstoinsight.org/tipitaka/an/an04/an04.036.than.html.

Thanissaro, Bhikkhu. "Anapanasati Sutta: Mindfulness of Breathing." *Access to Insight (BCBS Edition)*, 2006. Accessed June 20, 2020. http://www.accesstoinsight.org/tipitaka/mn/mn.118.than.html.

Thanissaro, Bhikkhu. "Maha-Saccaka Sutta: The Longer Discourse to Saccaka." *Access to Insight (BCBS Edition)*, 2008. Accessed June 20, 2020. http://www.accesstoinsight.org/tipitaka/mn/mn.036.than.html.

Thanissaro, Bhikkhu. "The Five Aggregates: A Study Guide." *Access to Insight (BCBS Edition)*, 2010. Accessed June 20, 2020. http://www.accesstoinsight.org/lib/study/khandha.html.

Thanissaro, Bhikkhu. "Affirming the Truths of the Heart: The Buddhist Teachings on Samvega & Pasada." *Access to Insight (BCBS Edition)*, 2011. Accessed June 20, 2020. http://www.accesstoinsight.org/lib/authors/thanissaro/affirming.html.

Thanissaro, Bhikkhu, ed. and trans. *Handful of Leaves, Volume Three: An Anthology from the Samyutta Nikaya*. Valley Center, CA: Metta Forest Monastery, 2015.

Thanissaro, Bhikkhu. "The Image of Nirvaṇa." *The Image of Nirvaṇa | Noble Strategy*, Accessed June 20, 2020. https://www.dhammatalks.org/books/NobleStrategy/Section0015.html.

Tirch, Dennis, Laura R. Silberstein, and Russel L. Kolts. *Buddhist Psychology and Cognitive Behavioral Therapy: A Clincian's Guide*. New York: Guilford, 2015.

Tolle, Eckhart. *The Power of Now: a Guide to Spiritual Enlightenment*. New World Library, 2004.

Trainor, Kevin, ed. *Buddhism: The Illustrated Guide*. New York: Oxford, 2004.

van Vugt, Marieke K. "Cognitive Benefits of Mindfulness Meditation." In *Handbook of Mindfulness: Theory, Research, and Practice*, edited by Kirk Warren Brown, J. David Creswell, and Richard M. Ryan, 190–207. New York: Guilford, 2015.

Walsh, Roger and Shauna L. Shapiro. "The Meeting of Meditative Disciplines and Western Psychology: A Mutually Enriching Dialogue, *American Psychologist*, 61 (2006): 227–239.

WBUR. "Conservationist Carl Safina's Ecosystem Wake Up Call." Conservationist Carl Safina's Ecosystem Wake Up Call | On Point. WBUR, January 28, 2011. https://www.wbur.org/onpoint/2011/01/28/conservationist-safina-ecosystems.

Whyte, David. *Three Marriages: Revisioning Self, Work, and Relationship*. Langley WA: Many Rivers Press, 2009.

Wilber, Ken. *A Brief History of Everything*. Boulder, Co: Shambhala, 2007.
Wilson, Jeff. *Mindful America: The Mutual Transformation of Buddhist Meditation and American Culture*. New York: Oxford, 2014.
Wilson, Timothy D., et al. "Just Think: The Challenges of the Disengaged Mind." *Science*, 345, no. 6192 (2014): 75–77. doi:10.1126/science.1250830.
Wright, Robert. *Why Buddhism Is True: the Science and Philosophy of Meditation and Enlightenment*. New York: Simon & Schuster, 2018.
Yalom, Irvin. *Existential Psychotherapy*. New York: Basic Books, 1980.
Yalom, Irvin. *The Schopenhauer Cure*. New York: Harper Perennial, 2009.
Young-Eisendrath, Polly. *The Self-Esteem Trap: Raising Confident and Compassionate Kids in an Age of Self-Importance*. New York: Little Brown, 2008.
Young-Eisendrath, Polly, and Shoji Muramoto. *Awakening and Insight Zen Buddhism and Psychotherapy*. Abingdon, Oxon: Taylor and Francis, 2003.

Index

Abhidhamma (Abhidharma), 53, 57, 71
affective heuristics, 95, 112
agency. *See* determinism, participatory; free will
aggregates, five (*upadana khanda*): adaptations and limitations of, 60; as Buddha's pedagogical goal, 35; as Buddha's psychological mind model, xliii; as contingency/clinging, 47, 58, 62, 71, 123; defined, xxxiii, 61–64; example of, 69; as not self, 88, 102, 123
Ananda, 6, 20, 122, 125–26
Anapanasati Sutta, 53–54
anatman. See not self
anatta. See not self
anicca. See impermanence
appamada, xi
ariya (noble), 34, 54. *See also* Four Noble Truths
asceticism, 12
Ascoli, Giorgi, 73–78, 83–84
atman. See essential self
aversion, 29–30, 33, 39, 89, 92
awakening: Brahma's reaction to, 14; Buddha's personal, xxxiii, 40, 56, 58; and consciousness, 113; democracy of, 14; difficulty of, xlvi, 42, 73, 78, 122; *vs.* enlightenment, xxxv, 56, 121; metaphors for, 29, 34; and mindfulness, xi, xxii; and three jewels, 25; and three poisons, 46; and well-being, 48
awareness. *See* consciousness
axiology, xxiii, 100

Batchelor, Stephen, viii, xvi, xxvii, xxxviii, xl, 1, 34, 39, 43–45, 47, 51–52, 85
bhava, xxv
Bodhisattva, vii, xii, xli, 58
Book of Eights, xxxviii, 29–30, 92
brain: architecture of, 74, 77; Ascoli's theory of, 73–80; complexity of, 32; and computation, 77, 98, 107; connectome, 76; and consciousness, 32, 70, 109; contextual processing, 78; and evolution, ix; and feeling (*vedana*) aggregate, 67; and form (*rupa*) aggregate, 64–65; functional specialization, 98; and fusiform gyrus, 104; and hallucinations, controlled, 82, 98; Hebb's axiom, 75, 77; interpreter module, 82; and learning, 64, 73–75; and memory, 75; and modularity, 98–99, 107; metaphorical perception, 74, 78; metaphorical (tree/forest) structure of, 73, 76; and *nirvana*, 47; and novelty, 83; and perception, 69, 71,

83; plasticity, 73, 75; probabilistic functioning, 77; as problem solver, general, 98; *projectome*, 76; redundancy, 75; and self, location of, 98; stability, 75; and volition (free-will), 100, 103
Brahma: as absolute consciousness, xvii, 38, 113; as Hindu god, 14, 20, 24
Brahmanism, xxxii, xxxv, xlvii, 19, 24, 28, 30, 58, 68, 93, 119
Buddha: 2.0, viii–ix, xiii, xl, 1; as antisocial, 15; avoidant personality of, 3, 21, 91, 123; before Buddhism, xix, 29–30; as bodhisattva, xli, 38, 58; *vs.* Buddhism, 2; on dogma, ix, xv, xxxvi, xxxviii–xxxix, xli, xliv, 2, 6, 25, 33, 127; end of life, 8, 15–16, 20, 30–31; evidence for, 1, 5–6, 23; fictionalized depiction of, viii, xii, xv, 5, 123; as fireman, xxix, xlii; hagiography, xii, xl–xli, 1–2, 28–29, 32, 49, 121–23; homosexuality question, 17, 91; human depiction of, 20, 30–31; intentions of, 2, 14, 23–24, 30; on joy (delight), 38–39, 42, 90; mythological, 7–21; narrative coherence of four signs, 9–10, 16–17, 25; non-literal (e.g., irony, satire) interpretations of, xxvii, 2, 24, 26–27, 42; as physician, xxxii, 34–35; as psychologist, viii, xv–xvi, xviii–xxi, xxxi, xli, 2, 5, 15, 48, 123; under the rose apple tree, 16, 21; as salvific religious figure, xviii, xxii, 14; solitude, importance of, 12–13, 17, 21, 25, 92; as *tathagata*, xxxvii, xl, 26, 48, 57, 113, 119
Buddhacarita, 18
Buddha's teachings. *See* dharma
Buddhism: American, viii–ix; Brahmanification of, 20; Ch'an, xxviii, 118; cultural appropriation of, viii, xii, xv, xliv; early, xv, xix, xxii, 29; and essence, xvi, 124; historical, x, xiii, 5–7, 15; Mahayana, xxii, xlvi; migration of, 5–6; and mindfulness, x–xiii, xvi; mythological, 24; naturalized (rational, scientific), xliv, 60; secular, viii, xiii, xv, 1, 126; Theravadan, xxii; Tibetan, viii–ix, xii, xxxiv, xlvi, 2, 57, 124–25; Vajrayana, xviii, xlvi; Western, viii–ix, xiii; Zen, xii, xliv–xlvi, 32, 57, 120, 124–25
buddho, 8, 14

Cajal, Santiago Ramon y, 74
categorization. *See* perception
chanda, 42
Chopra, Deepak, x
citta, 68
clinging. *See* desire
concentration. *See* jhanas
consciousness: absolute, xiii, xvi, 20, 24; and agency (volition), 110–11; aggregate of (*vinnana*), xxx, xxxii–xxxiv, 61, 63, 68–71, 109–14; and awakening, 113; and brain, 32, 75; as *cetana*, 77; conditioned nature of, xxviii, 113; disembodied, 104; and *dukkha*, 38, 40; and language, xxvi, 117; limitations, appreciation of, xvii, 109; metaphors for, xxv; mindfulness, distinguished from, 113; as not self, 110, 113; perception, accurate, and humility for, 64; perception of specialness, 110; as Presence (awareness), 105–6, 119; as press secretary metaphor, 100; role for mindfulness, 111–12; and *sankhara*, 71, 110; and self, 101; and thinking, 99, 107; to unconsciousness ratio, 109
contingency, xxxii–xxxv, xliii, 20, 37–39, 43, 46, 54, 56, 60–62, 64, 67, 88, 91–95, 120
craving. *See* desire

death, vii, xxvi, xxx–xxx ii, xxxiv, xliv–xlv, xlvii, 8, 11, 13, 19, 21, 26, 32, 43, 55, 90, 120, 123
delusion. *See moha*
dependent origination, chain of, xix, xliv, 14, 29, 77–78
deprivation. *See* asceticism
desire: aversion towards (asceticism), 8, 12, 61; dangers of, xxxiii; and the deathless, 118; and *dukkha*, 33; as evolutionary factor, xxx, xxxiii, 38, 60–61, 87–95; lust metaphors, xxxi; as Mara, 12–13, 43; *raga*, xxix; and self-ownership, xxxviii, xliii, 13, 106, 119, 123; as sensuality (sex), xxxviii, 88, 90–94, 122–23; wholesome (*chanda*), 90. *See also* fires, three
determinations. *See* fabrications
determinism, participatory, 110–12
Devadatta, xxxix, 8, 126
Dhammapada, xix
dharma, ix, xii, xviii, xix, xxii, xxvii, xxix, xxxvi, xxxviii, xxxix, xlvi, 1, 16, 25, 29, 34, 60, 118, 123–26
dharma wars, xi
dogma, ix, xii, xv–xvi, xxiii, xxxvi–xxxix, xli, xliv, 2, 6, 25, 28, 33–34, 124, 127
dosa. *See* desire
dukkha: causes of (e.g., contingency/craving/clinging/reactivity), xxxv, 41–44, 46–47, 62, 93–94, 106; *dukkha-dukkha*, 19, 37–39, 95; and essence, 105; and fabrications, 68, 119; and fires, xxi, xxxi; Four Noble Truths, part of, xxi, 34, 37–40, 56–57; and impermanence, xxxii; joy, compared to, xliv; and medical metaphor, 34–35; as metaphor, xx–xxi, 51; and *nirvana*, xxii; *sankhara dukkha*, 37–38; and self-concepts, xxiv–xxv, 102; as self-inflicted, 39; and sensuality, 90, 92; translation, difficulties of, xx; *vipariname dukkha*, 37–38

Eliot, T. S., 84
emotions (compared to feelings), 95
emptiness, xxxvii, xlvi, 117, 120
enlightenment. *See* awakening; *nirvana*
Epstein, Mark, xxviii
essence. *See* essentialism
essentialism, xxiii, 31, 57, 105, 126
essential self: and *atman*/soul, xvi; and awakening, 42; Buddha's denial of, 13, 25, 62, 106; and Capgras delusion, 104; and consciousness, 110–11; as controlled hallucination, 98; and emotional reactivity, 112; and environment, 105; and evolution, xliii, 105; and fires, xxxiii; and fundamental attribution error, xvii; as metaphor, 101–2; and mindfulness, 85; ownership and identification of, 106; and Presence, 120; and science fiction, 104; and self, 63, 68, 106
evolution: and aggregates, xliii, 61; evolutionary psychology, ix, xv, xxxiii, xlii, 60, 98–99, 101–3, 113; and feeling, xxx, xxxiii, 42, 66, 87–96; and fire metaphor, xxx, xxxvi, 59; and Mara, 12; and Presence, 121; and reactivity, xvi, 38; #resistevolution, ix, 61, 88, 97, 105; and teleology, xliv, 107; and wellbeing, 48
existential realities (sickness, aging, death), xxvii–xxviii, 8–12, 16–19, 25, 33, 37–38, 44, 57. *See also* four signs
existential responsibility, xv, xxxvi–xxxix, xli, 2, 28

fabrications: aggregate (*sankhara*), 67–69, 71, 78, 97–108; and brain, 78; Buddha's final words, 123; and consciousness, 110; FEAR acronym,

44; and fires, 122; limitations of language, 47; and mindfulness, 123; and reactivity, 42; and volition, 110
feeling: aggregate (*vedana*), 61–63, 66–67, 69–70, 87–95; and fabrications aggregate, 67, 97; and fire metaphor, xxxii, 64; and karma, 28; and mindfulness, four foundations of, 54; and perception aggregate, 66, 81, 110; and self, 106
fires, three (*dosa, raga, moha*): and aggregates, 59–71; and evolution, 88–89, 93; extinguishing, xxi, 45–47, 118, 121; Fire Sermon (The Way of Putting Things as Being on Fire), xxix–xxxi, xli, xlvi, 43; metaphors for, xxi, xxiii–xxv, xxvii, xxix, xxxi, xlii, 118; and mindfulness, 56, 111, 118, 123; and *nirvana*, xxi; and Noble Eightfold Path, xxi; *vs.* poisons, 122; reduced to embers, 123; and Vangisa, 122; *yagna*, xlvii
Flower Ornament Scripture, 19
form (*rupa* aggregate), xxx, 59, 61–65, 67, 70–71, 73–74, 84, 88
formations, mental. *See* fabrications
Four Noble Truths, xii, xxi, xlii–xliii, 1, 26, 33–57
four signs, 8–11, 25, 44. *See also* existential realities
free will: as agency, xxi, xxviii, xxxvi, 9, 38, 78, 83, 106, 112, 116; illusion of, 63, 103, 111; Nesbitt and Wilson experiment on, 100; and post-hoc reasoning, 99–100; Spinoza on, 111

Goenka, S. N., vii, 65, 78
Gombrich, Richard, xvi, xxv, xxvii, xxix, xxxiii–xxxvi, xli, xliii–xliv, 6, 14, 23–24, 30–31, 45, 71

hallmarks of existence, three (*dukkha, annicca, anatta*), xx–xxi, xxxv, xlv, 39, 121
hindrances, five, 58

Hinton, David, 105–6, 117–20
hiri, 53
homelessness, psychological, xxxviii, xlvii, 85, 119

ignorance. *See moha*
impermanence, xxi–xxii, xxxix, 31, 38, 46, 76, 85, 91–92

Jaynes, Julian, xxvi, 107, 109–10, 117
jhanas. See concentration
jivan, 20

Kabat-Zinn, Jon, x–xi, 31, 52
Kalama, Arada, 11
karma, xii, xxviii, 14, 28
khanda. See aggregates

Lakoff and Johnson, xxvii, xxxi, 84, 101–2
language, limitations of, xxiv, xxvi–xxix, 42, 45–47, 86, 95, 97, 113, 116–21
liberation. *See* awakening

magga. See Noble Eightfold Path
Malunkyaputta, 26
Mara, 12–13, 16, 43, 49, 58, 61, 93
meditation, ix–x, xiii, xvii, xxxvii, 8, 12, 15, 18, 21, 29, 34, 43, 51–53, 55, 61, 64–65, 86, 90, 105, 112, 117, 126
mental formations. *See* aggregates
metaphor: as Buddha's pedagogical device (*upaya*), xxvii, xli–xliii, xliv, 2, 33; conceptual, xxxi, 78, 82, 84, 105, 110, 118–19; and language, xxvi; and similes, xxvii, xlv
metaphysics: and awakening, 121; and belief (dogma), xxvi; and Buddhism, xii, xxxviii, 6, 24; and cosmology (ontology) xlvii, 1, 20; *vs.* empiricism, ix, xvi, 2, 25–26; and non-harmfulness, 31; and science, xxiii; and wholeness, intrinsic, 32

mind, computational modules, xliii, 60, 71, 82, 98–100, 105, 107, 112
mind, model. *See* aggregates
mindfulness: in *Abhidharma* (*Abhidhamma*), 57; and aggregates, 63–64, 94; and *Anapanasati Sutta*, 53–54; *appamada* aspect of, xi; and awakening, 48; as *bhavana*, 55; of the body, viii, 56; brain findings, 95; Buddha origins of, xiii, xv, 57–58; and categories, 84; compared to Transcendental Meditation (TM), xiii–xiiv; and concentration, 53; and consciousness, 111, 113; defined, xi, 52–53; and essentialism, 105; and ethics (dharma wars/McMindfulness), xi–xii, 56; four foundations of, 54, 58; and happiness, xxii; as Heidegger's Care (*bessinung*), 53; and intrinsic wholeness, 31; Langer's approach to, 53; and language, 119; MBI—mindfulness based intervention, x; meditation (insight/vipassana), xiv, xvi–xvii, 48; meditation retreats, 55; movement, ix–xiii, 35, 53, 126; in Noble Eightfold Path, 51–52, 57; and participatory determinism, 70, 111–12; and psychotherapy, 18; and *Satipatthana Sutta*, 54, 58; as secular religion, x; and wisdom, 42, 58, 123
moha (delusion, ignorance, confusion), xxiii, xxix–xxxii, xlvi, 25, 38, 45, 60, 89, 103, 118. *See also* fires, three
morality/ethics (*sila*): and conscientiousness, 34, 53; and Eightfold Path, xxi, 51–52, 56–57, 61; and feeling (*vedana*), 67; and fires, xxi; and mindfulness, xi; and personal responsibility, xxxix; and pragmatism, xxxviii, 14, 31; and self-bias, 104; and spirituality, xxii
mukti, 20, 56
My Dinner with Andre, 84

Neruda, Pablo, 65
Nesbitt and Wilson experiment, 100
nibanna. *See nirvana*
Nietzsche, Friedrich, 115–16
nimttakarano (sign-making), 118
nirvana, xxi–xxii, xxxii, xxxiv, xlii–xliii, xlv–xlvi, 13, 19, 26, 35, 45–49, 55, 60, 85, 91, 117
Noble Eightfold Path, 51–56
Noble Quest, 28
not self, xvii, xxiii–vi, xxxv, xli, xlv, 21, 39, 52, 62, 73, 81, 87, 98, 102–3, 110–13, 124

On Fear and Dread, 28
ottapa, 53

Pali Canon, xxvii, xli, xlv, 2, 5–6, 23–24, 29–30, 57, 64. *See also* dharma
papanca (proliferation), 41–42
paranirvana, xxxii, 123
patticca samupada (*pratitya-samutpada*). *See* dependent origination
Peacock, John, xvi, xx, 33, 38, 41, 53, 118
Penner, Hans, 5, 7, 19, 24
perception: aggregate (*sanna*), xxx, 61–66, 81–86; and brain, 75, 84; and consciousness, 68–69; as controlled hallucinations, 82; as creative act, 84–86; and evolution, 89; and fabrication, 67; and feeling, 69, 104, 112–13; as metaphoric process, 115–17, 120; and not self/self, xliii, xlv, 68, 81, 106, 112; and objectivity, xliii, 69, 83, 112; and openness, xlv; T. S. Eliot on, 84; and volition, xliii. *See also* aggregates, five
Percheron, Maurice, 5, 8–9
poetry: in Buddha's teaching, xxvii, xxxvii, 28; and experience, xxvii, 85, 117–18
poisons, three, xlvi, 122. *See also* fires, three

praxis, viii, xxiv, xxix, xlii, 1–2, 25, 29, 34–35, 59, 62, 65, 123
Presence, xiv, 82, 117, 120–21
primordial moment, 86, 115
psychology, science of, x, xiii, xix, xxii, xliii, 14, 28, 33, 67, 71, 86

raga. *See* aversion
Rahula (Buddha's son), 20–21
Ramaputra, Udraka, 11
reactivity. *See* contingency
rebirth: and bodhisattvas, vii; as common cosmological belief, xii, 19, 27, 126; and confirmation bias, 32; as metaphorical rhetoric, xxxiv, 28–29, 123; as metaphysical speculation, 28, 126; and past and future lives, 7, 26, 118; and *samudaya*, 41. *See also* Wheel of Life
refuges, three/triple (*Buddha, dharma, sangha*), 25
reified self. *See* not self
renunciation. *See* asceticism
Rilke, Rainer Maria: "Eighth Duino Elegy," 120; on existential insecurity, xxxix; "The Swan," 85
rupa. *See* form

samsara, xvii, 38
samudaya (arising), 34, 41, 43–44
samvega, 25
sankhara. *See* fabrications
sanna. *See* perception
satchitananda (being-consciousness-bliss), 68
sati, 53–54, 57. *See also* mindfulness
Satipatthana Sutta (The Way of Mindfulness), 54, 58
Sayadaw, Ledi, 15, 26
Schopenhauer, Arthur, 89
science: of happiness, xxii; naturalizing Buddhism/mindfulness, x, xii, xix–xxx, xliii–xliv, 25, 59–60; philosophy of, xix–xxx, xxiii, 2, 86, 124

self: agency (volition, free will), 116; and aggregates, 73–74, 81–82, 87–88, 98; attunement to, 121; bias towards, 100, 103–7; and brain damage, 100, 103; brain location, xxv, 98; coherence and confabulation, 100–101, 103; decision making, 99–100, 103, 110–11; and environmental exchange, 86, 105; folk-psychological, xxiv–xxvi, 102–3; hierarchical organization of, 99–100; illusion of, 13, 60, 102; impression management, 103; language, created by, xxvi–xxix, 116–21; metaphor for, xxiv–xxvii, xlvi, 100–101, 106, 115–17, 119; modularity of, 97–108; as noun, xxiii–vi, 116; and personality, xxiv, 100; post-hoc reasoning, 99–100; press secretary metaphor, 100; reified, xxiii, xxv, 60–61, 97, 101, 105–6, 124; Self Determination Theory, xlv; selfing, xxvi, xxviii; as sense of ownership/possession of/identification with experience, xxiii, xxviii, xxxviii, 39, 46, 66, 68, 88, 94, 106, 113, 116, 119; as soul, xvi, xxiv, xxvii, xxxv, xlvi, 13, 20, 26, 61, 101–2, 119, 124, 126; as storytelling, xxviii, 97; subselves and evolutionary functions, 98–99; true (authentic) *vs.* false, 101–2
sex, xxx, xliv, 9, 12, 21, 66, 87, 89, 91–92, 95
Shaivism, Kashmir, xvi–xvii, xlvii
Siddhartha: as honorific title, xii; Hermen Hesse novel, xl
Siddha Yoga, xvi
soul. *See* essential self
Spinoza, B., 111
spirituality, vii, xv, xxi–xxiii, xxv, xxxvi, xlv, 8, 10–11, 15, 19–20, 56, 58, 119
spiritual materialism, 120

storytelling animals, xxvi, xxviii, 97
stress. *See* dukkha
suffering. *See* dukkha

tanha, 41–43, 45, 47
Tao Te Ching, 118
tat tvam-asi, 11, 19
this-that causality. *See* dependent origination
Transcendental Meditation (TM), x

unbinding. *See* awakening
Universal Monarchs, 7
upadana (upadana-khanda), xxxii, xxxv, 47. *See also* fires, metaphors
upaya, xxvii

vedena. *See* feeling
vinnana. *See* consciousness
vipassana, vii, ix–x, xiv, xvii–xviii, 20, 55, 57, 114
viveka, 91
volitions. *See* fabrications

Wheel of Life, xx–xxi, xxvii–xxviii
wisdom (*prajna*), xvi, xxi, xxxvii, xxxix, 14, 33–34, 42, 45, 51–52, 56–57, 62, 64, 123. *See also* Four Noble Truths
Wittgenstein, Ludwig, 98
Wright, Robert, ix, xliv, 60, 105

yagna, xxxv, xlvii
Young, Shinzen, 46–49

About the Author

Arnold Kozak, PhD, is a licensed psychologist and clinical assistant professor in psychiatry at the University of Vermont Larner College of Medicine. He is the author of *108 Metaphors for Mindfulness, Mindfulness A to Z, The Awakened Introvert, The Everything Essentials Buddhism Book, Buddhism 101,* and *Timeless Truths for Modern Mindfulness*. He also contributed a chapter to *Pseudoscience: The Conspiracy Against Science*. He is an artist and has been practicing yoga and meditation for nearly forty years and is dedicated to translating the Buddha's teachings into secular and readily accessible forms.

Website: http://arniekozak.com/

Social Media:

https://www.facebook.com/DrArnieKozak
https://twitter.com/arniekozak
https://www.linkedin.com/in/arniekozak
https://www.goodreads.com/author/show/2806266.Arnie_Kozak
https://www.instagram.com/arniekozak/

www.ingramcontent.com/pod-product-compliance
Lightning Source LLC
Chambersburg PA
CBHW020121010526
44115CB00008B/925